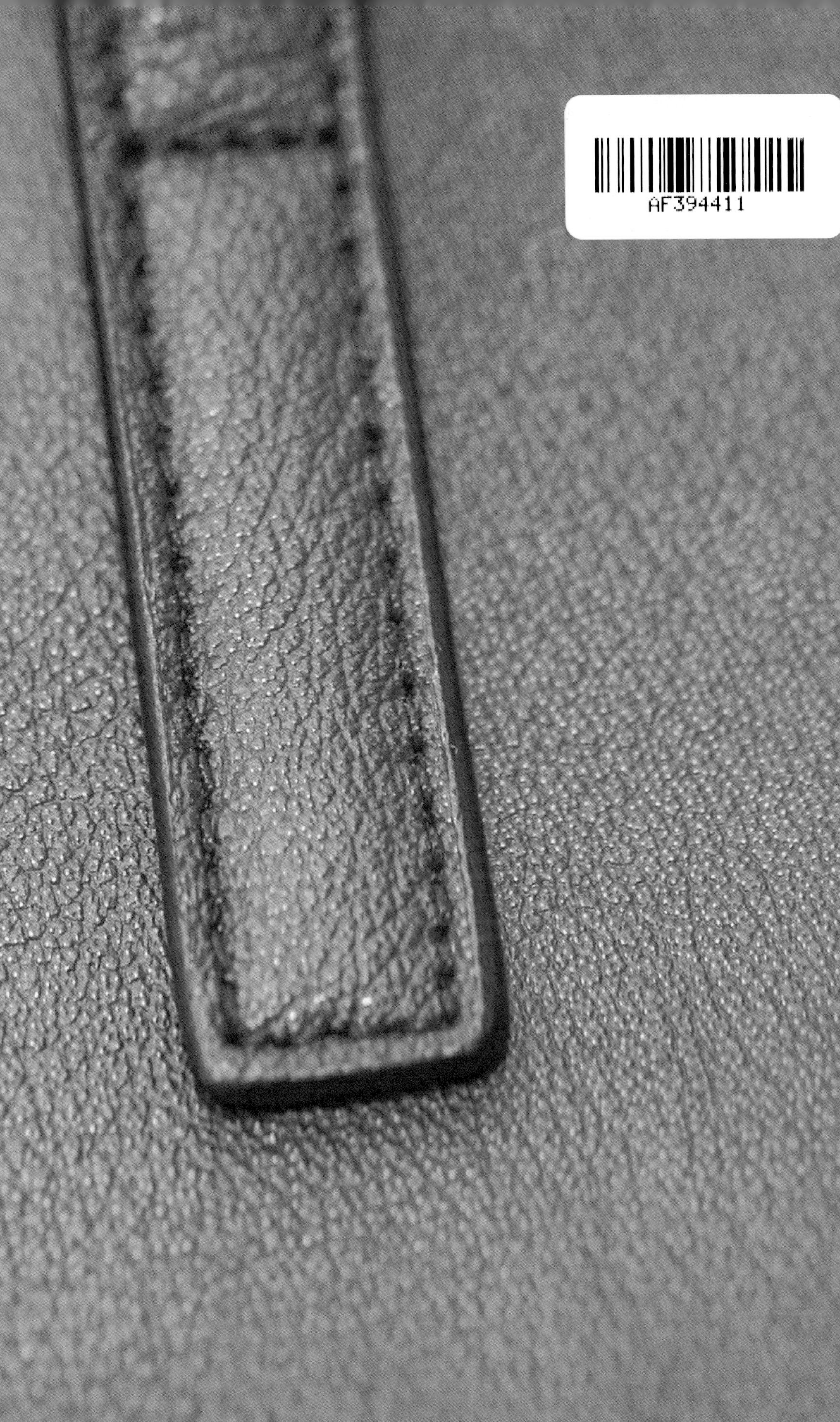
AF394411

THE FASHION ICONS

YVES SAINT LAURENT

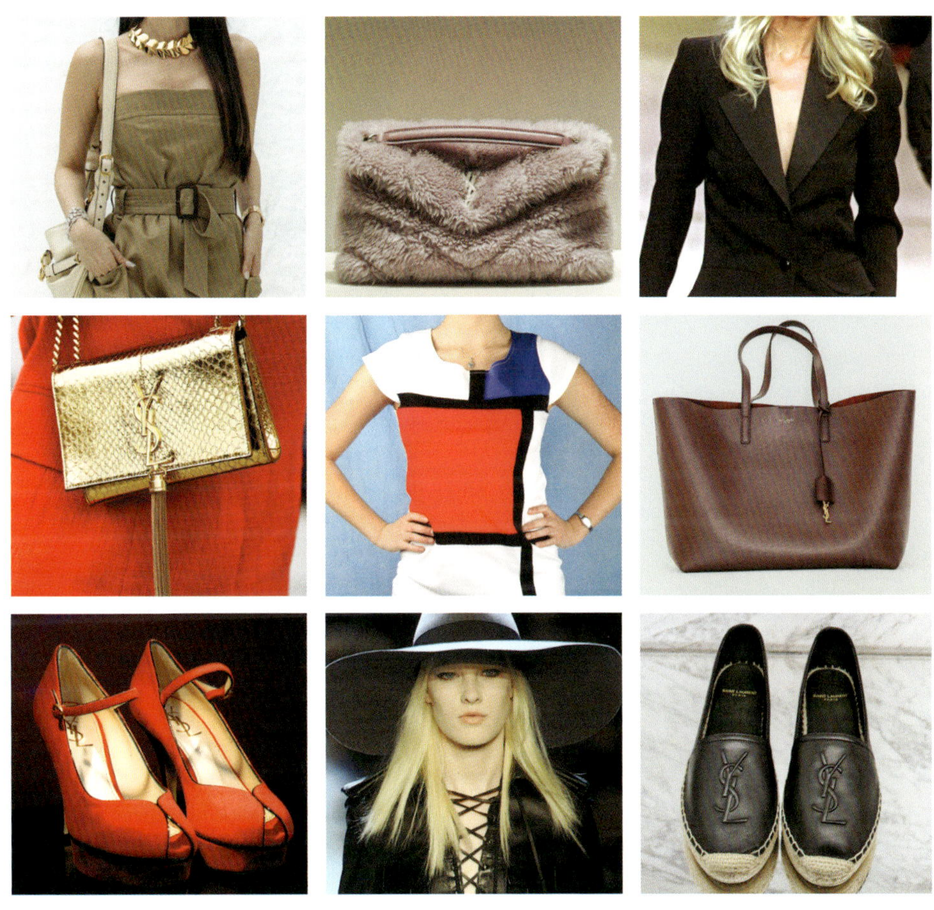

Alison James

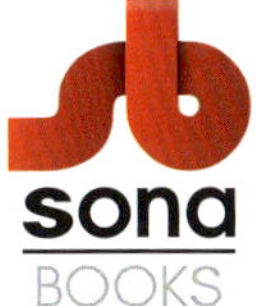

sona BOOKS

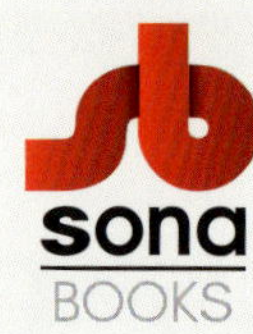

sona
BOOKS

CONTENTS

INTRODUCTION

"Fashions fade, style is eternal"
Yves Saint Laurent

Yves Saint Laurent was more than a fashion designer - he was a visionary who changed the way the world dresses. Over a career spanning four decades, he redefined elegance, introduced new silhouettes and challenged conventions of gender, art and culture through clothing. From the creation of the iconic tuxedo for women to his ground-breaking ready-to-wear line, Saint Laurent shaped modern fashion in ways that continue to influence designers and inspire admiration around the world.

This book is a celebration of his work and his legacy. Through archival photographs, sketches, runway moments and reflections, it explores the creativity, daring and refinement that defined his work. From Paris to Marrakech, from haute couture salons to museum exhibitions, Yves Saint Laurent's spirit lives on - in every sharp line, bold colour and timeless design.

Welcome to the world of a true master.

RIGHT: Yves Saint Laurent with Betty Catroux (left) and Loulou de la Falaise outside his newly opened Rive Gauche boutique in London, 13 September 1969

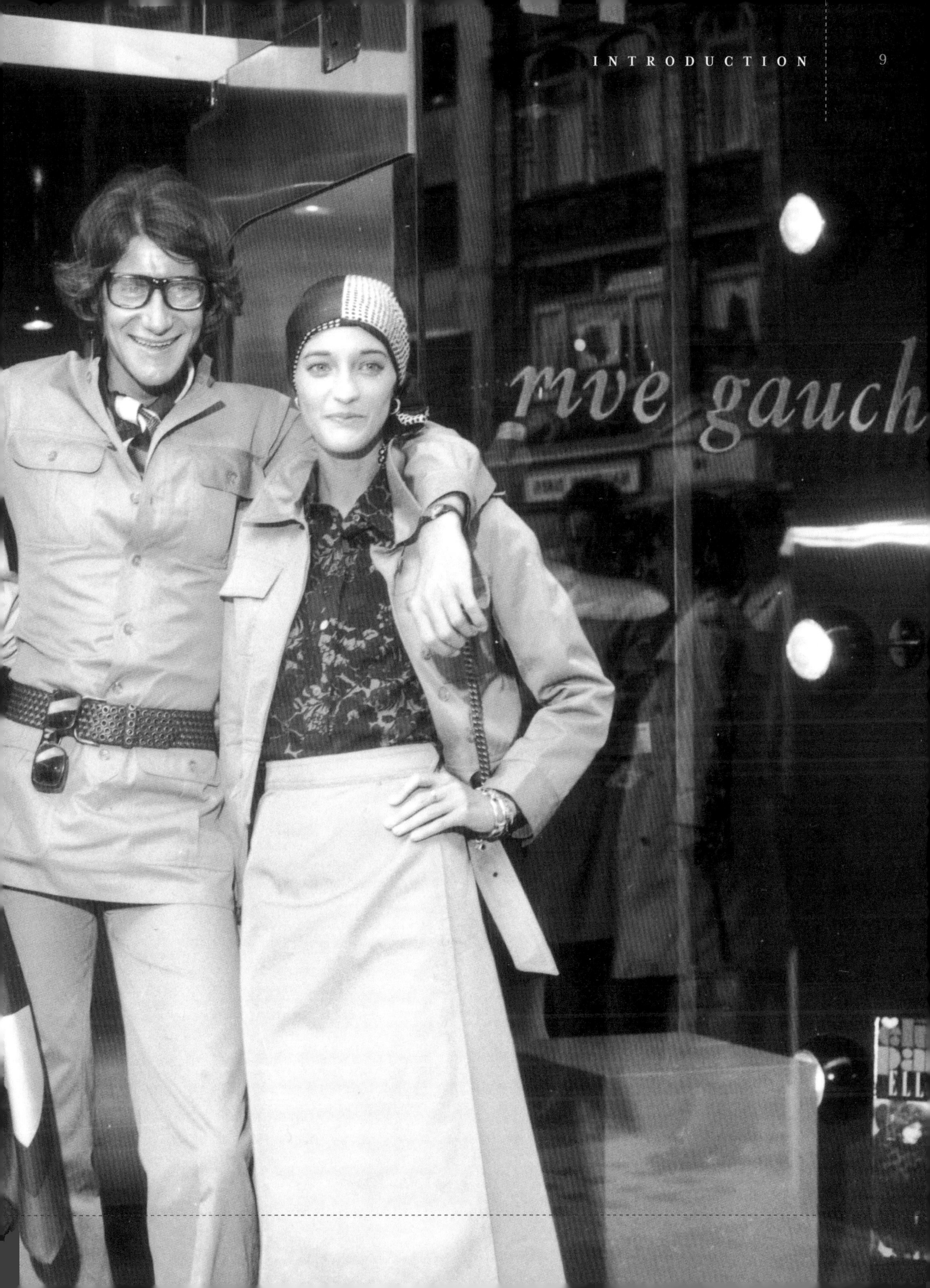

rive gauch

EARLY YEARS

"Oran, not Paris, was our world at the time. Oran, a cosmopolitan place made up of merchants from everywhere and especially somewhere else, was a city that sparkled in a multicoloured patchwork under the calm North African sun"

Yves Saint Laurent

Yves Henri Donat Mathieu Saint Laurent was born on 1 August 1936 in Oran, a vibrant coastal city in what was then French Algeria in northern Africa. He was the only son of Lucienne, a stylish socialite, and Charles Mathieu Saint Laurent, the manager of an insurance company and owner of a chain of cinemas. Raised in an affluent and cultured household, it was a family that valued elegance and refinement, with Yves, and his younger sisters Michèle and Brigitte, growing up among the society people of Oran. From an early age, it was clear that he possessed a unique sensitivity and an artistic inclination that set him apart from his peers.

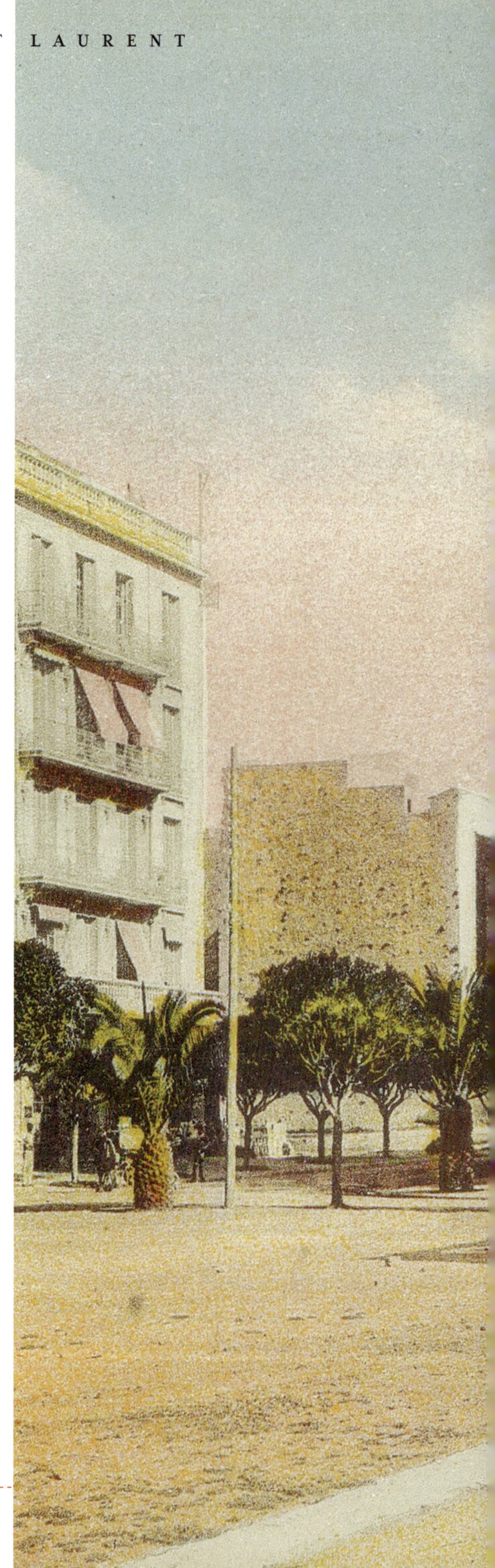

RIGHT: Province of Oran

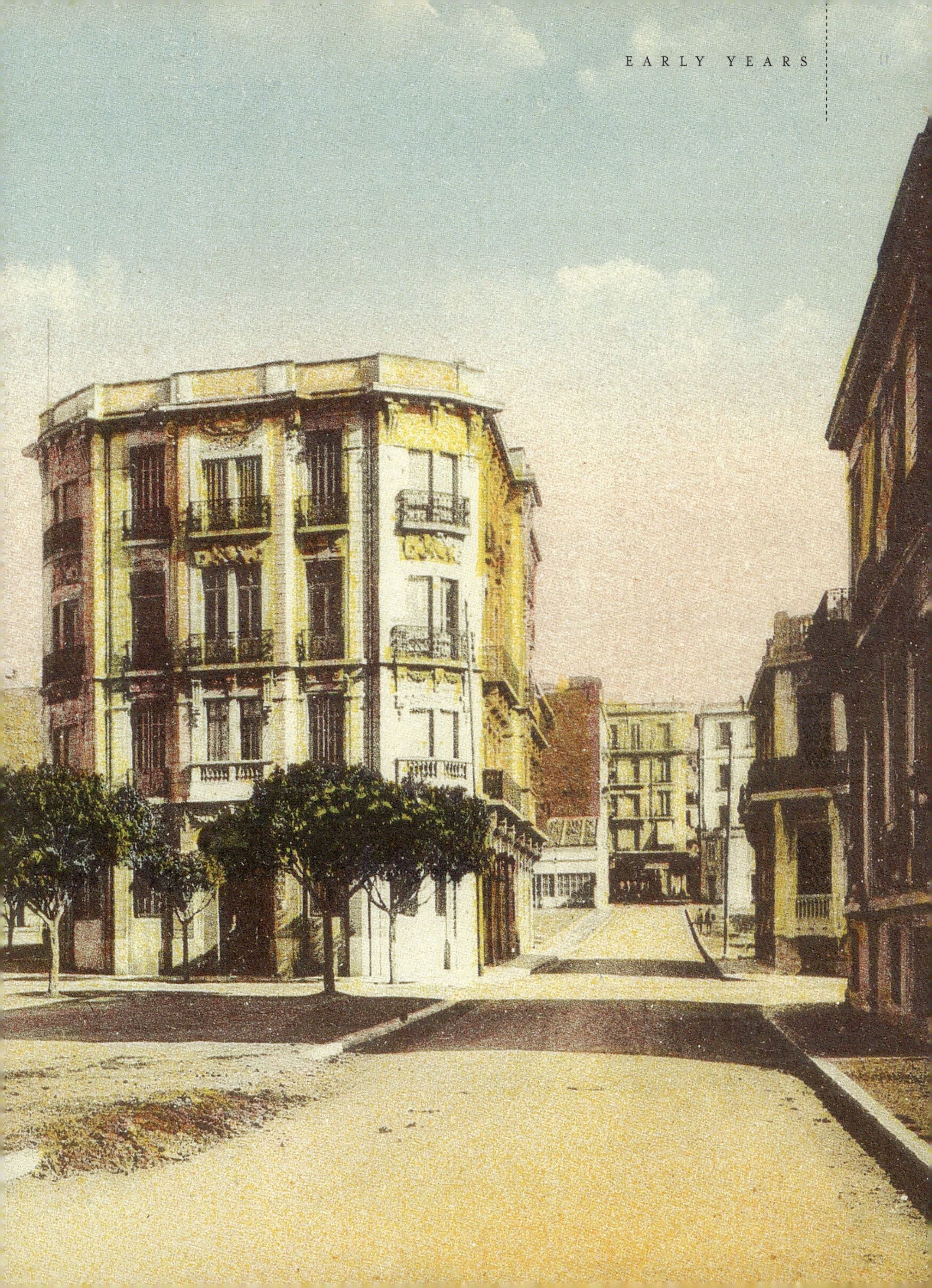

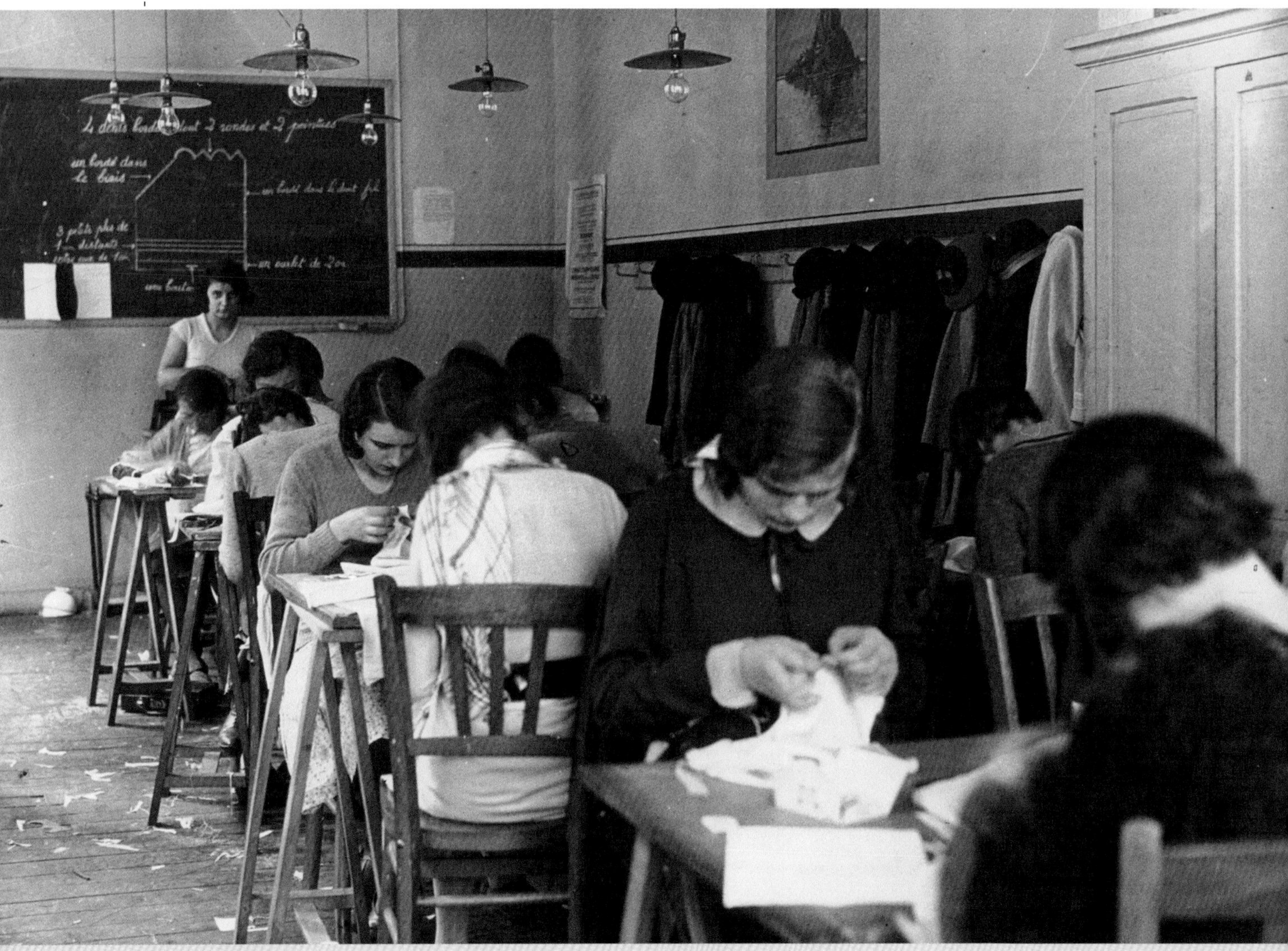

ABOVE: Students at ECSCP, the world-renowned Parisian couture school, 1931

A shy, somewhat introverted child, Yves showed little interest in sports or outdoor activities, preferring instead to immerse himself in drawing and sketching. His early artistic endeavours were encouraged by his stylish mother who recognized his talent and nurtured his passion for creativity. School life was not easy for Yves. His delicate demeanour and artistic nature often made him a target of bullying. He used art and his creativity as an escape from these harsh realities. However, his talent did not go unnoticed by his teachers who encouraged his artistic leanings. Yves would spend hours drawing and sketching – in addition to devouring his mother's fashion magazines for inspiration. He was especially fond of designing and crafting paper dolls which he would dress in exquisite gowns he had drawn. Then, aged 13, he had something of an epiphany.

'I saw a performance of Moliere's "École des Femmes" (School for Wives) starring Louis Jouvet,' he

OPP PAGE: (TOP TO BOTTOM): *Vogue* magazine from 1948, a 1943 Christian Bérard fashion sketch, and Jean Marais' 'La Machine Infernale'

would later recall. *'The set was by Christian Bérard, an immense artist. It had a major impact on me. At the time, the touring theatre productions were outstanding. That was how I discovered Jean Cocteau's "Infernal Machine" starring Jean Marais, Elvire Popesco and Jean-Pierre Aumont, with a set by Bérard.'*

Following this life-changing discovery, Yves Saint Laurent created his 'Illustre Petit Théâtre', a miniature stage set for a series of cardboard characters who wore costumes he designed. This passion for the theatre went hand-in-hand with an interest in literature. He began writing his first poems and spent time transcribing and illustrating Alfred de Musset's 'Les Caprices de Marianne' (Moods of Marianne) and Gustave Flaubert's 'Madame Bovary'. During his adolescence, Saint Laurent also discovered Marcel Proust, whose work would continue to fascinate him throughout his life.

In 1953, aged 17, Yves entered a fashion design competition organized by the International Wool Secretariat. He submitted a series of elegant sketches that caught the attention of the judges. As a result, he moved to Paris enrolling at 'École de la Chambre Syndicale de la Couture Parisienne' (ECSCP), the most prestigious couture industry school in Paris at the time. His talent was such that he stayed for just three months – his skills already far beyond anything the school could teach him. Within weeks, he had been taken on by the iconic fashion house of Christian Dior...

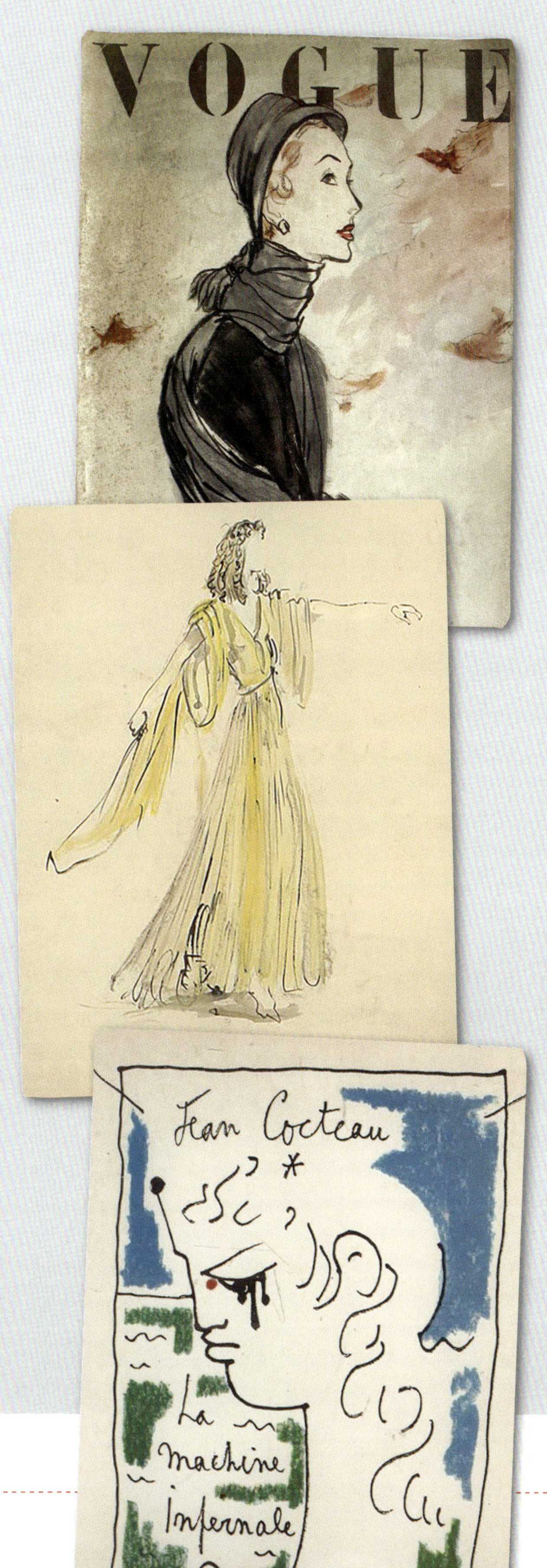

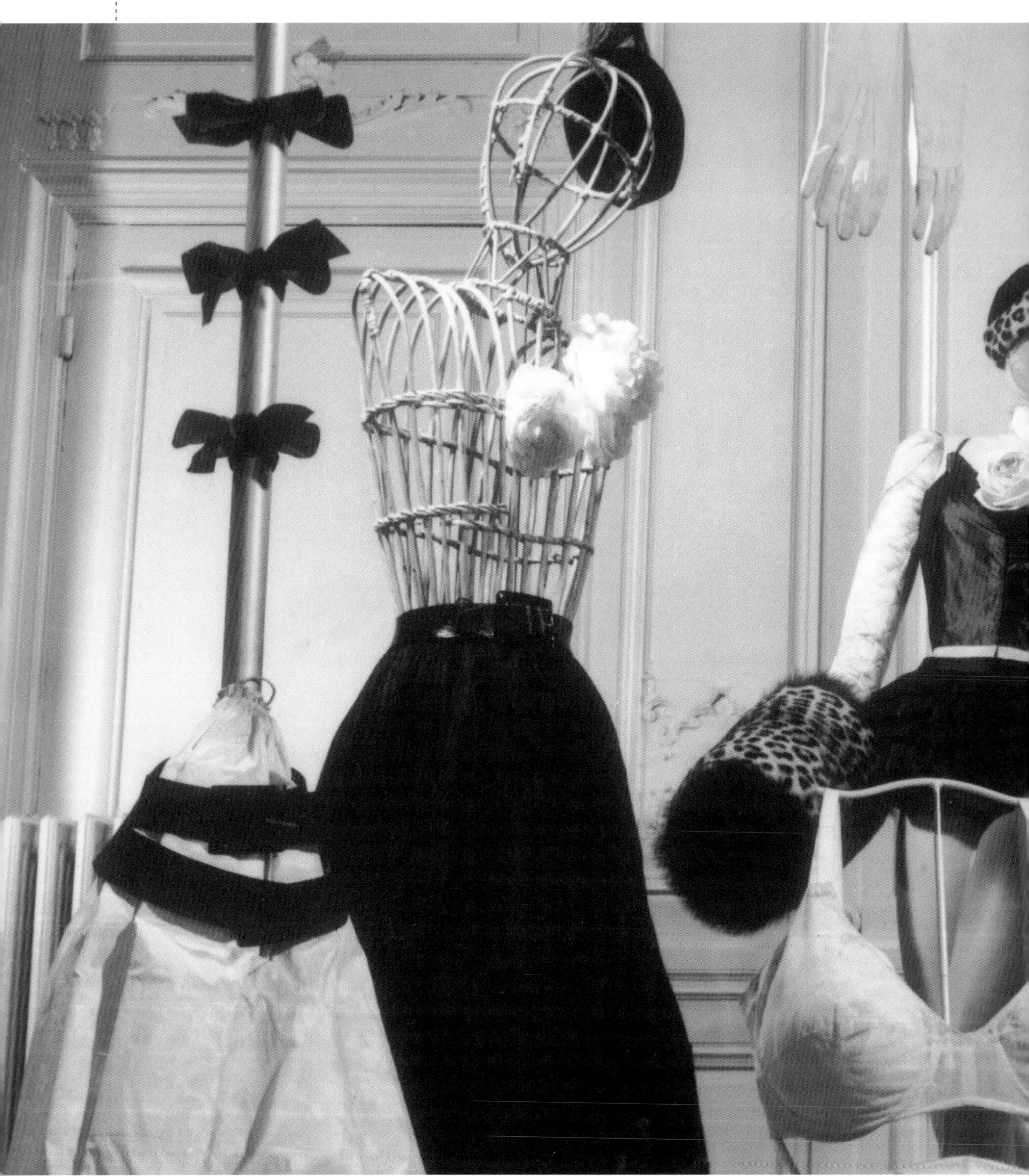

ABOVE: Yves Saint Laurent's first employer, fashion designer Christian Dior, standing in a showroom with samples of his accessory designs in 1955

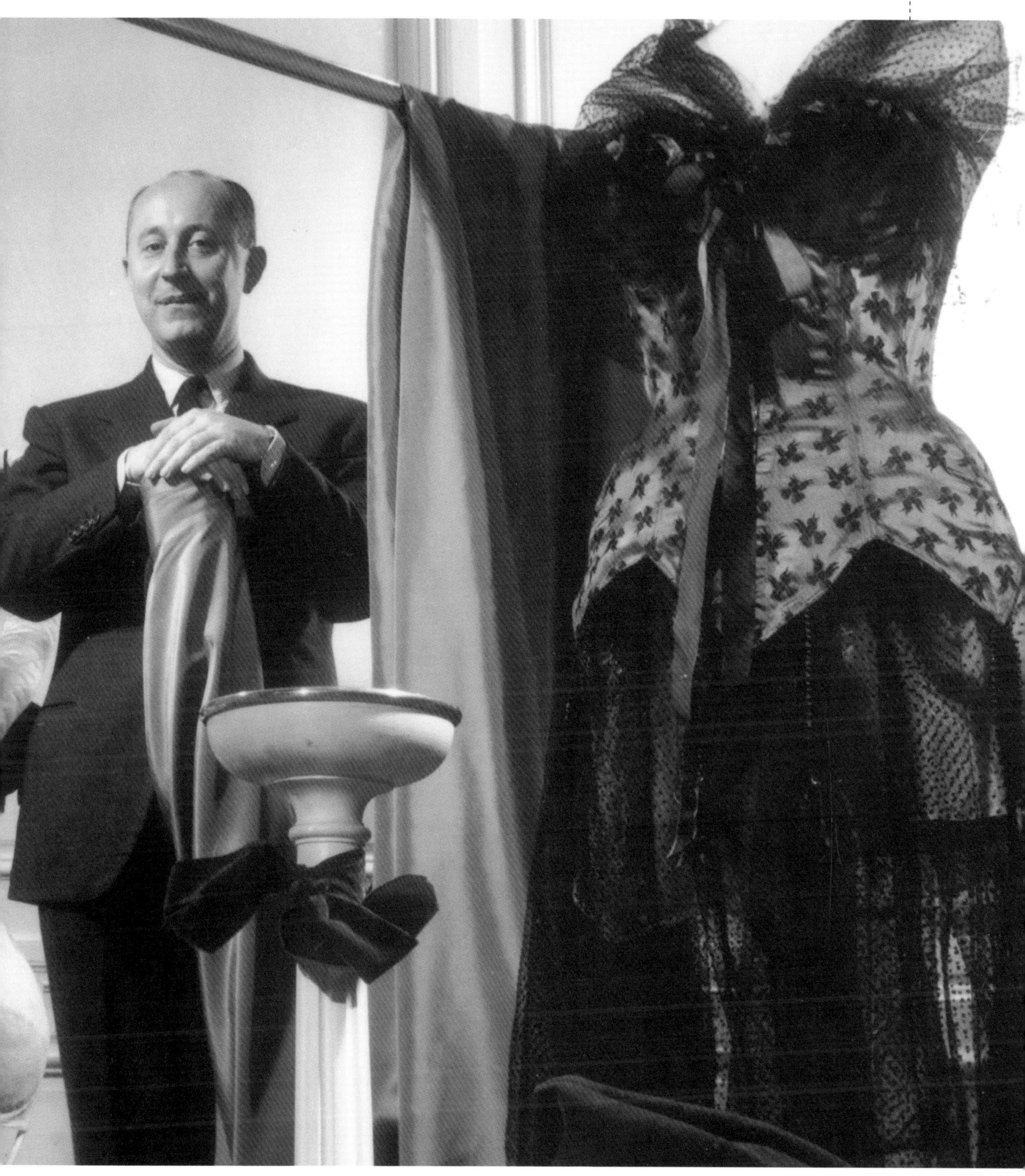

DIOR

"Yves Saint Laurent is young, but he is an immense talent. In my last collection, I consider him to be the father of 34 out of the 180 designs. I think the time has come to reveal it to the press. My prestige won't suffer from it"
Christian Dior

It was Michel de Brunhoff, a contact of Yves father's and also the editor of *Vogue Paris*, who introduced the 19-year-old to legendary designer Christian Dior in 1955. De Brunhoff and YSL had initially made contact two years earlier with the influential journalist suggesting the prodigiously talented teen continue with his studies. In letters, Saint Laurent had asked de Brunhoff for advice about his future career.

'As you recommended, I paint profusely and also continue to design scale models, sets, and costumes as well as dresses.' Saint Laurent wrote.

On being shown Yves' drawings and sketches, de Brunhoff was immediately taken by the young

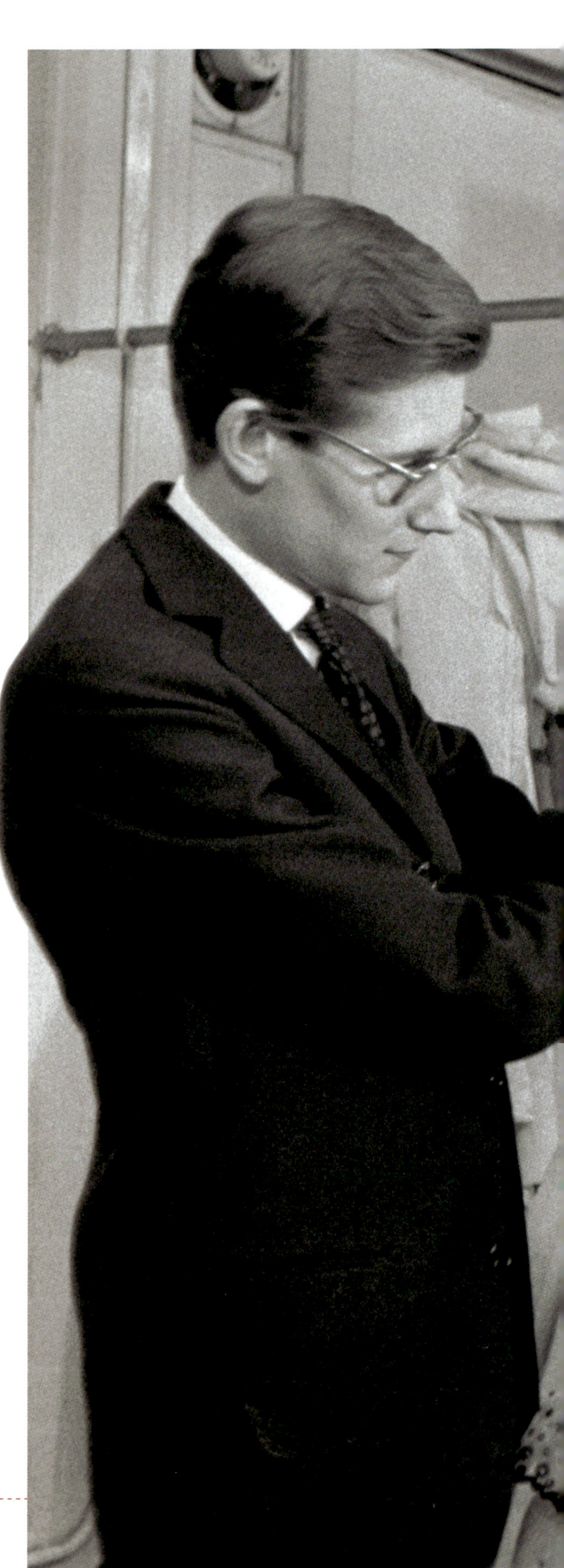

RIGHT: Dior designer Yves Saint Laurent puts the finishing touches on a dress worn by model Kouka Denis, 1959

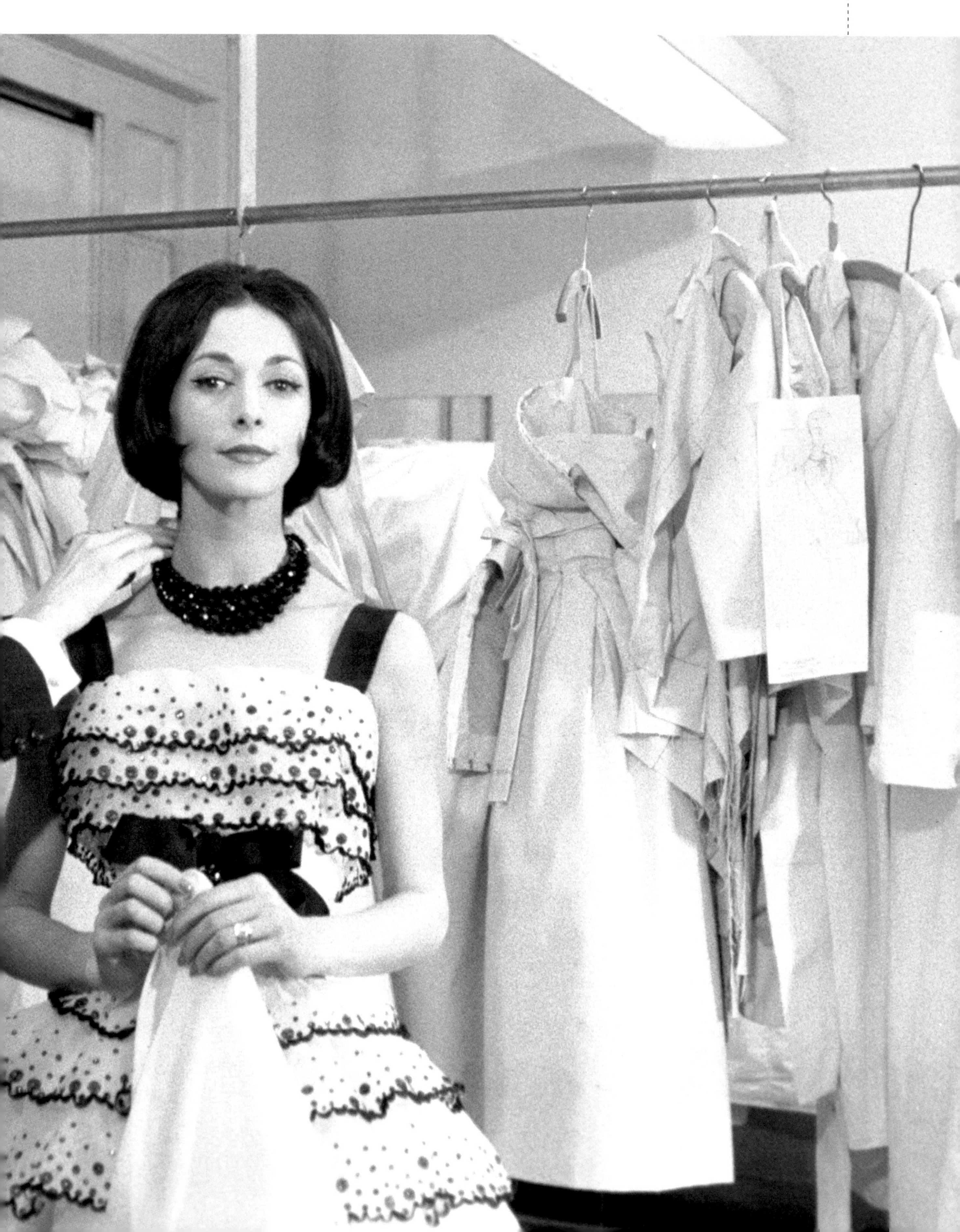

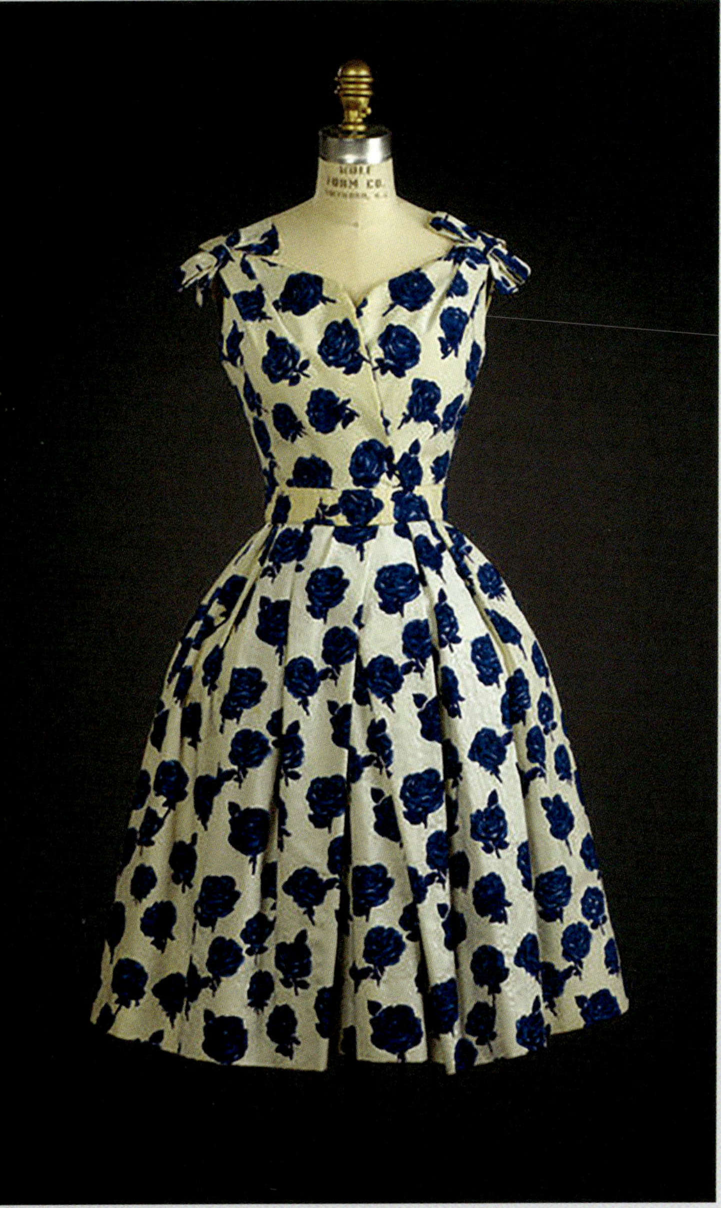

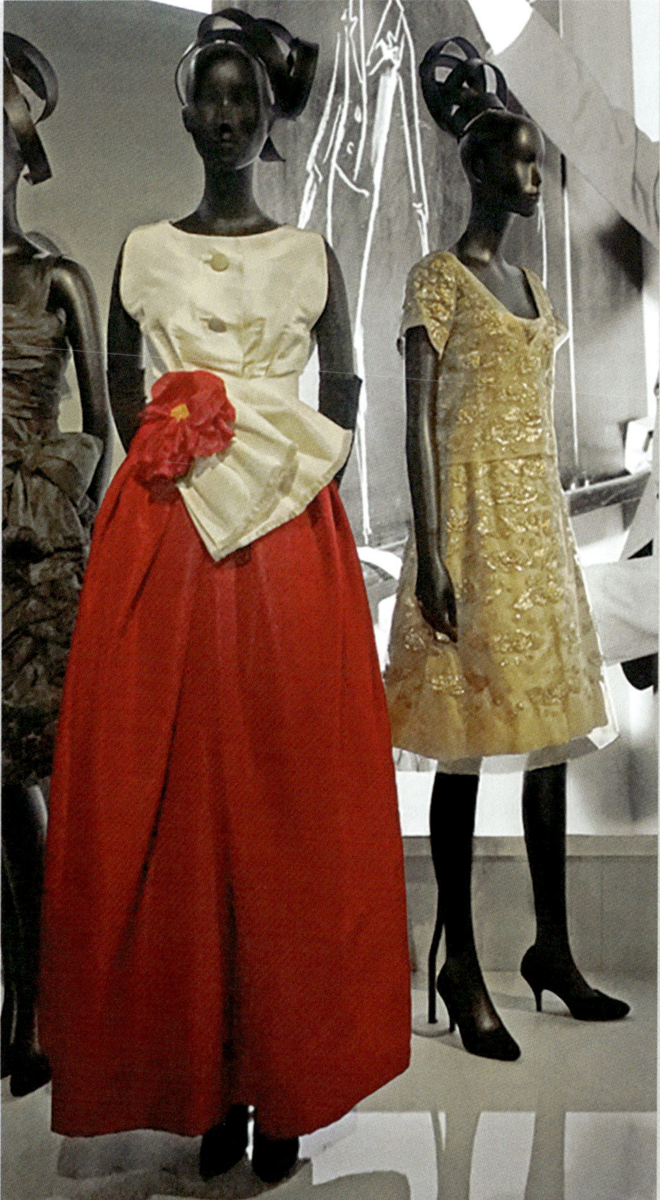

man's talent and the close resemblance between his drawings and Christian Dior's A-line designs. He immediately contacted Dior.

'I have never in my life met anyone more gifted. If the young man grows up to become a great man, have a thought for me...' de Brunhoff wrote.

He arranged for Saint Laurent to meet Dior at 30 Avenue Montaigne, the label's premises, where YSL was immediately hired to work in the legendary couturier's studio. Dior saw the teenager as a kindred spirit with the potential to one day become his successor. Saint Laurent was initially entrusted with decorating the Dior boutiques but under the 'New Look' icon's instruction, he absorbed

ABOVE: (LEFT) 1960 cocktail dress in printed cotton by Yves Saint Laurent for Dior. (RIGHT) Haute couture dresses by Yves Saint Laurent for Christian Dior, 1957–1960
OPP PAGE: Black silk tissue taffeta dress by Yves Saint Laurent for Christian Dior, July 1959

the master's techniques and aesthetic philosophy while contributing sketches and refining his own sense of proportion, silhouette and fabric. He also helped create a number of haute couture dresses. Earning Dior's trust, he was given more and more responsibilities. Dior, known for his romantic and feminine designs, took Saint Laurent under his wing, recognizing his gift for innovation while ensuring he understood the house's legacy. It was during these formative years that Saint Laurent honed his skills, preparing for an eventual leadership role. Yves Saint Laurent spent two years working alongside Christian Dior, learning the secrets of haute couture from the master himself.

'He taught me the essentials,' Saint Laurent wrote in 1986. *'Then came other influences that, because he had taught me the essentials, blended into a wonderful and prolific terrain, the necessary seeds that would allow me to assert myself, grow strong, blossom, and finally exude my own universe.'*

In October 1957, tragedy struck when Christian Dior passed away unexpectedly from a heart attack. The fashion world was left in shock, and the future of the house was uncertain. Just weeks later, at the age of 21, Yves Saint Laurent was named Dior's new artistic director. Entrusting the most prestigious fashion house in Paris to someone so young and inexperienced was an unprecedented move but YSL's first collection would soon silence any doubts. For this outing, Saint Laurent set himself apart from his late mentor. Using less fabric than Dior's signature 'New Look' cinched waist style and

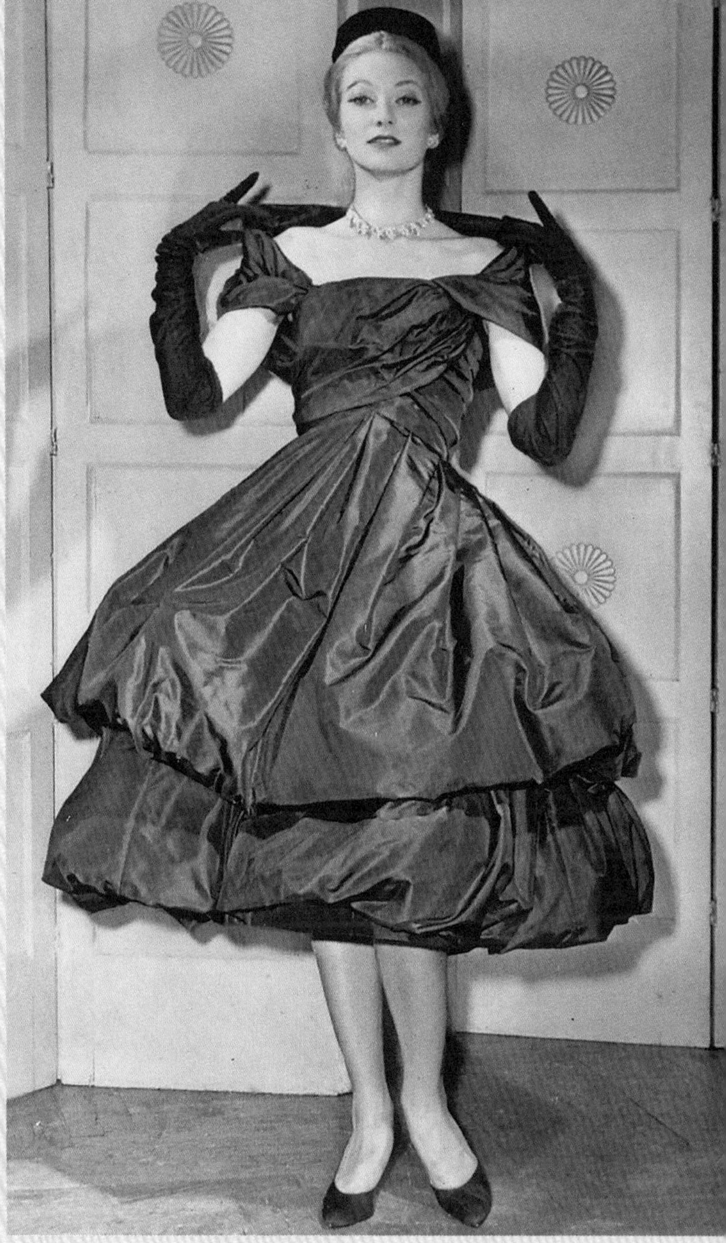

employing a lighter approach, YSL created a softer and more fluid, more subtle silhouette which allowed for greater movement and ease. Voila! The Trapeze line was born. It was an instant success, hailed as a modern evolution of couture and solidifying Saint Laurent's

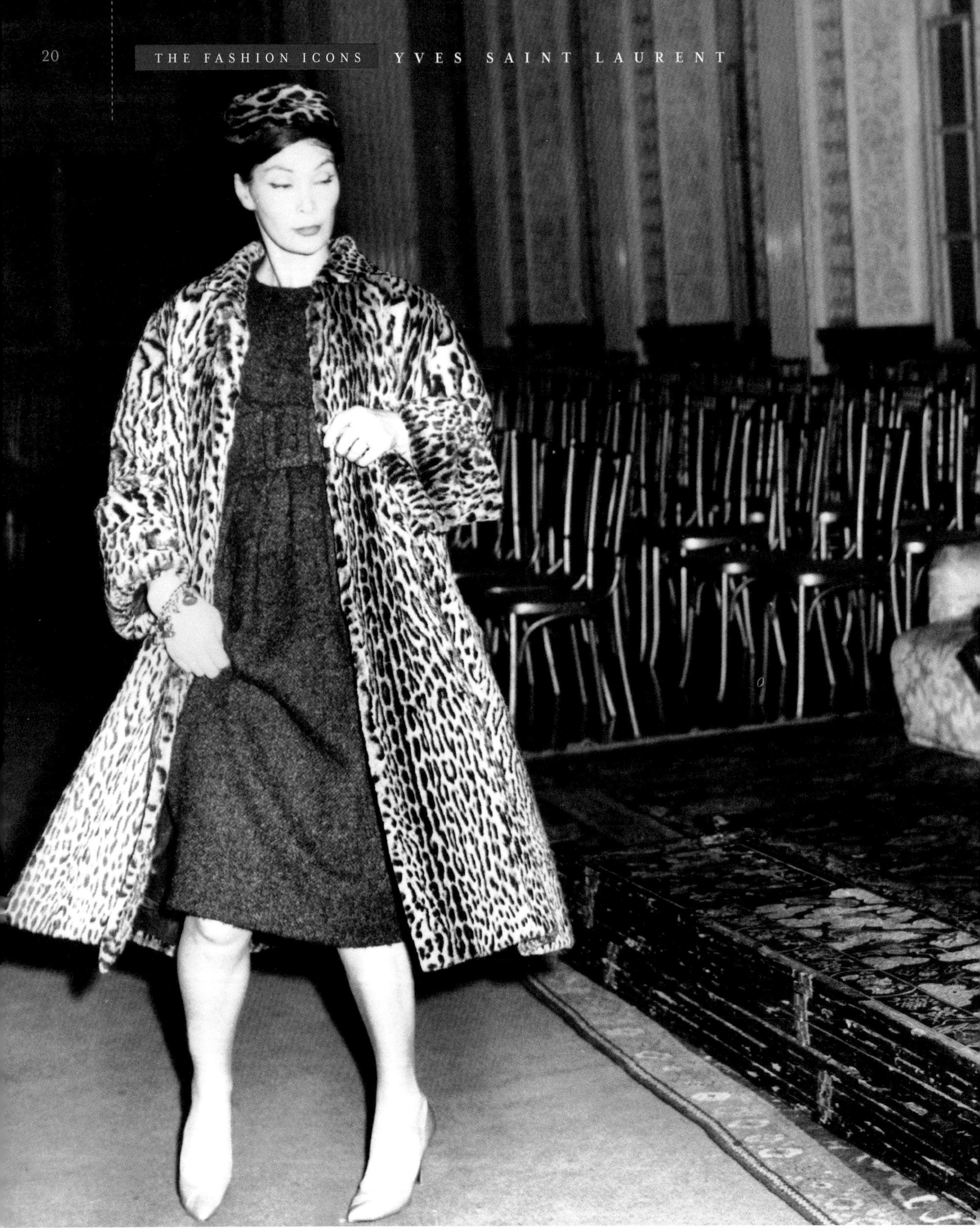

ABOVE: Yves Saint Laurent, of the House of Christian Dior, preparing to unveil the Paris winter collection at Blenheim Palace, 1958

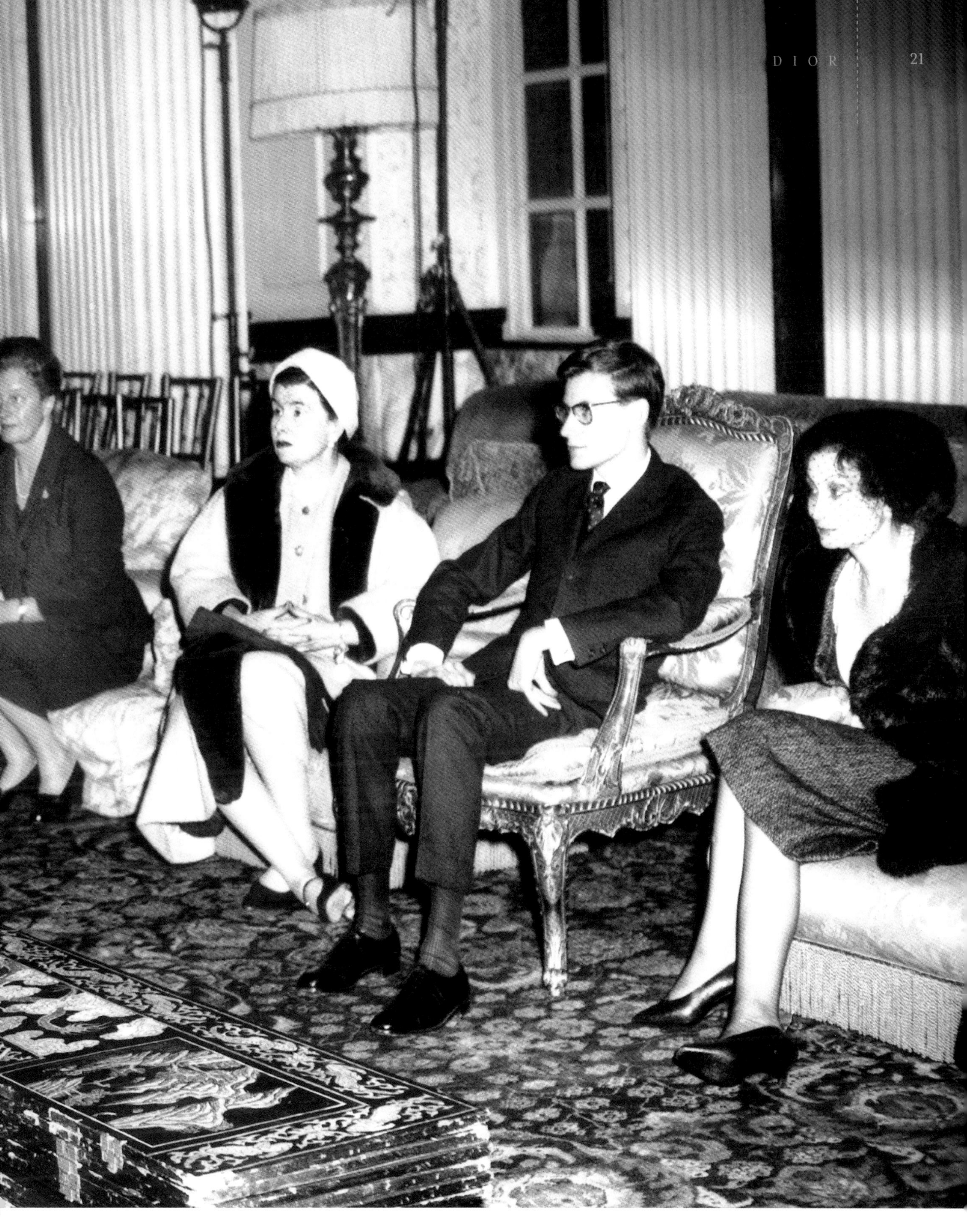

reputation as a visionary. Fashion editors who dubbed YSL as *the little prince of fashion*, clients, and celebrities flocked to Dior to embrace this fresh perspective on femininity and style. It was at the collection's launch that Yves Saint Laurent first became acquainted with business man Pierre Berge who would become his future partner in both a personal and professional capacity.

However, Saint Laurent's second and third collections were not received so well. The designer was in his early 20s and wished to imbue haute couture with a more youthful and contemporary feel. He simplified designs, ignoring the more conventional dictates of haute couture fashion. In his view, style had to evolve from collection to collection and he sought inspiration from the fashion he saw on the streets of Paris. This would lie at the root of his first setback. His 1960 'Beat Look' collection – officially entitled *Souplesse, Légèreté, Vie'* (suppleness, lightness, life) - was influenced by the emerging beatnik movement and 'Rive Gauche' bohemians, and made use of leather and dark colours. Indeed, Saint Laurent was the first to propose a leather jacket as an haute couture piece. However, neither the press nor Dior customers were convinced. The edgy, rebellious designs were met with resistance from both Dior's traditional clientele and the media.

'The figure was lost in favour of style,' opined one critic.

The Dior management grew increasingly uneasy. In September 1960, as conflict in Algeria intensified, Yves Saint Laurent was drafted for military service. It was not a good fit. He lasted only three weeks in the French Army before he suffered a nervous breakdown. Bullied by fellow soldiers for being delicate and different, extreme stress had triggered serious psychiatric problems. After his breakdown, he was hospitalised in a military hospital, where he was subjected to harsh treatments, including electroshock therapy and heavy sedation. His stay there deeply traumatized him. Eventually, through the intervention of his friends, lawyers and also his partner Pierre Bergé, he was medically discharged from the military. However, there would be no return to Dior. The House decided to fire him and replace him with more traditional designer Marc Bohan. When Pierre Bergé delivered the news, Saint Laurent said, *'We will found a haute couture house together, and you will manage it'*, to which Bergé replied, *'That is what we will do.'* It was a vow that would become a reality.

Saint Laurent's years at Dior had already cemented his legacy. He had proven himself a force to be reckoned with, showcasing his talent for blending elegance with innovation and setting the stage for his own eponymous brand. The Dior years were both a blessing and a curse for Saint Laurent. They had provided him with an unparalleled platform, but also subjected him to immense pressure at a young age. Yet, his time at the House remains one of the most significant chapters in fashion history - a moment when a young genius reshaped couture and laid the foundation for modern style.

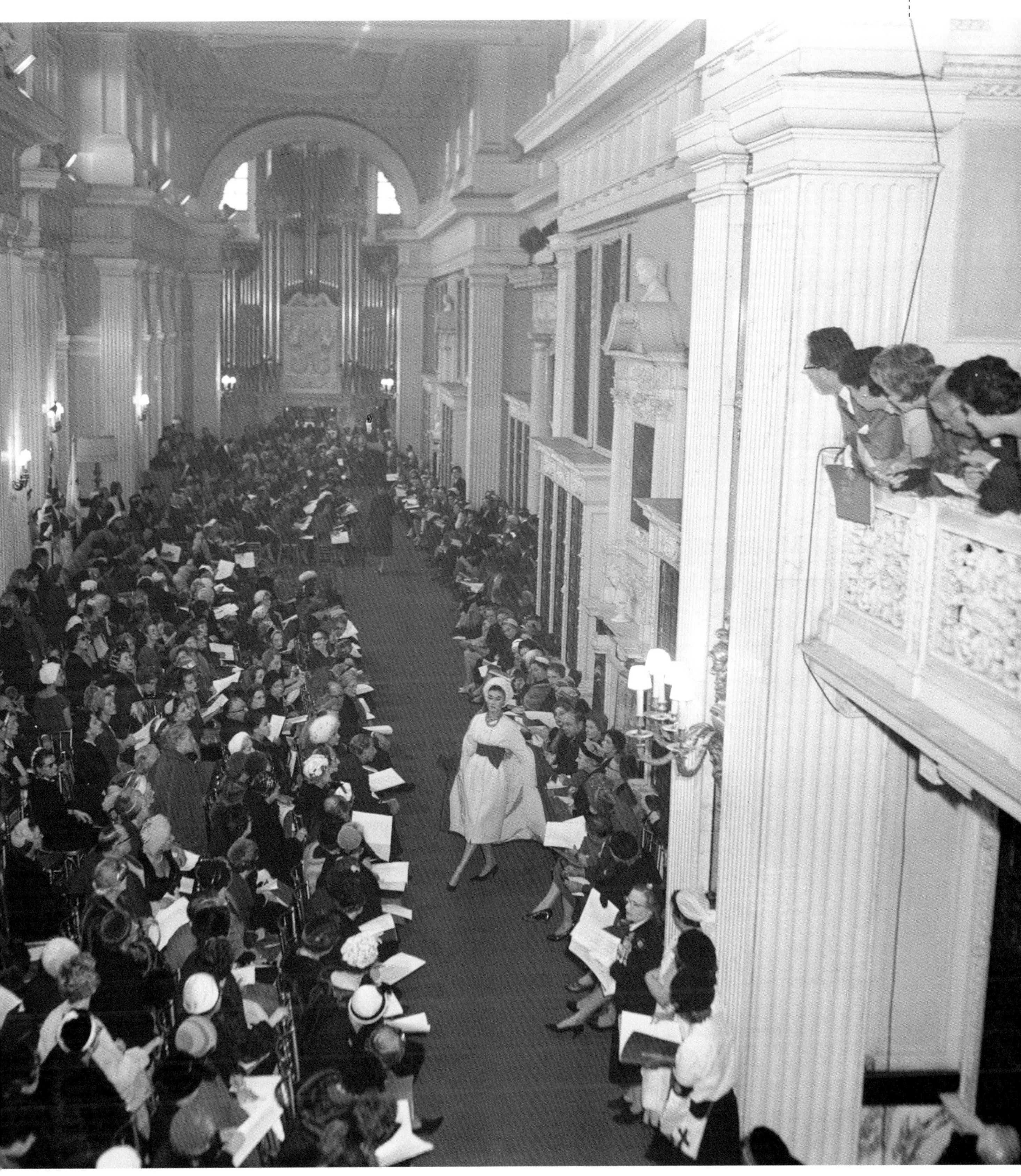

YSL

"Fashions fade, style is eternal"
Yves Saint Laurent

With Pierre Bergé's support, Yves Saint Laurent pursued legal action against Dior, citing his sacking as a breach of his employment contract. He was successful, winning the lawsuit and being awarded approximately $60,000 (worth over 10 times that today) in damages. With these funds, along with financial backing from an American source, Saint Laurent and Bergé founded the House of Yves Saint Laurent (YSL). It was a partnership that would not only redefine Yves' career but also influence the future of fashion.

YSL's first premises were located at 30 bis Rue Spontini in the 16th arrondissement of Paris. The space was elegant but relatively modest compared to the grand luxury houses of the time. It was a reflection of Saint Laurent's modern, innovative approach to fashion - intimate yet sophisticated. The embryonic label's logo, entwining the initials 'YSL', was designed by French graphic artist Adolphe Jean-Marie Mouron, better known as 'Cassandre'. This original form of the logo continues to be used as part of the House iconography today.

RIGHT: Yves Saint Laurent creation on a model beside
a logo-branded car for the new boutique, circa 1961

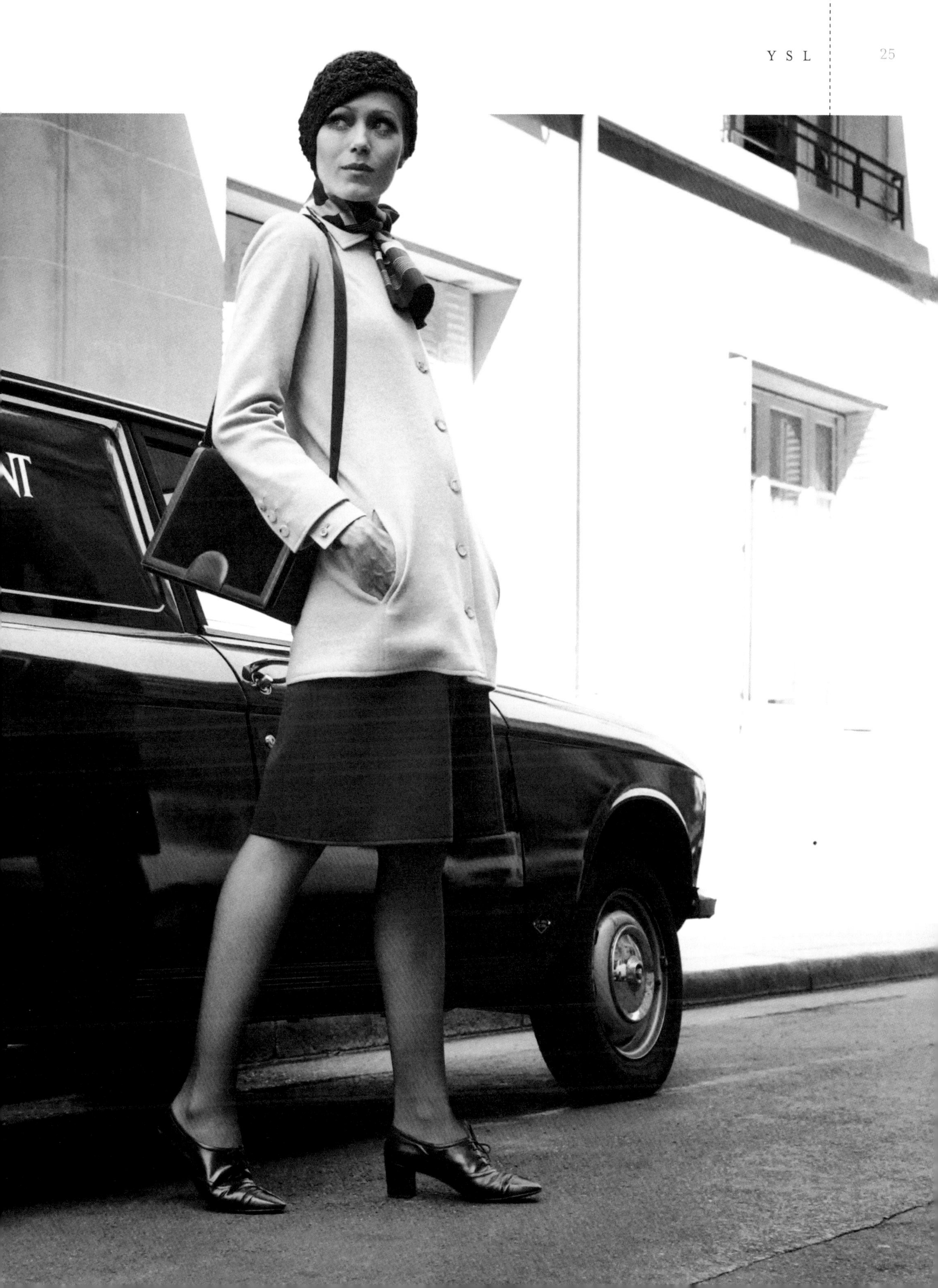

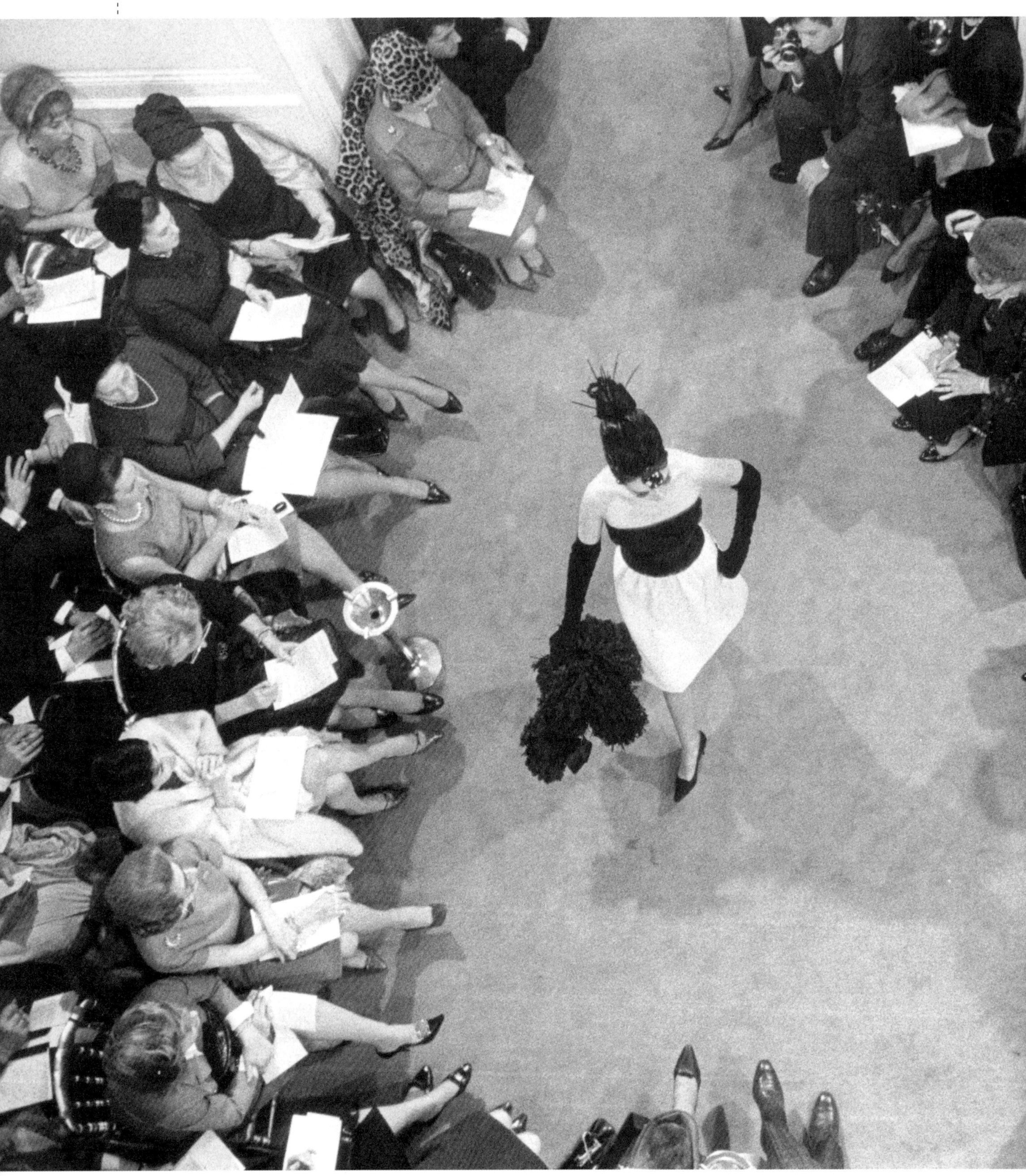

ABOVE: Presentation of the first collection from the Yves Saint Laurent house, 29 January, 1962

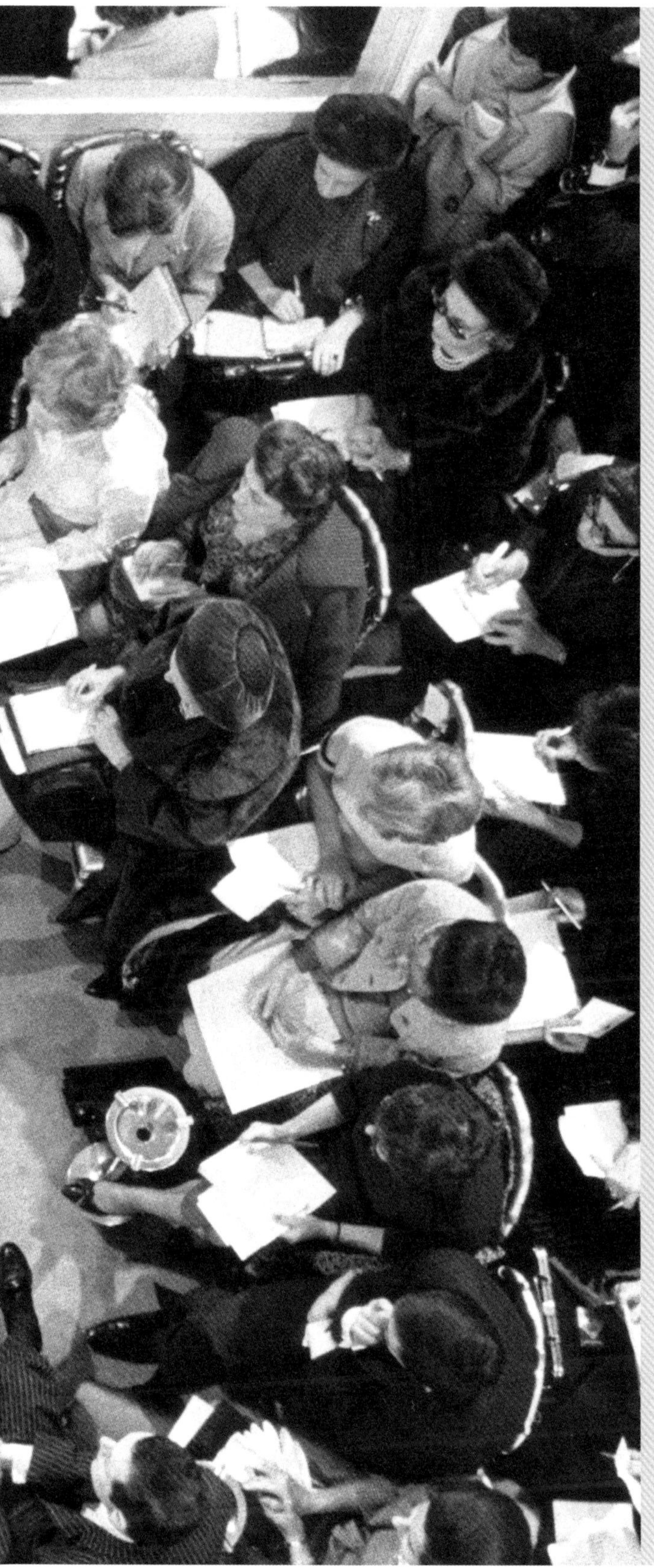

In January 1962, Saint Laurent presented his inaugural collection for Spring/Summer at 30 bis Rue Spontini. The Countess of Paris, Princess Margaret, the Baroness de Rothschild, Roland Petit, Zizi Jeanmaire, Geneviève Fath, Françoise Sagan, and members of the fashion industry came to witness the comeback of *the little prince of fashion'*. Saint Laurent later admitted he was terrified before this first show, knowing full well that everyone would be comparing him to Dior. He worried that if it failed, he wouldn't just lose a show — he would lose everything he had built post Dior and potentially lose his future.

'I was fighting not only for my life but for my vision of what fashion could be,' he said.

The collection was a marriage of old school sartorial style embued with a spirit of youthful rebellion, living up to his vision of it being *'a love letter to youth, freedom, and real life'* which would *'give women the freedom to move, to live, to be themselves'.*

Sleek, modern and elegant, key pieces included pea coats and trench coats inspired by menswear, tailored suits with a softer silhouette than previous more rigid couture styles, shift dresses that embraced a youthful and relaxed aesthetic, and stylishly simple knee-length skirts in contrast to the fuller silhouettes of the previous decade. It was a fresh and youthful take on Parisienne chic and largely well received, although some of the fashion old guard felt it too modern, too casual, for haute couture.

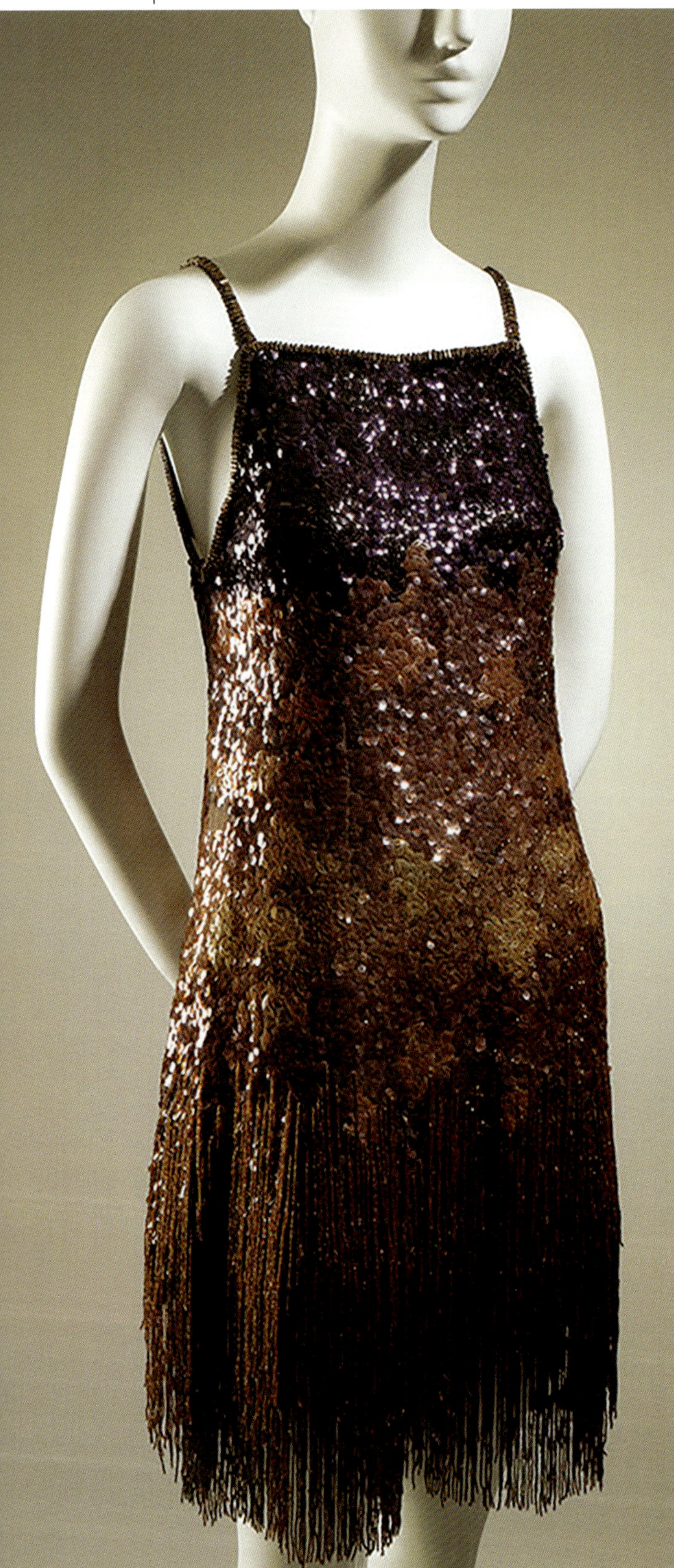

Harper's Bazaar wrote that Saint Laurent could **'***lead fashion into a new decade***'**, *French Vogue* opined the collection was *'a confident debut'* while *The New York Times* claimed the collection was *'bold and divisive'*. However French newspaper *Le Figaro* maintained it was *'the rise of fashion for the street not the salon'*.

With his second collection (Fall–Winter 1962), Yves Saint Laurent responded to the critics by showing more 'serious' haute couture craftsmanship. However, he didn't give up on his youthful, 'Rive Gauche' aesthetic – rather he refined it. He demonstrated he could still create luxurious, classic couture — but with a twist. The collection incorporated beautiful tailoring, sharper silhouettes and rich fabrics – velvet, brocade and heavy silks. The palette leaned toward black, which would evolve as a YSL lifelong signature shade, deep navy, plum, and charcoal — all of which gave the garments a moodier, more intellectual feel. The pea coat design from the first YSL collection continued to feature but with a more elegant feel incorporating softer shoulders and more luxurious detail. During this second collection, Saint Laurent first experimented with masculine/feminine tailoring, sowing the seeds of his 'Le Smoking' tuxedo which would come to fruition in 1966. Some coats and jackets from this collection already had an edge of crisp, androgynous sharpness. Though not as pop-art-inspired as later collections, this second collection hinted at YSL's love of art and minimalism, which would explode with the iconic Mondrian dress in 1965. *Elle* and *Harper's Bazaar* praised his **'***brilliant future***'**

ABOVE: 1969 Yves Saint Laurent beaded evening dress
OPP PAGE: *Harper's Bazaar* magazine, 1960s

and called the collection *'youthful with poise'*. It was felt that while Yves Saint Laurent had matured, he hadn't lost his modern vision. This second collection proved he wasn't a 'one-hit wonder', demonstrating he could be both radical and classic at the same time — a tough balance to pull off. The thinking was that Yves Saint Laurent was not merely designing clothes, he was also designing the future.

The role of Pierre Bergé in the brand's burgeoning success cannot be underestimated. While Yves was the visionary behind the label, Bergé was instrumental in managing the business aspects, ensuring the brand expanded globally and that Yves' designs reached international markets. Together, they became a formidable team, with Bergé often serving as Yves' stabilizing force. By the mid-1960s, Yves Saint Laurent's name was synonymous with cutting-edge fashion. His brand's international expansion began with boutiques in cities like New York and London. This period also saw the advent of major fashion shows, which were more than just showcases for clothing. They were carefully curated spectacles that brought new concepts of creativity and artistic expression to the fashion world. The YSL brand became a symbol of sophistication, elegance and intellectualism, attracting not only fashion elites but also cultural figures from across the world. The founding of Yves Saint Laurent wasn't just a business venture - it was part of a larger cultural revolution in the 1960s. Yves understood the changing times and his work was deeply intertwined with the social upheavals of the era. His designs for women challenged the status quo, and

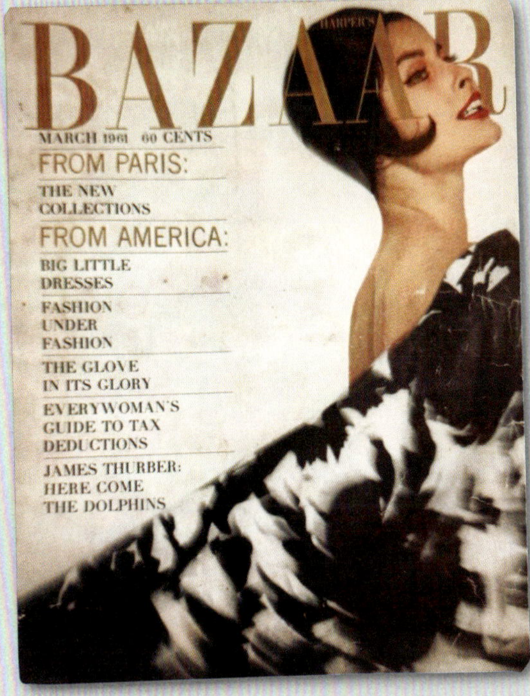

he quickly became an ally of the feminist movement, advocating for women's freedom and empowerment through fashion. From the outset, Yves Saint Laurent created practical, bold, and beautiful clothing that reflected the modern woman's desires. He never stopped evolving, and the Yves Saint Laurent brand would continue to be a benchmark of innovation, style, and cultural relevance for decades to come.

Yves Saint Laurent's decision to establish his own fashion house was a pivotal moment in the history of fashion. It wasn't just about creating beautiful clothes; it was about creating an identity, a movement and a lasting legacy. His partnership with Pierre Bergé ensured that his vision came to life and the early collections laid the foundation for what would become one of the most influential and iconic fashion houses in the world.

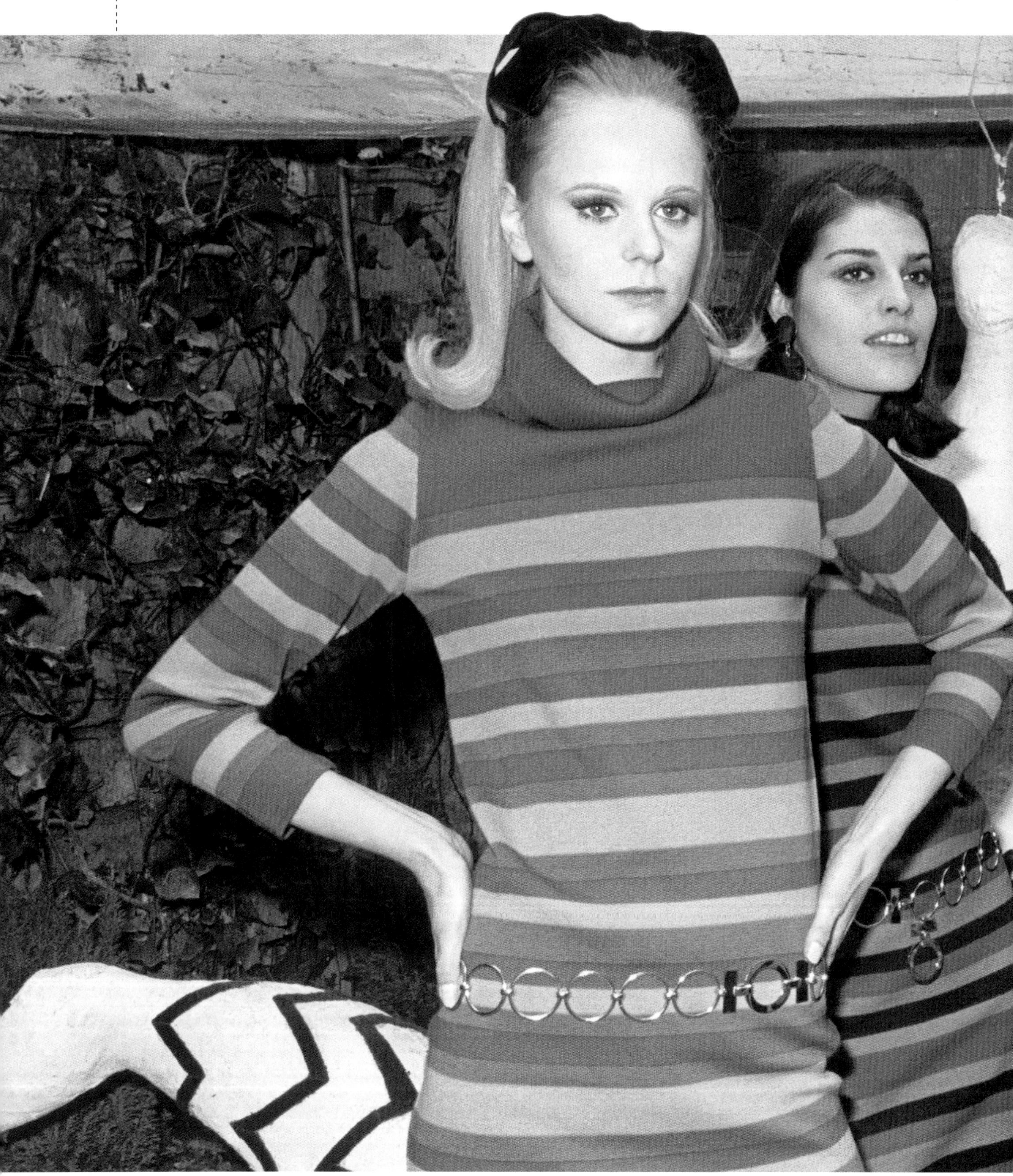

ABOVE: Yves Saint Laurent with three models at the inauguration of his first boutique on Rue de Tournon, 1966

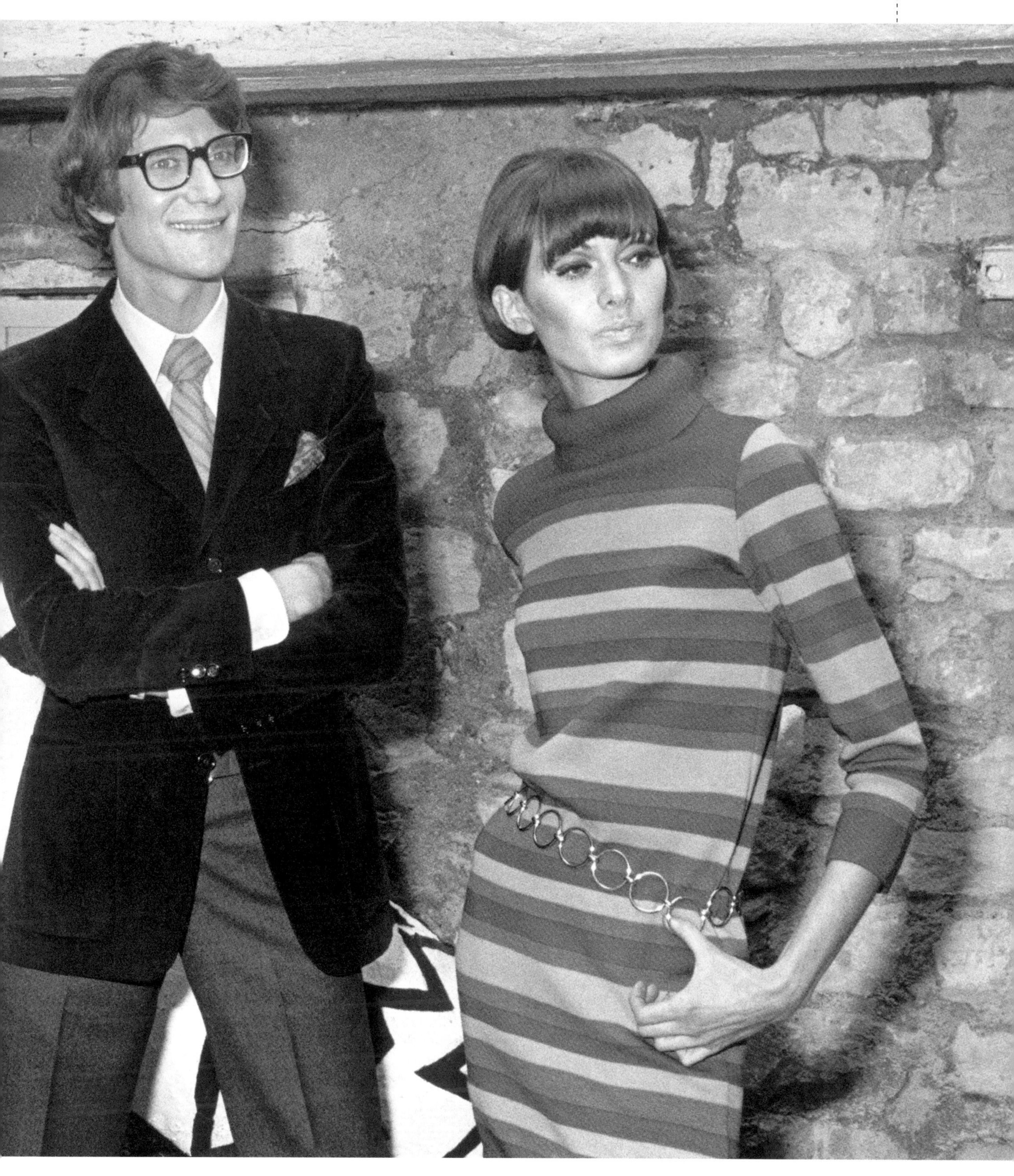

HOMAGE TO MONDRIAN

"The Mondrian dresses are examples of my efforts to approach fashion as art"

Yves Saint Laurent

In 1965, Yves Saint Laurent created one of the most iconic garments of the 20th century - the Mondrian dress. It was part of his Fall/Winter haute couture collection of that year and inspired by the paintings of Dutch modernist artist Piet Mondrian (1872-1944), known for his abstract works - grids of black lines and blocks of red, blue, white and yellow. Yves had been introduced to Mondrian's work by his mother who gifted him a book on the Dutch artist's work – 'Piet Mondrian Sa Vie, Son Oeuvre' by Michel Seuphor - in the 1950s. YSL was particularly taken with Mondrian's ability to paint with absolute 'purity'.

'I love Mondrian. I love the rigidity, the cleanness, and the directness of his work,' he commented.

Out of 160 models who walked the runway for Yves Saint Laurent in the Fall/Winter 1965 show, 26 sported Mondrian looks – quite an achievement when the dresses were, in fact, created only a month prior to the show. Although the design of the Mondrian dress looked simple — clean black lines and flat blocks of colour — the construction required incredible precision and technical mastery. Rather than simply printing the iconic Mondrian design onto plain fabric, YSL constructed each garment to mimic the artist's exact style. In effect, turning a knee-length, sleek, sleeveless, A-line designed dress into a three-dimensional form constructed as a kind of patchwork

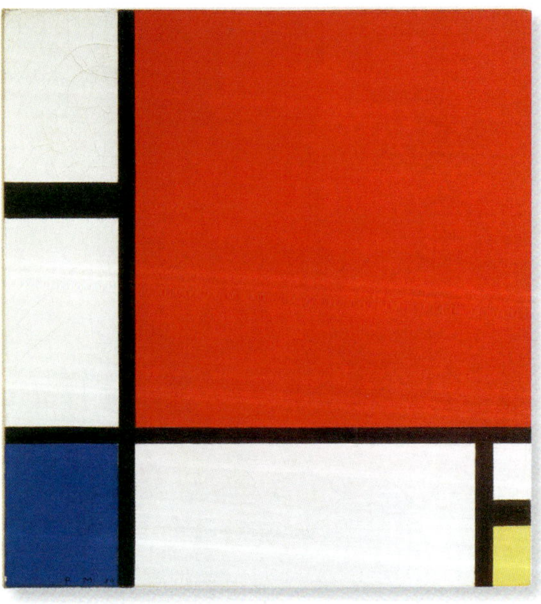

ABOVE: Composition II in Red, Blue, and Yellow by Piet Mondrian, 1930

OPP PAGE: A model in an Yves Saint Laurent Mondrian-style mini-dress

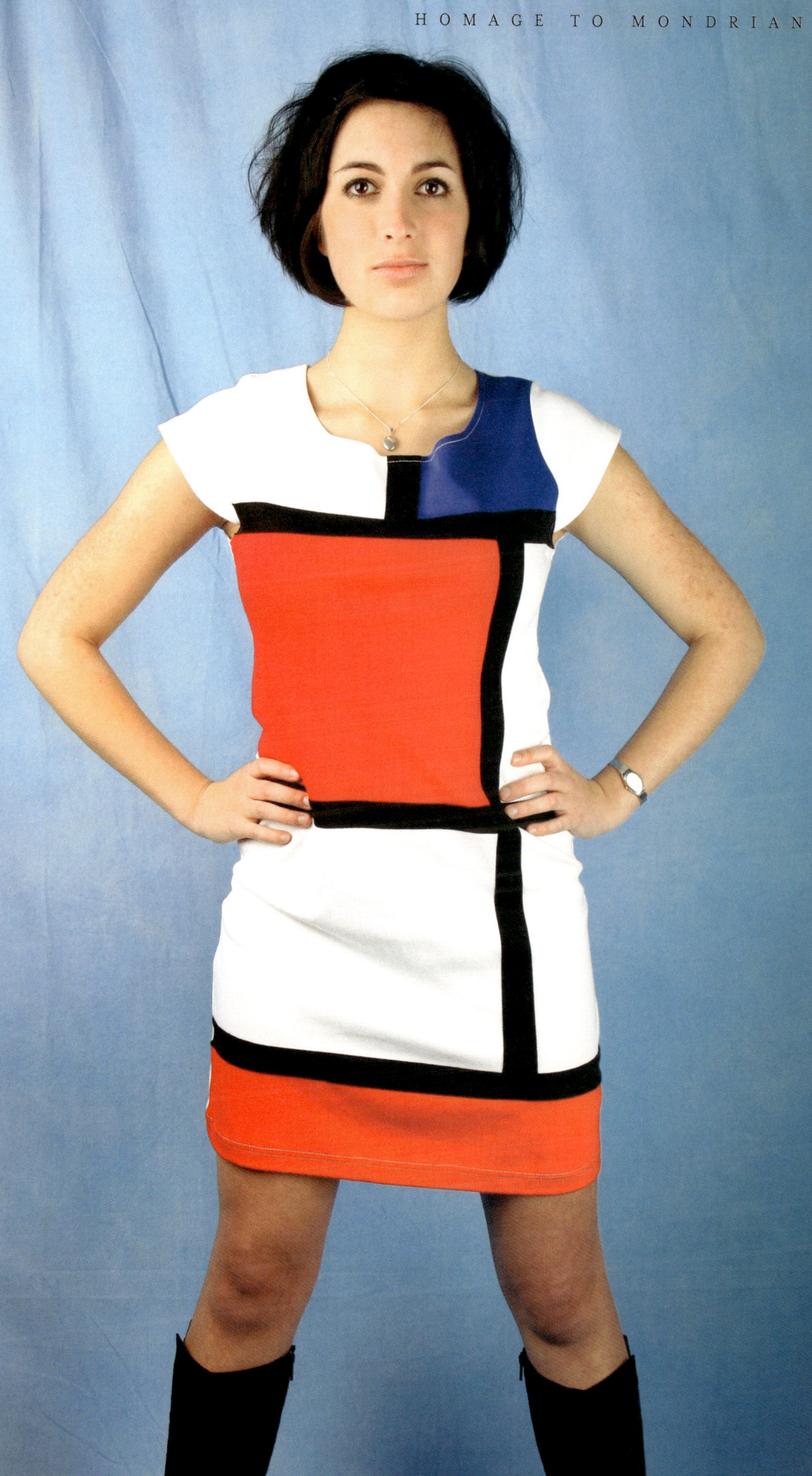

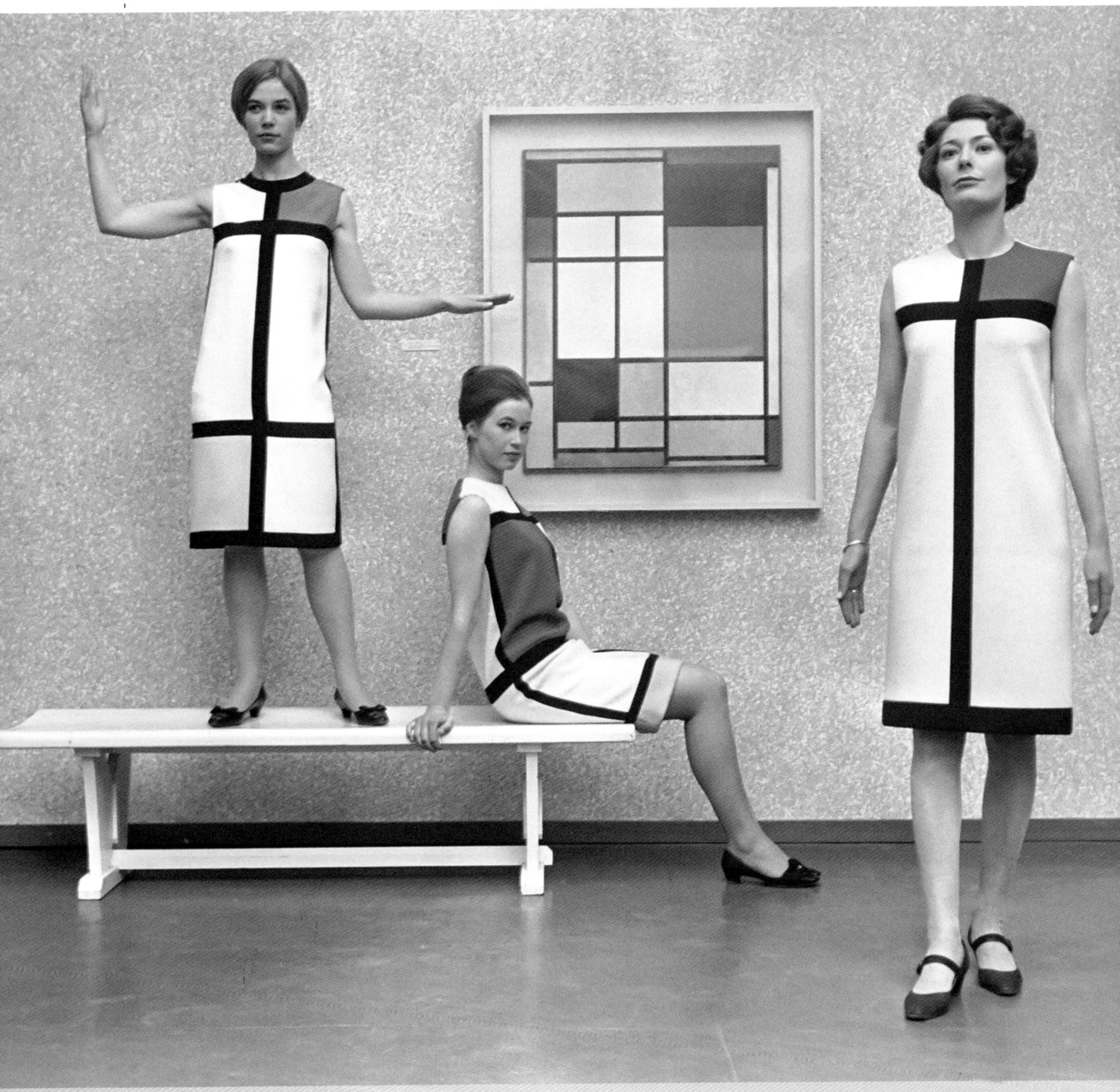

or puzzle. Each block of red, blue, yellow and white, and each black line was a separate piece of fabric, with Saint Laurent cutting and sewing each piece individually. This method gave the dress structure, texture and a richness that printing would never have achieved. Seam lines were carefully hidden under

ABOVE: Mondrian dresses by Yves Saint Laurent shown with a Mondrian painting in 1966
OPP PAGE: 1965 Mondrian dress

the black bands, mimicking Mondrian's painted black lines. This made the garment appear like a genuine work of art. Saint Laurent selected structured-but-pliable wool jersey fabric for the design as it provided the clean, smooth surface required for the colour blocks. Jersey also allowed the dress to hold its shape without wrinkling easily - critical for maintaining a canvas-like flatness. The dress was carefully lined to balance the weight of the fabric pieces and prevent sagging at the seams. Any distortion would have ruined the illusion of perfect geometric lines. Every measurement and cut of fabric had to be exact - even a tiny mistake in aligning the black lines or matching colour blocks would have been glaringly obvious. The geometric balance required mathematical accuracy, almost like engineering a piece of architecture. YSL's construction techniques honoured Mondrian's strict philosophy of order and harmony — turning couture into wearable, living art.

This was one of the many reasons the Mondrian dress was exceptional. By blurring boundaries, the unique design fused fine art and fashion in a way that had never been done so boldly. It elevated clothing into the realms of high art, suggesting that fashion could be just as intellectually and culturally significant as painting or sculpture. The Mondrian's clean lines and bold, primary colours also perfectly matched the zeitgeist of the 1960s — a decade obsessed with modernity, simplicity and breaking old rules. The dress captured that spirit and it became a became a defining symbol of the 'Swinging Sixties'. It remains one of the most recognizable and celebrated fashion designs in history.

The reaction to Yves Saint Laurent's Mondrian dress was overwhelmingly positive with both the fashion world and the public. Fashion critics were amazed by how Saint Laurent merged fine art and haute couture. It wasn't just inspired by Mondrian — it seemed to embody the spirit, the very essence, of modernism. The precision of the coloured blocks and clean lines were seen as revolutionary in addition to being fresh, modern and accessible. Photographed by David Bailey, the dresses appeared on the covers of major magazines such as *Vogue* – where the design was dubbed *'the dress of tomorrow'*, *Harpers Bazaar* and *Elle*, becoming instantly iconic. Diana Vreeland raved about them in the *New York Times*, deeming this *'the best collection'*, while *Women's Wear Daily* hailed Saint Laurent as the *'King of Paris'*. So successful was the dress – and the numerous imitations it subsequently spawned – it gave Saint Laurent the impetus to open his 'Rive Gauche' boutique at 21 Rue de Tournon on Paris' bohemian Left Bank in 1966. This was the first 'ready-to-

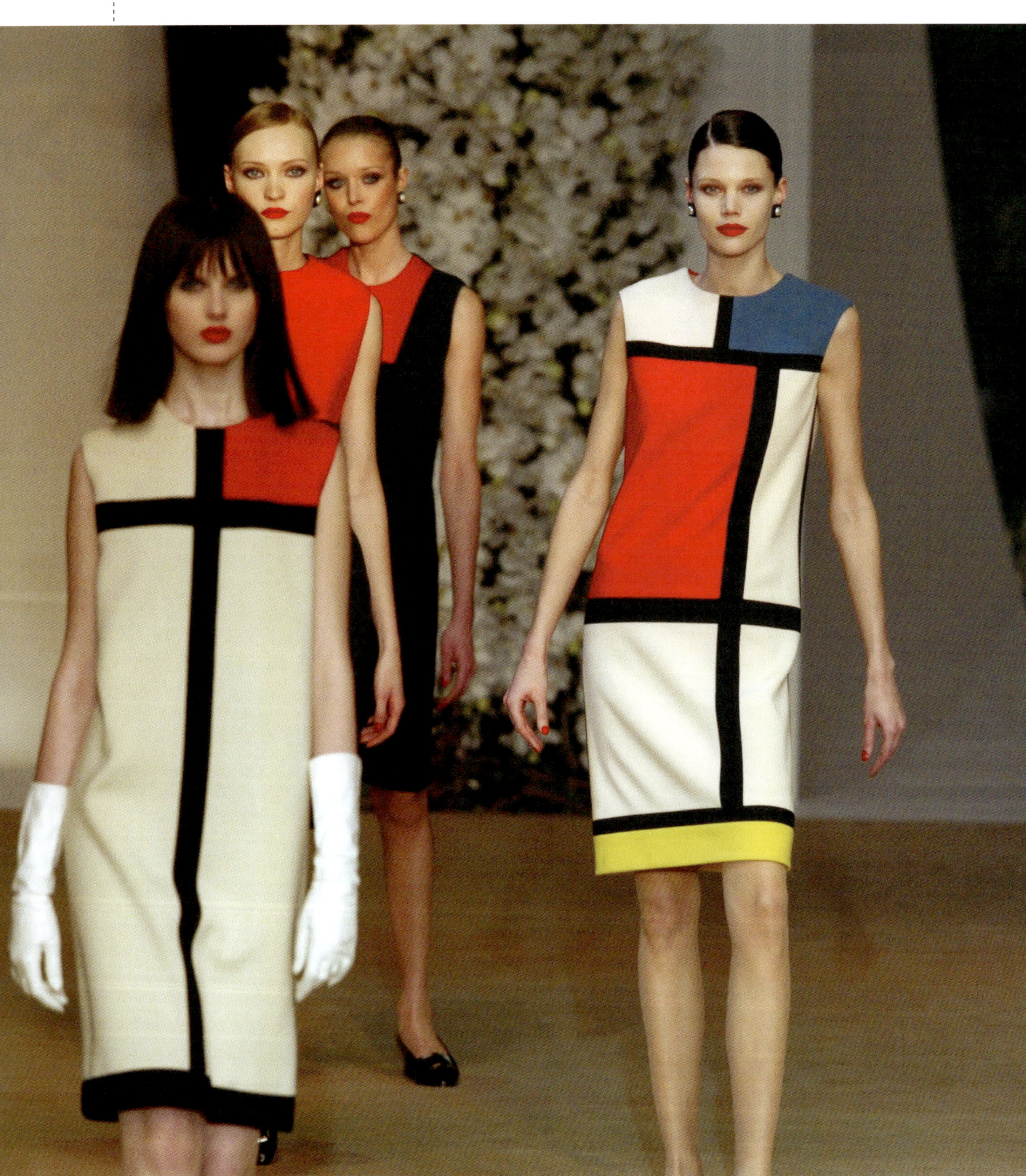

ABOVE: Showcase of the dresses at a 2022 Yves Saint Laurent show, drawing on the iconic 1965 designs inspired by Dutch painter Piet Mondrian
OPP PAGE: Roger Vivier square buckle pumps

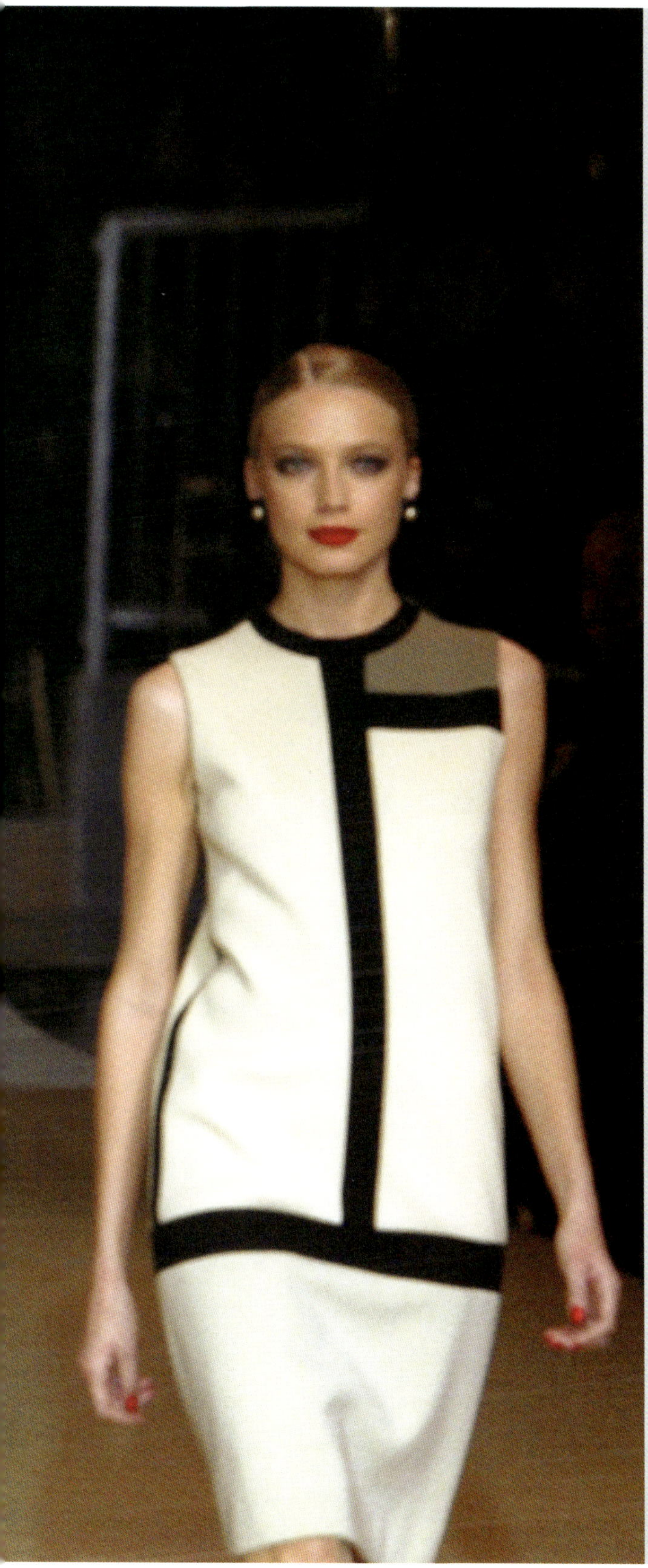

wear' store to be opened by a high-end couturier, setting the trend for other designers to follow suite.

The Modrian collection also saw YSL's first range of footwear come to fruition. To accessorise the iconic dresses, Saint Laurent sketched a series of shoes - classic black pumps decorated with a large square buckle in gold or silver metal - that were made by designer Rogier Vivier. These shoes would later become famous in their own right when actress Catherine Deneuve wore them in the world-famous 1967 film, 'Belle du Jour'.

Other items in the YSL Fall/Winter 1965 collection included minimalist tunics and trousers with clean, architectural lines; graphic monochrome, often boldly contrasting, looks; shorter hemlines which had become de-rigeur in this ground-breaking-in-so-many-ways decade; and the 'Russian Doll' inspired woollen wedding dress which closed the show. However, henceforth this collection would be forever known by fashionistas and the world at large as The Mondrian Collection. It would go on to be the inspiration for YSL to create further 'art' collections over the years – 33 in all – which included works by Goya, Picasso, Léger, Matisse, and Van Gogh.

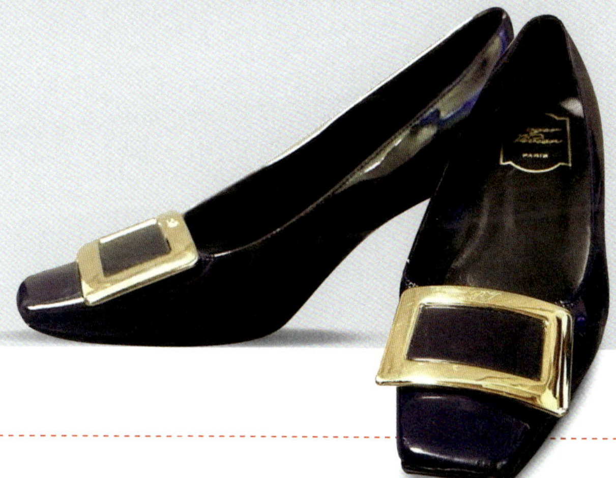

L'ATELIER

"I am not a designer, I am a craftsman.
A manufacturer of happiness"
Yves Saint Laurent

L'atelier (the workspace) of Yves Saint Laurent was more than just a place where clothes were made - it was the very heart and soul of his creative process. It was within these walls that ideas came to life, artistic visions translated into reality and where some of the most iconic garments in fashion history were conceived and then brought to life.

For Yves Saint Laurent, fashion was never just about clothing, rather creating a complete experience - an artistic expression - that told a story, reflected cultural movements and captured the essence of beauty, elegance, and innovation. His workroom was the crucible of this creativity. Where he and his team of skilled artisans turned concepts into finished designs. It was here that visions were sketched, patterns drawn, fabric selected and seams stitched to create pieces that would break barriers and go on to make fashion history.

L'atelier itself was designed to be both functional and inspirational. Saint Laurent's attention to detail was meticulous and he carefully curated the atmosphere

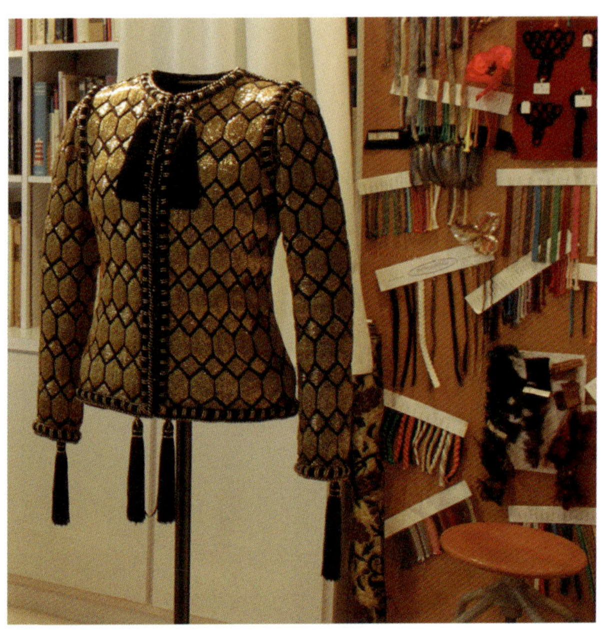

to inspire those around him, encouraging an environment of collaboration, focus and innovation. The workspace had a calm yet focused atmosphere, reflecting Yves Saint Laurent's own personality and working style. Yves was a man of delicate sensibilities - he had a deep understanding of beauty and artistry but he also possessed a quiet yet intense commitment to perfection. The space was always well-lit, with sunlight streaming through large windows to create an inspiring environment, and was

ABOVE & OPP PAGE: The office workshop of Yves Saint Laurent as seen at the Yves Saint Laurent Museum in Paris

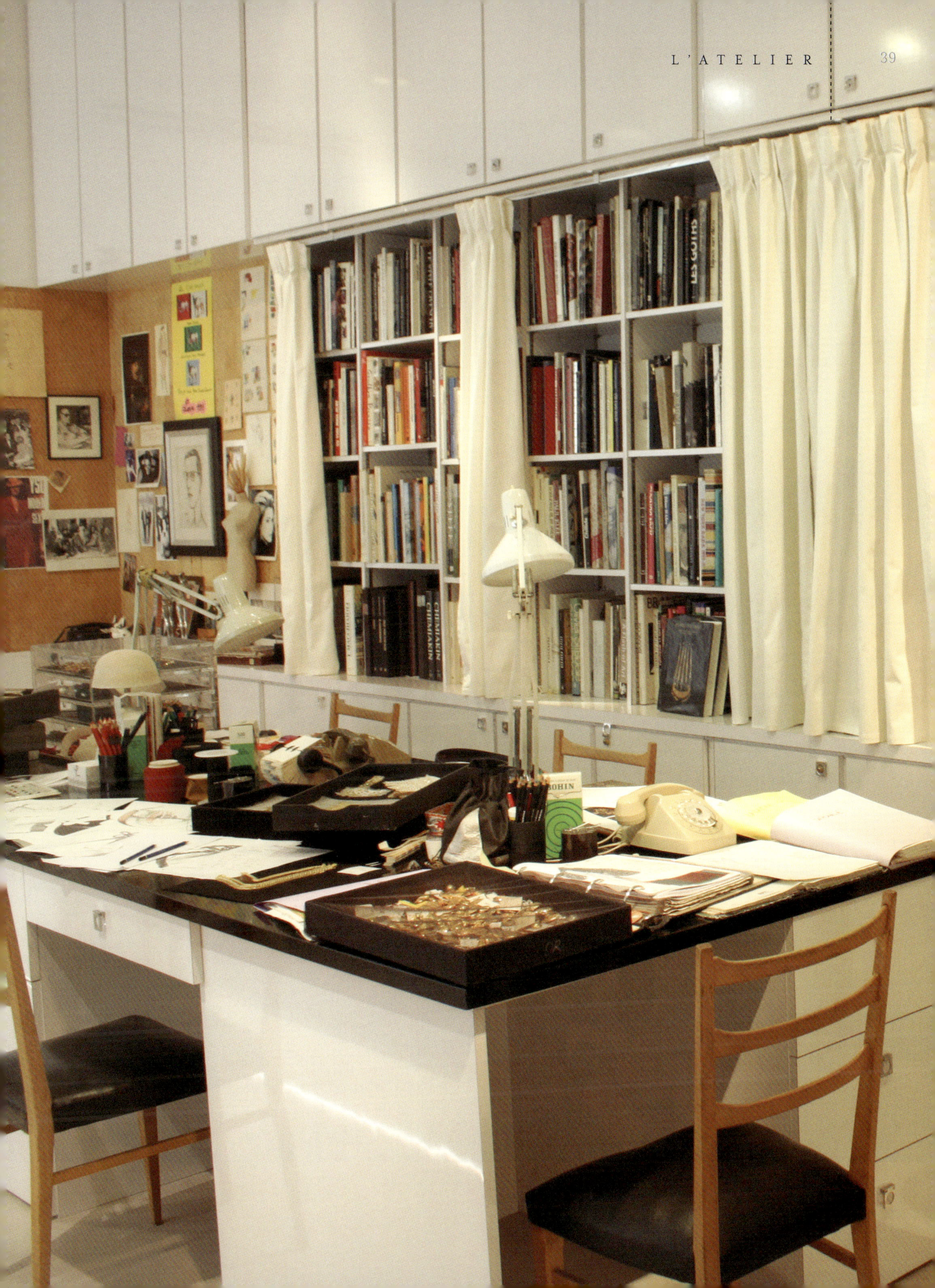

often filled with muses and models in addition to the team of dedicated artisans who worked tirelessly to bring the designer's creative visions to life.

Saint Laurent was known for being deeply involved in every aspect of his creations and this showed in the workspace. He was hands-on - sketching his ideas, revising them and collaborating with his team of tailors, seamstresses and patternmakers – many of whom were with him for years. The team were vital to his success. He surrounded himself with talented individuals who were experts in their respective fields and who ensured that each garment and accessory met his high standards of craftsmanship and quality. Saint Laurent's ability to work so closely with his team allowed him to translate his vision into wondrous reality.

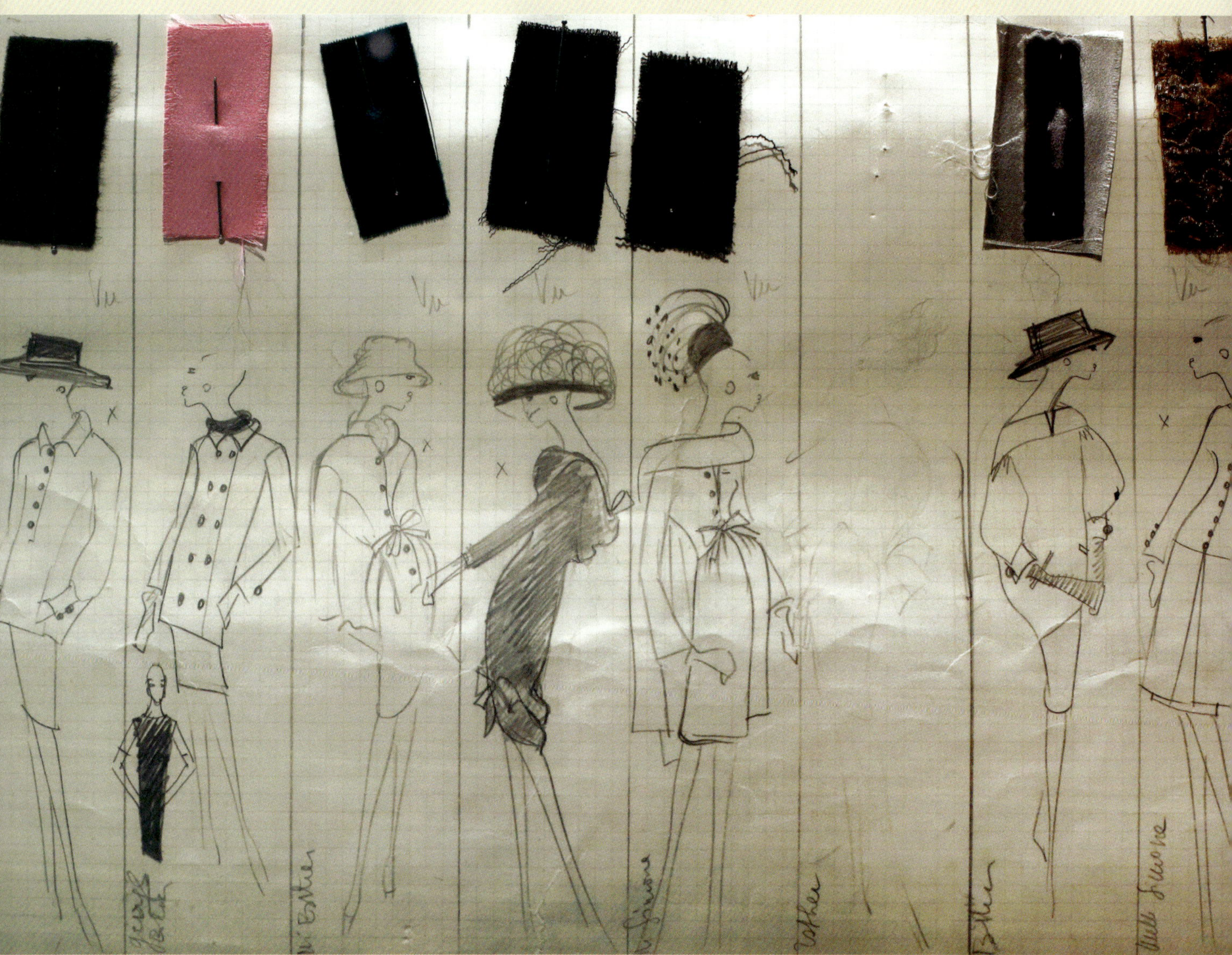

ABOVE: Drawings and samples by Yves Saint Laurent
OPP PAGE: L'atelier wall display and desk featuring fashion drawings, photographs, and portraits, including a Bernard Buffet drawing and a photograph of Catherine Deneuve

Every collection began with inspiration. Saint Laurent was deeply attuned to the world around him - whether that be the arts, literature, travel, history, street style... These influences often fed directly into his collections. He would begin by sketching ideas, using pencils and markers to create quick drawings. These sketches were not necessarily detailed but they captured the essence of the piece he wanted to create. The patternmakers would begin the process of creating patterns from Saint Laurent's sketches. Once made, a 'toile' (prototype garment in muslin) would be produced. The toile served as a test version to perfect the cut, drape, and construction of a design before it was made in its final fabric. These muslin versions were crafted by the première d'atelier (head of the atelier) and were fitted on models or mannequins in the designer's studio. Saint Laurent would then make adjustments personally, often drawing or pinning directly on the toile to finalise how he wanted the garment to eventually look. Saint Laurent believed that fabric was the foundation of every design. In his workroom, a wide range of luxurious materials - from silk to velvet to leather - was available, and the choice of fabric was crucial in determining the structure and flow of the final garment. He often chose fabrics that were rich in texture and colour, and that would complement the designs he had in mind. Whether it was the heavy brocades of his Russian-inspired collection or the fluid silks of his African-inspired designs, fabric selection played a huge role in bringing his vision to life. The fabric chosen was carefully cut based on the corrected

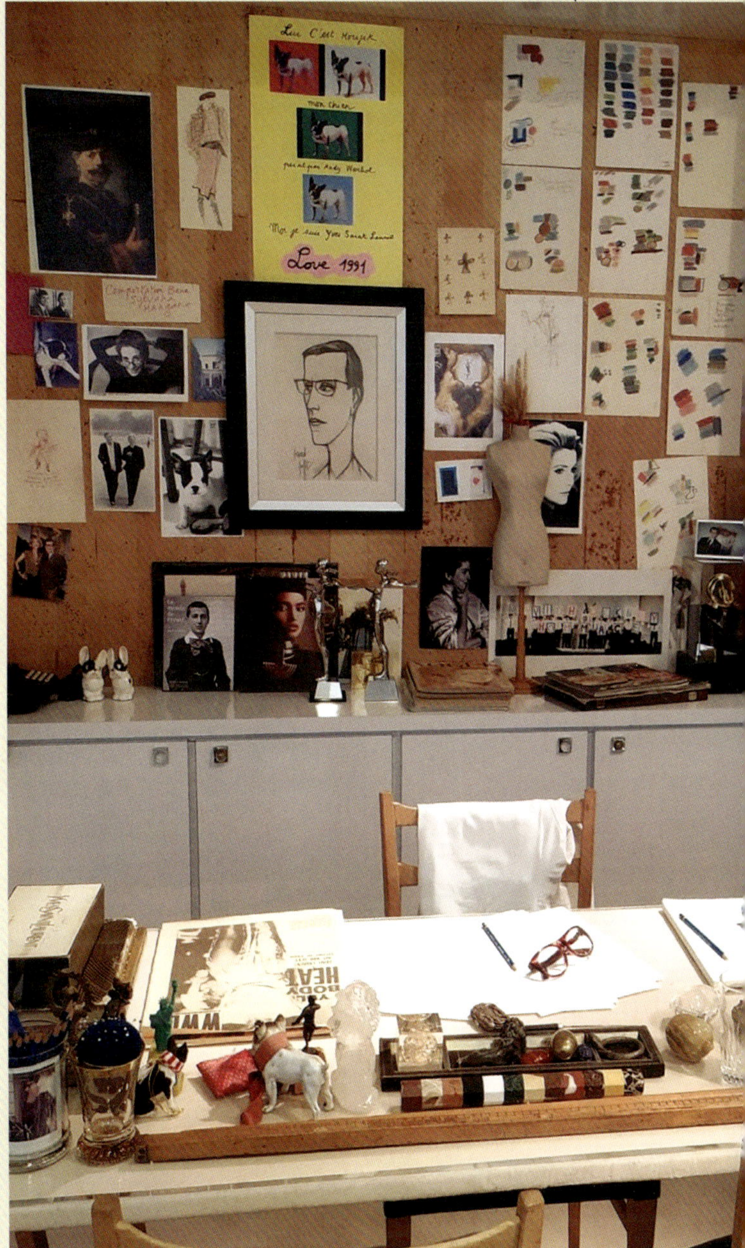

toile pattern of the garment. After this, it would undergo multiple fittings on models and sometimes on Saint Laurent's trusted muses. Saint Laurent was known to be hands-on during the fittings, constantly revising and fine-tuning. Fittings were also a chance to assess how the garment moved, how it fit the body, and whether

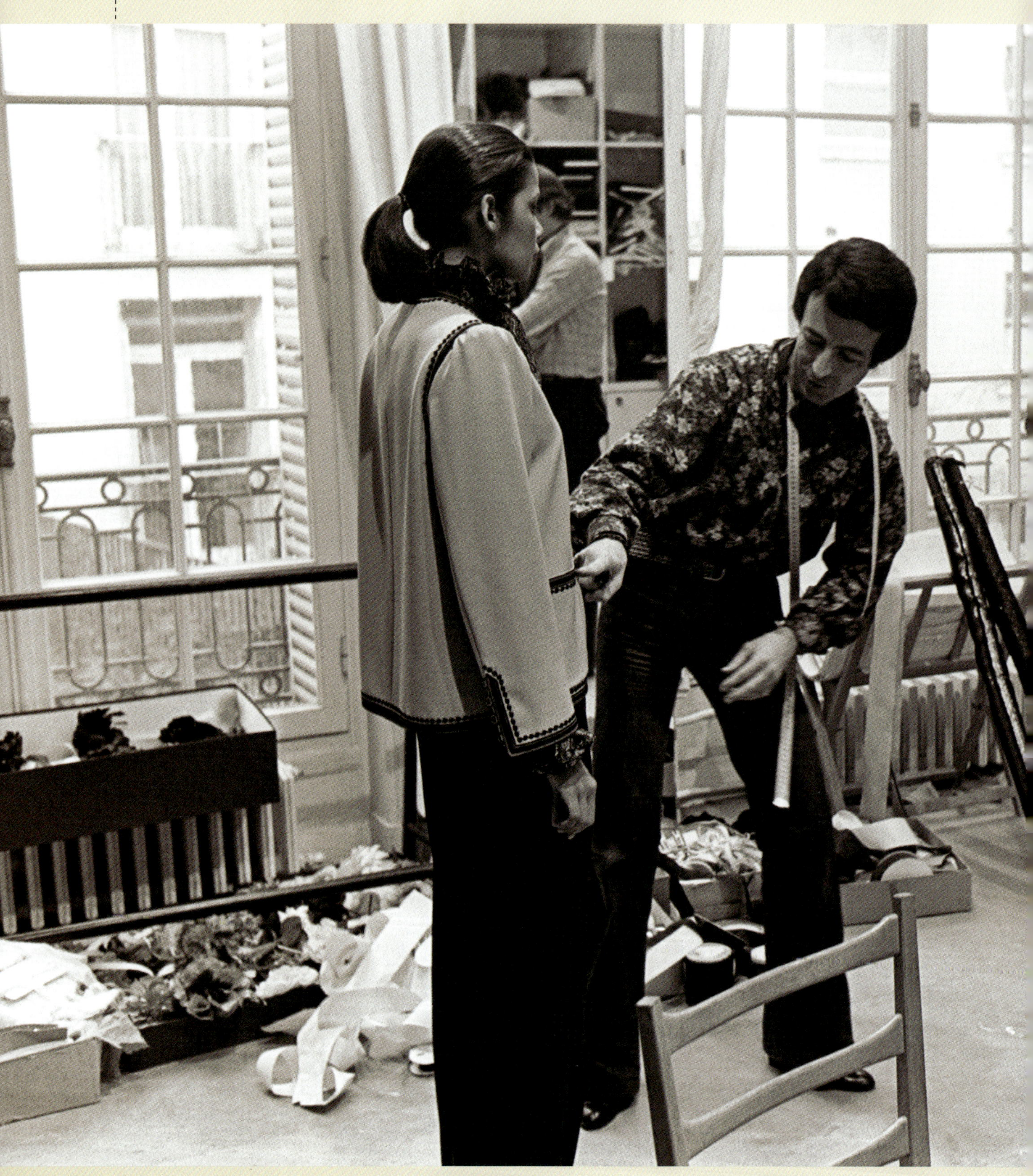

ABOVE: Yves Saint Laurent and his assistants fit an outfit on a model in his Paris atelier in 1977

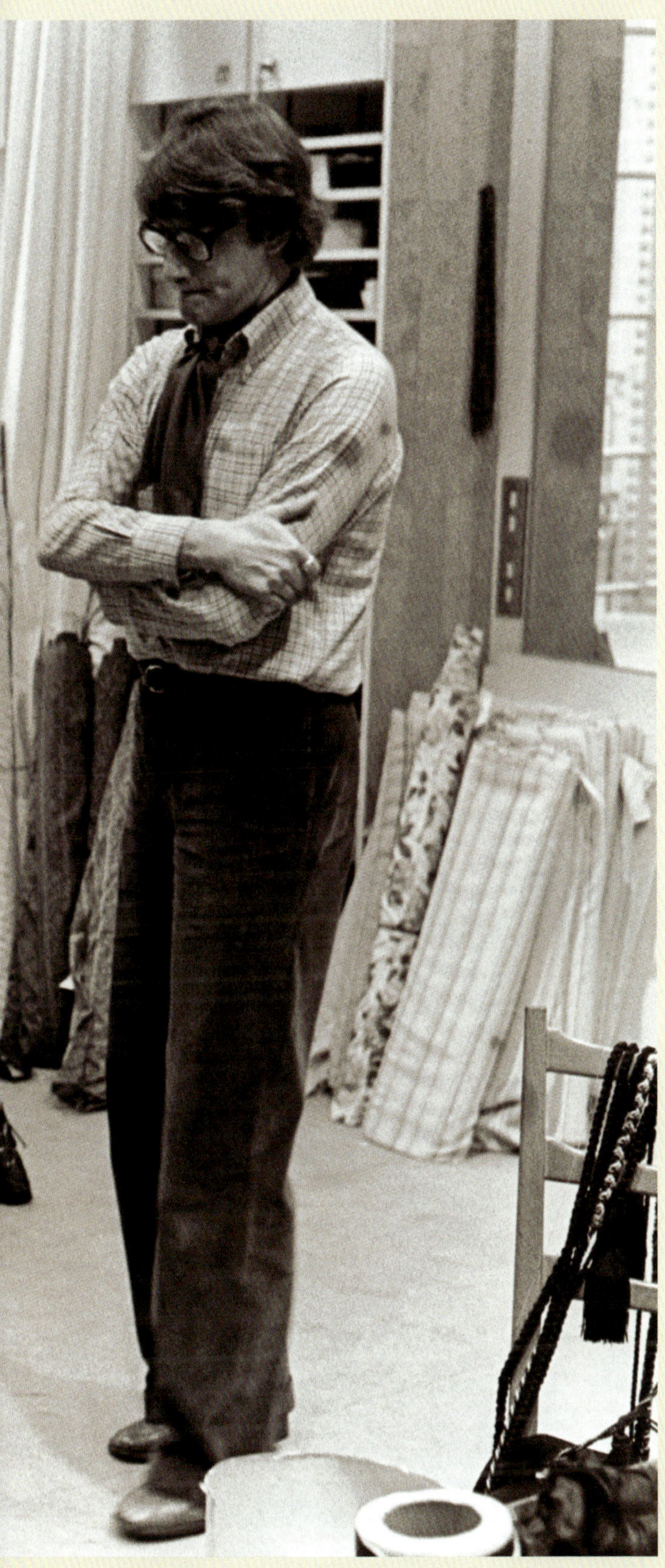

it was in harmony with the design concept. Saint Laurent's meticulous attention to how clothes draped on the body meant that the fitting process was often long but the results were always worth it.

Once the garment had been perfected, it was assembled by highly skilled artisans before the workroom would focus on the final touches - such as adding embellishments, beading or embroidery. The meticulous nature of this process ensured that the finished product was of the highest quality, showcasing craftsmanship that stood out in the world of high fashion.

Today, the workroom of Yves Saint Laurent is remembered not only as a place of design and production but as a symbol of the craftsmanship that defined the house. The legacy of the YSL workroom lives on through the continued focus on quality and detail in Saint Laurent's modern collections. It also stands as a testament to Saint Laurent's genius as both an innovator and a master craftsman, who always maintained the highest standards of luxury.

The Yves Saint Laurent Museum in Paris, which opened at the brand's former premises – 5 Avenue Marceau - in 2017, has meticulously restored the atelier to its original state, preserving the ambiance and details of the workspace as it would have been when YSL created there from 1974 to 2002. Visitors can see Saint Laurent's desk with his personal items, sketches, fabric samples and other elements that offer an intimate glimpse into his creative process.

RIVE GAUCHE, READY-TO-WEAR AND A FASHION REVOLUTION

"Rive Gauche is more than a boutique, it is a way of life"

Yves Saint Laurent

While his haute couture collections dazzled the Paris elite, it was Yves Saint Laurent's ground-breaking venture into ready-to-wear—'prêt-à-porter'—that truly reshaped the landscape of modern fashion. In 1966, Saint Laurent crossed over the Seine to the left bank, and in doing so, changed the fashion world forever. Until that moment, the fashion industry had been uber exclusive - haute couture existing in a rarefied world of salons and social hierarchy. But Saint Laurent believed style should belong to every woman, not just celebrities and the ones with chauffeurs and château addresses.

Rive Gauche—named after the bohemian side of Paris known for its cafés, intellectuals and revolutionaries—was the first ready-to-wear boutique launched by a couturier under his own name. It was a radical idea - designer fashion made in factories, sold in shops and at a price point working women, students and self-made Parisians could afford. A new era of fashion was born. But what made the Rive Gauche experiment so transformative wasn't just its business model. It was the clothes themselves - innovative, ground-breaking, never-seen-before pieces that redefined how women could dress, move, work, love and live.

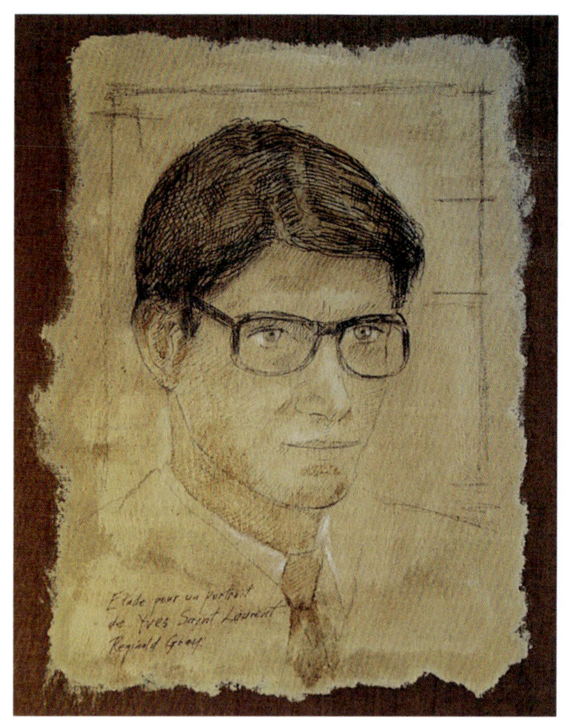

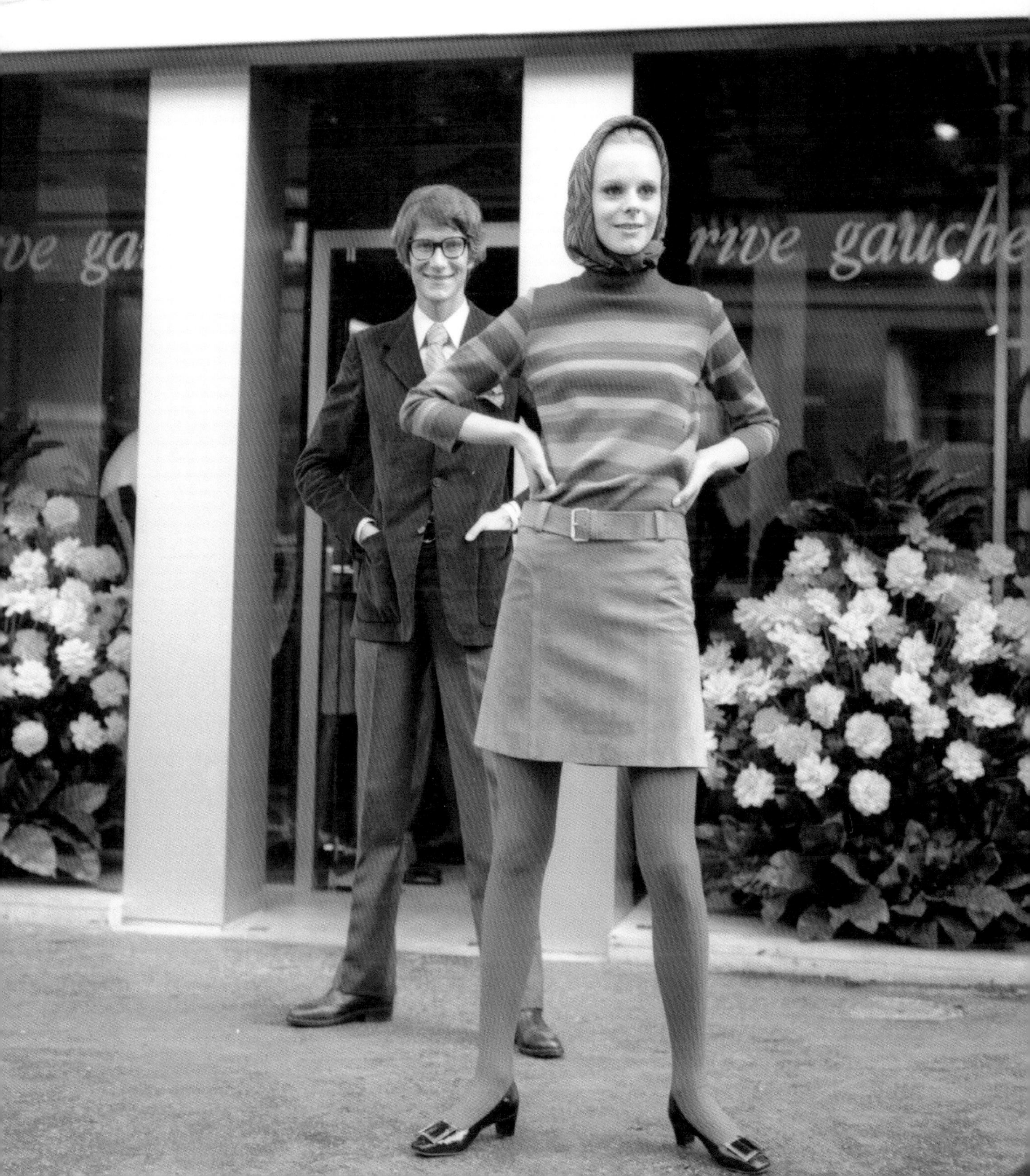
SAINT LAURENT
rve gauche
rive gauche

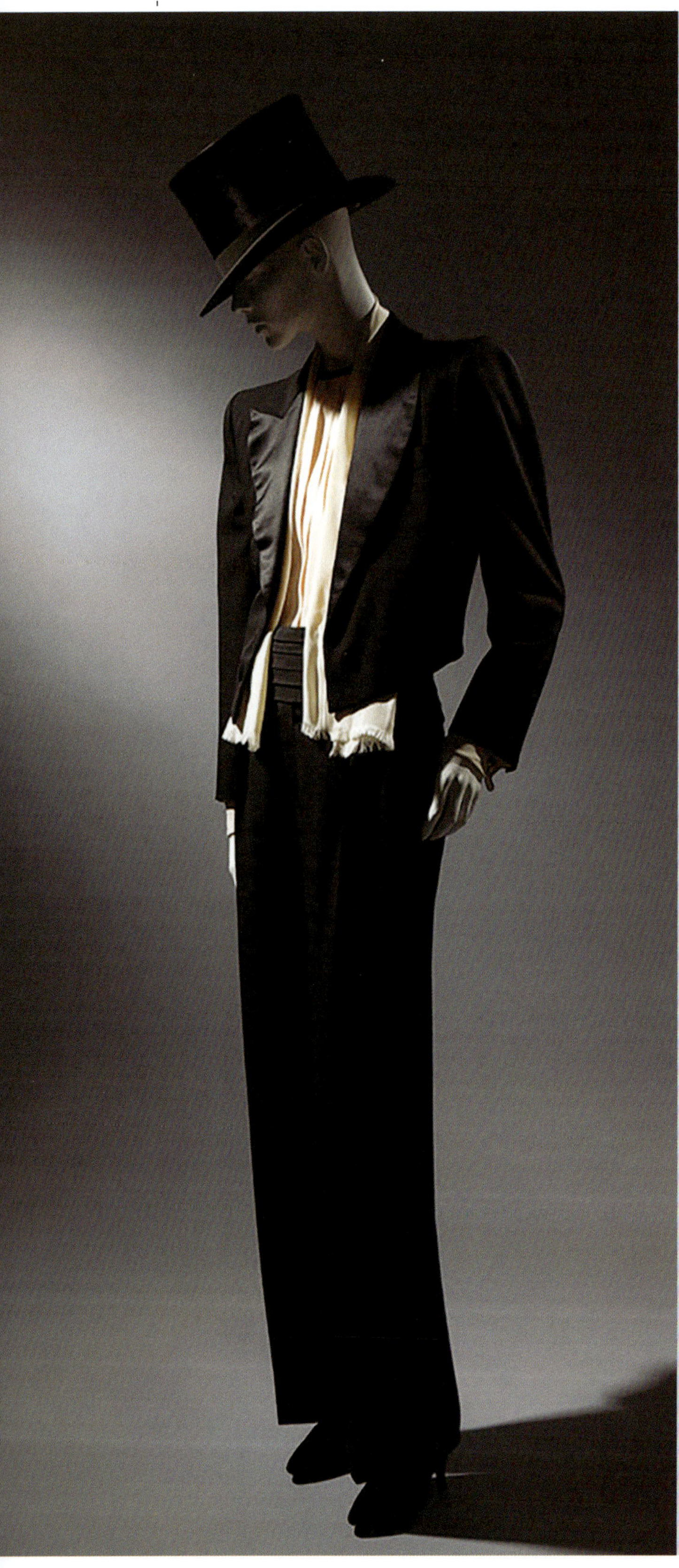

'LE SMOKING' - THE TUXEDO THAT CHANGED THE RULES

When Yves Saint Laurent introduced his 'Le Smoking' in 1966, it wasn't merely a suit - it was a provocation. A woman in a tuxedo - with crisp lapels, tailored trousers and a silk bow tie - was truly radical. At a time when women were still being denied entry to certain establishments if they weren't wearing a dress or skirt, YSL offered not just a look but a kind of uniform. Saint Laurent gave women their own version of the suit – reimaging traditional menswear for the female form. The debut of 'Le Smoking' under the Rive Gauche label was deliberate. It meant that this revolution in women's fashion was not confined to the world of couture but could be purchased, worn and lived in by women of the real world. The design itself was deceptively simple - black wool or satin trousers, a sharply cut jacket, a white ruffled blouse or nothing at all underneath. Saint Laurent softened the masculine lines without compromising structure. He tailored 'Le Smoking' to highlight the waist, to suggest hips, to assert femininity... The shock of it became its allure. In one infamous incident, New York socialite Nan Kempner was turned away from an establishment for wearing the suit. Her response? She removed her trousers and walked in wearing only the blazer which was long enough to serve as a mini dress! But the real genius of 'Le Smoking' was its timelessness. It reflected the zeitgeist – of the independent, working woman who was her own person and didn't need a ball gown to command a room. It is as relevant today as it's always been.

ABOVE: 'Le Smoking' in the Museum at FIT, New York
OPP PAGE: Claudia Schiffer walks the runway at the Yves Saint Laurent Spring/Summer 2013 fashion show during Paris Fashion Week

THE TROUSER SUIT - TAILORING A NEW ORDER

Long before 'power dressing' became a thing, Yves Saint Laurent gave women the trouser suit. Emerging from the same fashion roots as 'Le Smoking', the ready-to-wear version of the suit was for the professional, working woman. As with 'Le Smoking', YSL's trouser suit feminised the masculinity of the traditional suit – waist-hugging jackets, trousers cut in such a way they elongated the leg, more subtle fabrics.... In the 1970s, when women were pushing against boundaries in the workplace and beyond, these pant suits became their extremely chic and modern uniform. What made them revolutionary wasn't the cut alone, but the idea that a woman didn't have to exaggerate her femininity to be noticed. With the Rive Gauche trouser suit, she could step into a man's world on her own terms.

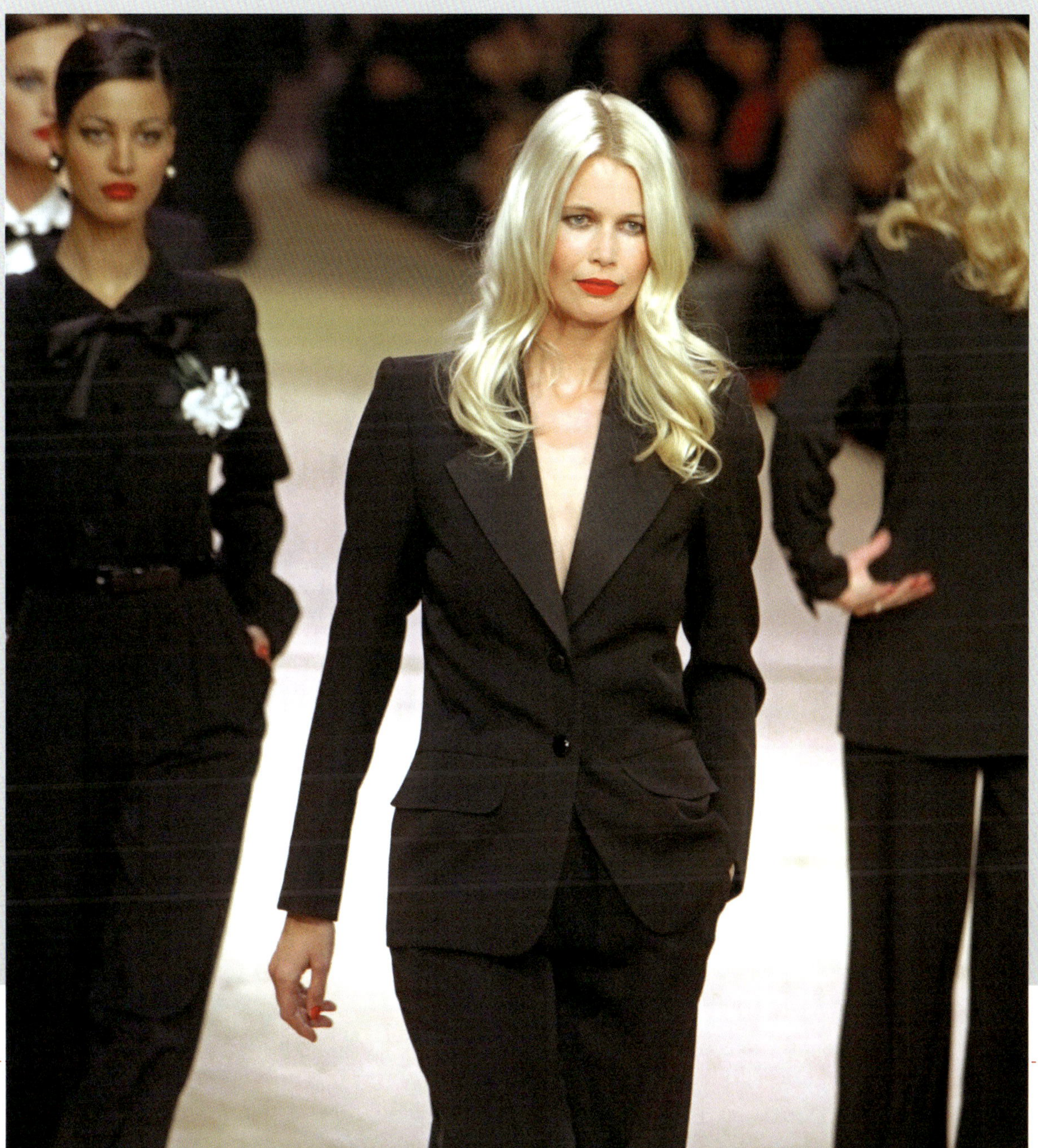

THE TRENCH COAT - UTILITY WITH A PARISIAN TWIST

In Yves Saint Laurent's hands, the trench coat - long a military staple and British classic - became sleek, sculpted and undeniably French. The cut was everything with YSL refining the proportions in order to flatter – cinched waist, fluid drape, double-breasted... Like so many of his designs, the trench worked on multiple levels. It protected and revealed, covered and seduced. And it became yet another item that women could buy off the rack and make entirely their own. Whether worn over a dress, slung off the shoulder, or paired with nothing but heels and a red lip, it had an air of provocation masked as practicality.

THE SAFARI JACKET - A GLAMOROUS FRONTIER

In 1968, fashion editor Diana Vreeland declared, *'Yves does safari clothes better than anyone'*. She wasn't wrong. The safari jacket, first appearing in the Rive Gauche collection and immortalized in a *Vogue* photo of model Veruschka in the African bush, melded together exoticism, functionality and sex appeal. It was a garment inspired by colonial uniforms - but transformed. Structured yet soft, belted at the waist, with oversized pockets and rolled-up sleeves, it projected a sense of adventure while staying deeply chic. In the ready-to-wear context, it was genius - women could buy it, wear it over jeans or bare legs, and instantly embody the worldly glamour of Saint Laurent. The safari jacket marked Saint Laurent's shift toward global influences - Moroccan djellabas, Russian peasant blouses, Chinese tunics... Yet it was always Parisian in attitude. Practical enough to be worn by day, seductive enough for evening.

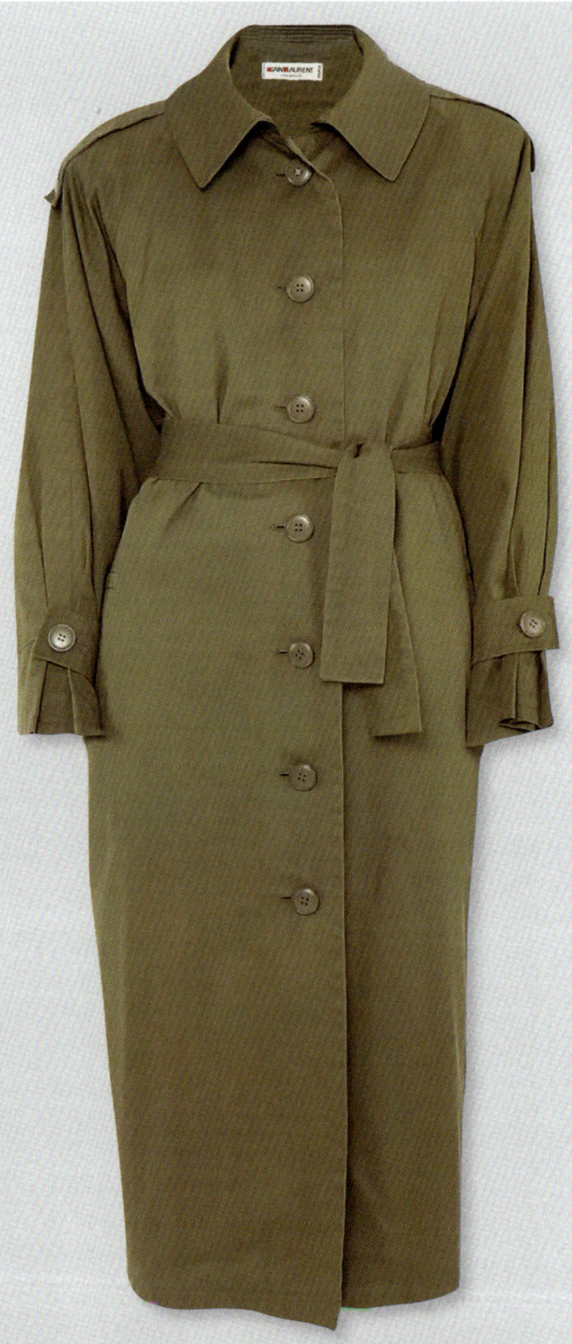

ABOVE: 1970s Classic Belted Rive Gauche Trench Coat
OPP PAGE: 1968 Saint Laurent Safari Jacket

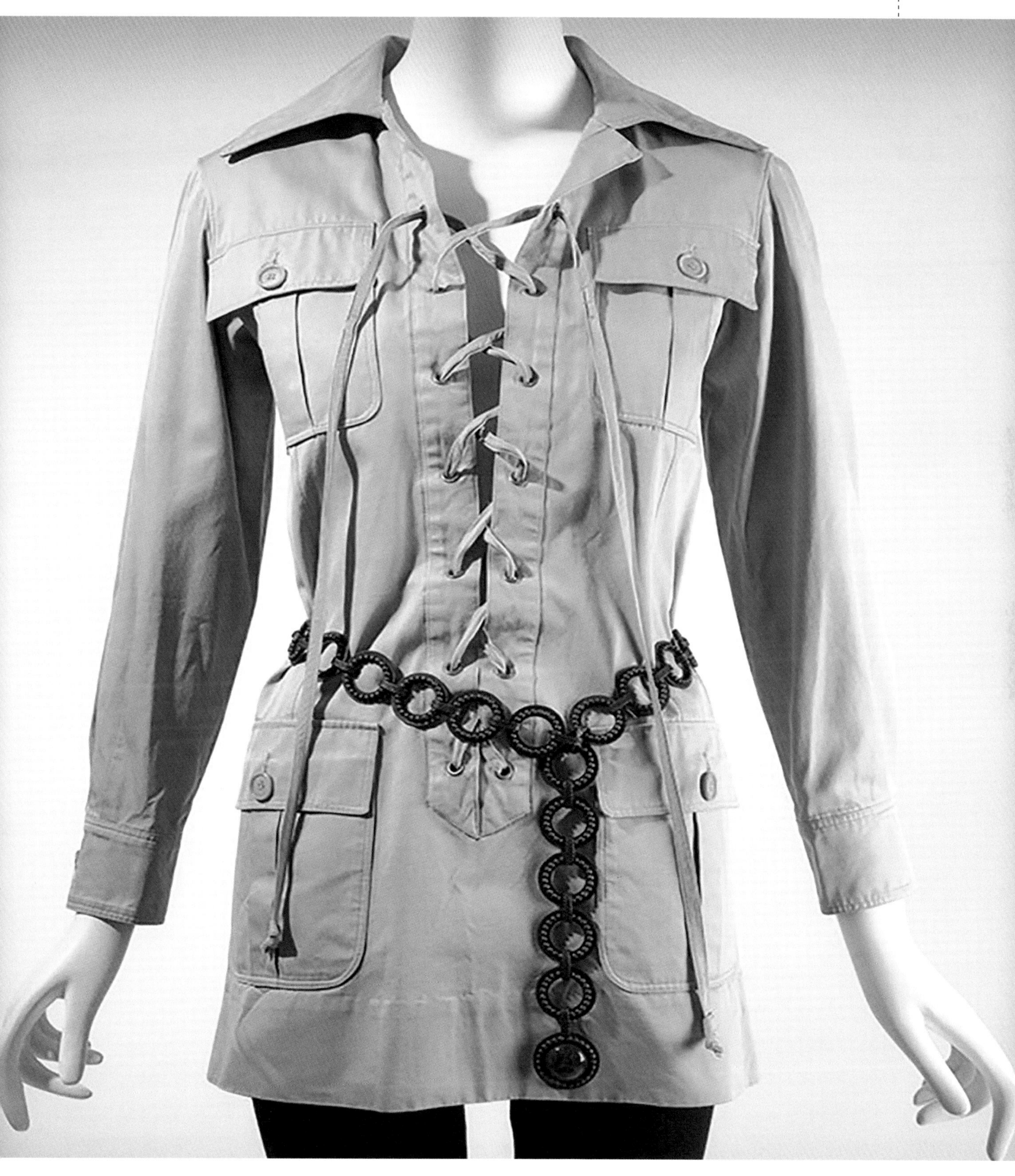

SHEER BLOUSES - SENSUALITY WITHOUT APOLOGY

Saint Laurent's sheer blouses, which appeared throughout his Rive Gauche collections in the late 1960s and 70s, were scandalous by design. Diaphanous silk, barely-there sleeves, and frequently worn braless - they made headlines, turned heads, and shifted the rules of modesty in fashion. However, these were not garments meant to provoke for the sake of it. Saint Laurent's vision was for women to own their sensuality. Light, soft, and beautifully constructed, these blouses put the female body back into fashion—and on the woman's terms. Worn tucked into high-waisted trousers, under jackets, or floating freely, the blouse was the perfect balance of provocation and elegance.

Other standout Rive Gauche pieces included peasant-inspired blouses, military jackets and Mondrian-print dresses - all emblematic of Saint Laurent's ability to draw from diverse sources and make them chic, modern and accessible. The clothes weren't watered-down versions of couture but powerful statements in their own right.

Rive Gauche wasn't just about fashion, it was also about choice. A woman could walk into the boutique and find a tuxedo, a trench coat, a sheer blouse, a tailored suit or a safari jacket - clothes that defined an era - all designed with the same respect, intellect and artistry as couture. It was a true turning point and soon replicated by other designers the world over.

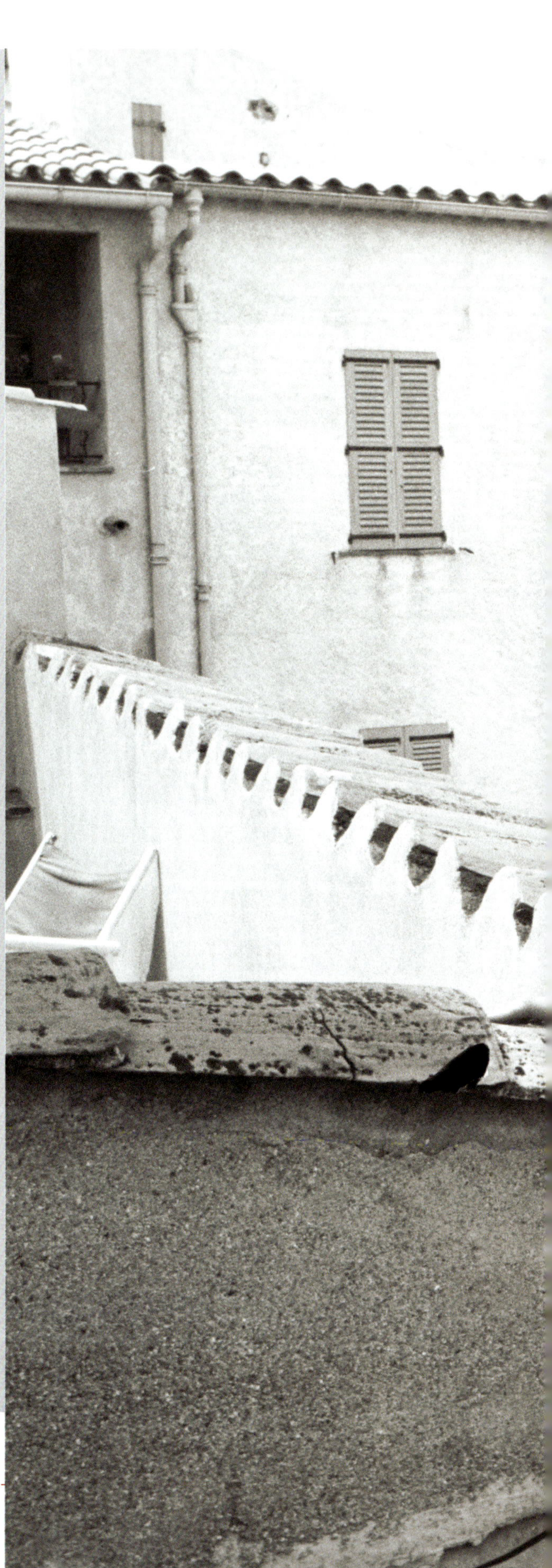

RIGHT: In Saint-Tropez, actress Anny Duperey poses on a rooftop, dressed in a gypsy skirt and sheer blouse from the Yves Saint Laurent Spring/Summer collection, May 1971

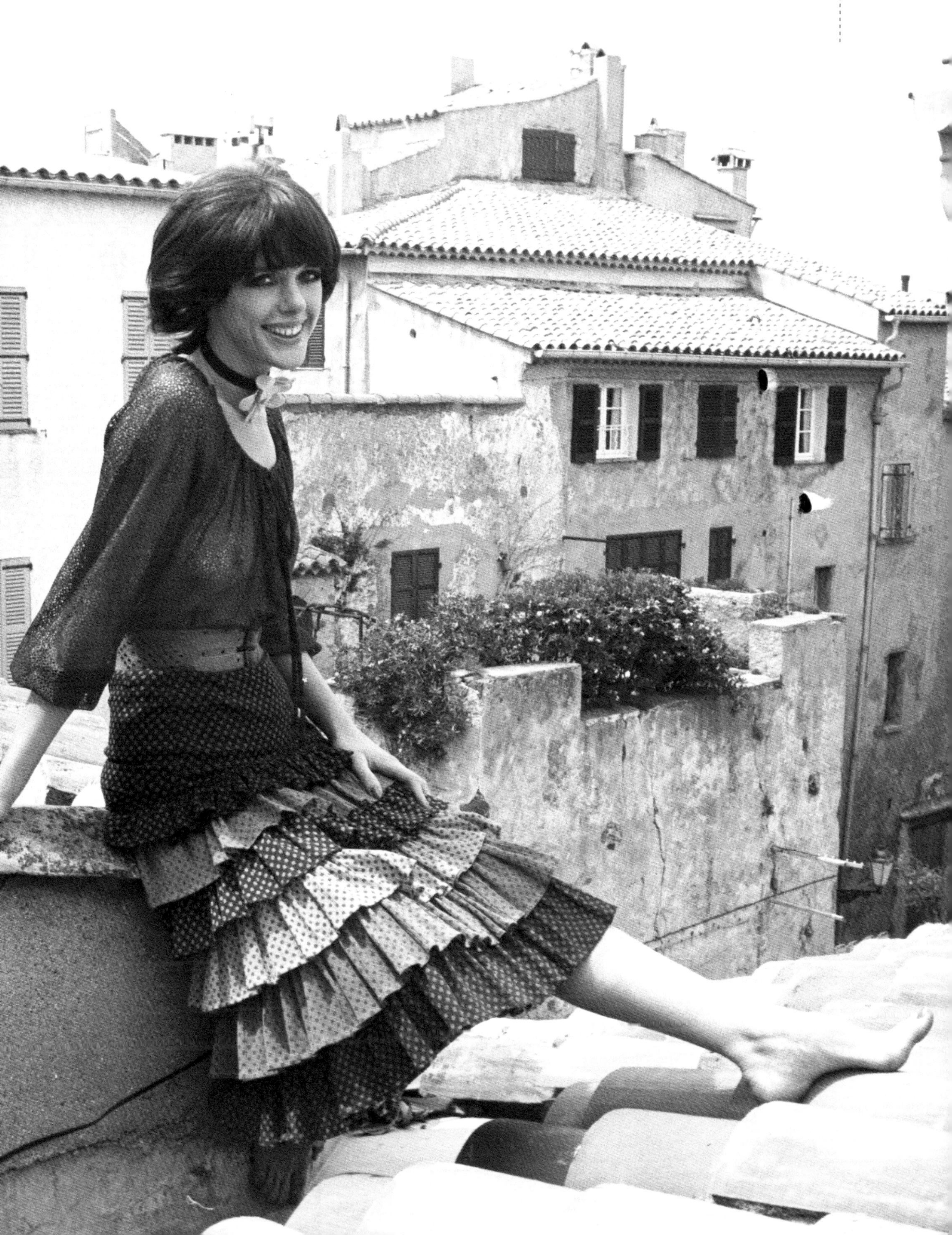

MARRAKECH

*"Before Marrakech,
everything was black"*
Yves Saint Laurent

When Saint Laurent and Pierre Bergé first visited the Moroccan city of Marrakech in 1966, they were instantly seduced. It was the most wonderful assault on the senses - ochre walls glowing in the desert sun, huge blue skies, the endless labyrinths of the medina, the call to prayer echoing through the evening air, and lush, secret gardens tucked behind ancient doors... Marrakech offered a vibrant contrast to the often-restrained world of Parisian haute couture. It also reminded Yves of his childhood and adolescence spent in the neighbouring north African country of Algeria. In Marrakech, the designer felt free and inspired. The city ignited his fascination with colour in ways he had never known before. The electric blues, fiery reds, saffron yellows and rich emerald greens of the Moroccan landscape and, also its textiles, would go on to feature in his collections, energizing his designs with boldness and sensuality. These hues - once seen as too daring for Western fashion - became his signature.

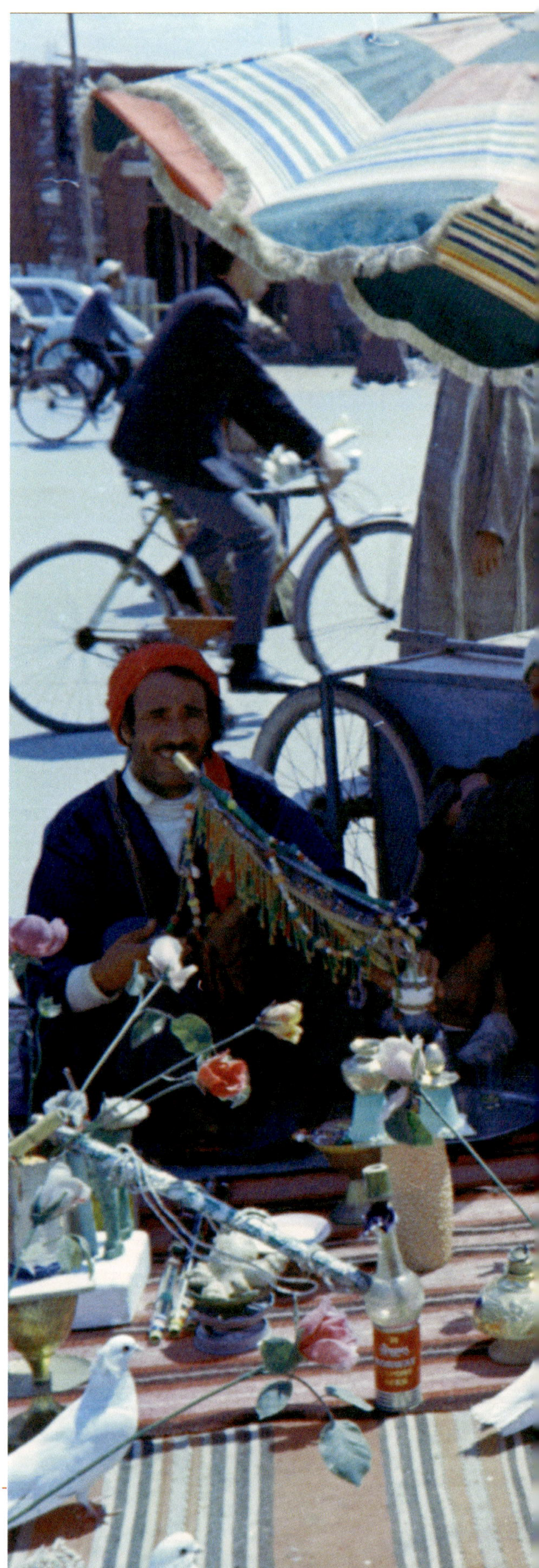

RIGHT: Yves Saint Laurent and Pierre Bergé in a Marrakech market, 1972

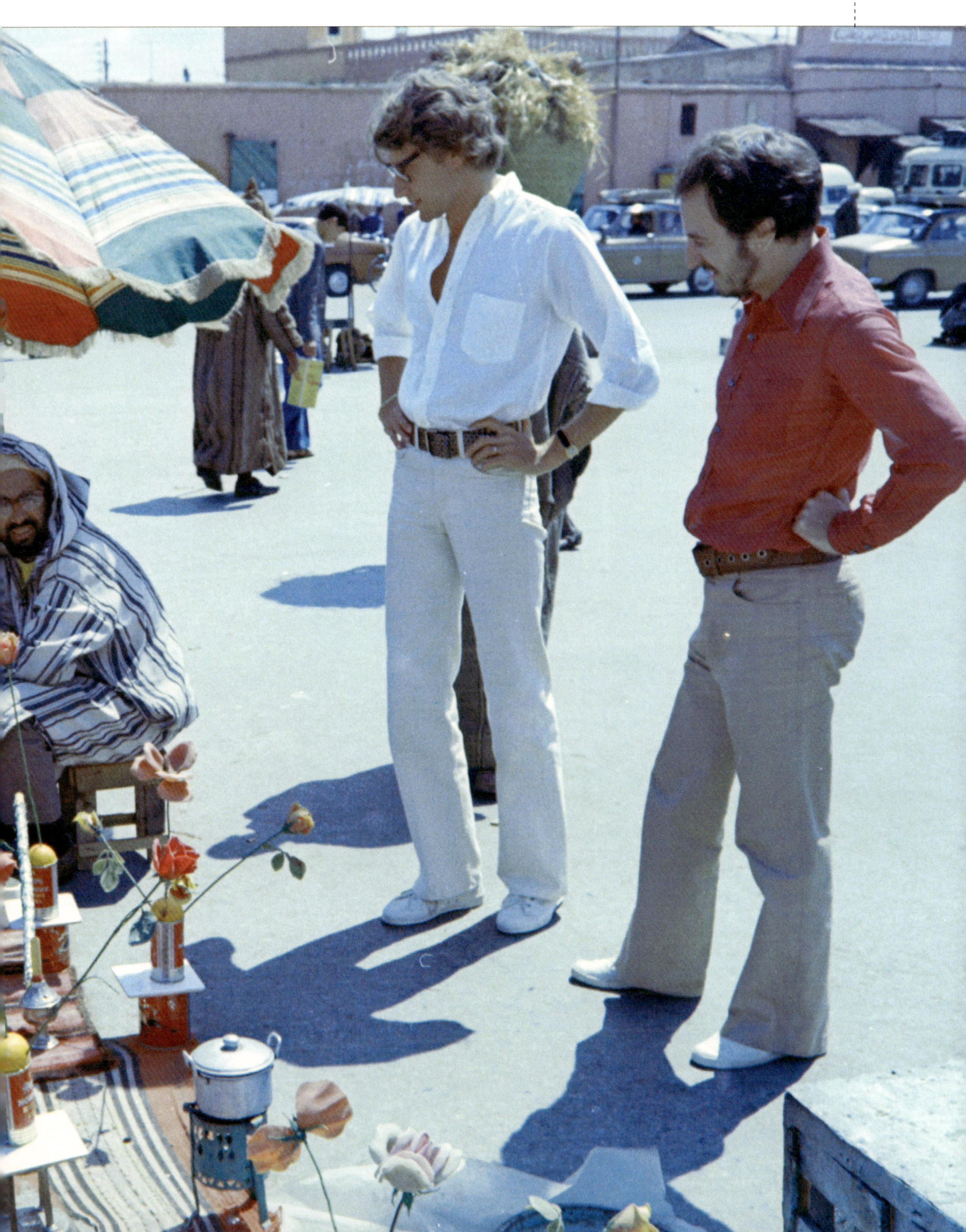

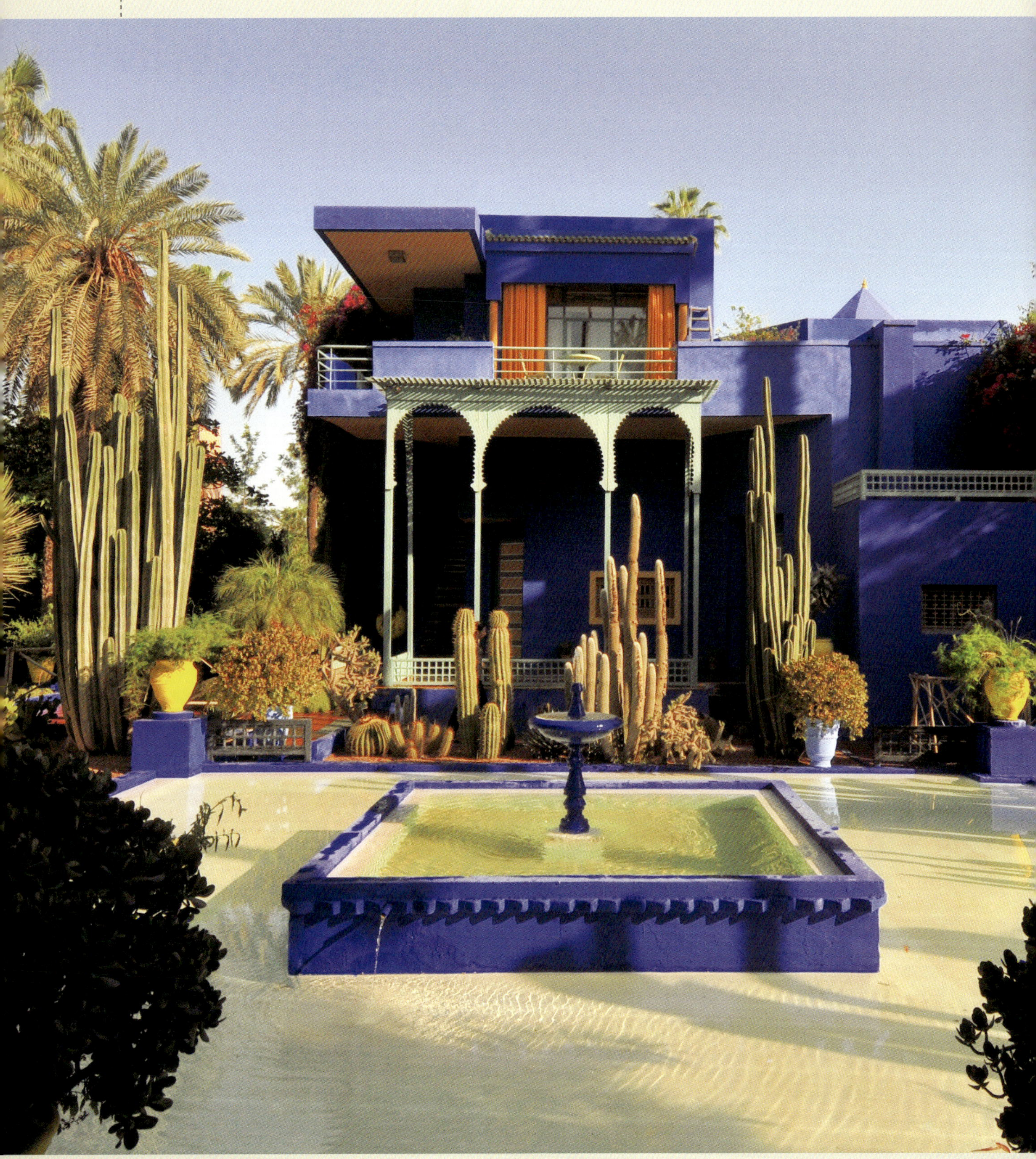

ABOVE: Jardin Majorelle
OPP PAGE: The vibrant colours of clothes on display at a market stall in Marrakech

More than just inspiration, Marrakech also became a creative refuge. Whenever the pressures of Paris overwhelmed him, Saint Laurent retreated to the sanctuary of his Moroccan home - a traditional riad hidden within the city's ancient walls. There, surrounded by palm trees, ceramics and Berber rugs, he sketched, dreamed and recharged. The city's rhythm slowed his pace and soothed his nerves, offering a kind of emotional and spiritual escape that was essential to his process. Not that it was always so serene. In addition to being Yves' haven at times, Marrakech, particularly during the hedonistic 1970s, was often party central.

Perhaps no symbol of his bond with Marrakech is more enduring than the Jardin Majorelle. Originally built in the 1920s by French artist Jacques Majorelle, the garden had fallen into disrepair by the time Saint Laurent and Bergé discovered it. Enchanted by its cobalt-blue buildings, rare plant collections, and calm, painterly composition, in 1980 they purchased and lovingly restored the property. It became their retreat and a source of endless inspiration. The shade of blue used throughout the garden—now famously called 'Majorelle Blue' - became inextricably linked to Saint Laurent's palette.

In many ways, Yves Saint Laurent belonged to two cities - Paris and Marrakech. The tension and harmony between those two worlds - urban sophistication and bohemian soul - defined his style and made him not only a couturier but a cultural alchemist.

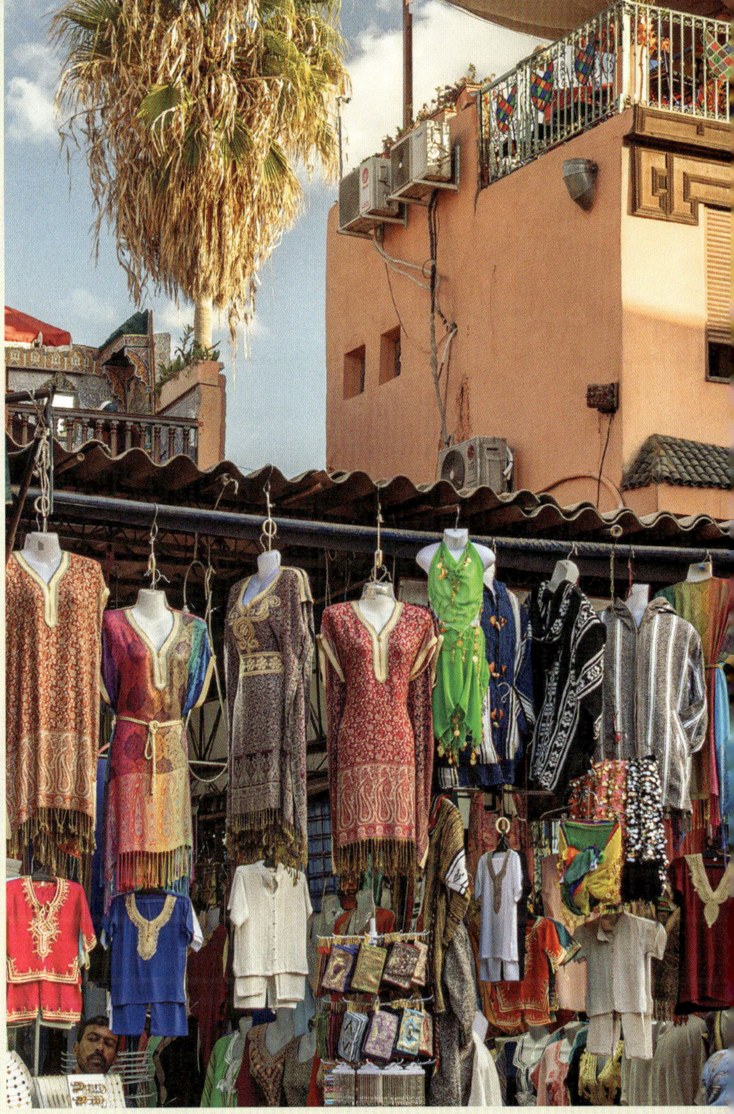

After his retirement from fashion in 2002, Saint Laurent continued to return to Marrakech, drawn again and again to its mystery and vitality. When he passed away in 2008, his ashes were scattered in the rose garden of the Jardin Majorelle. Today, the garden is not only a pilgrimage site for fashion lovers but also home to the Musée Yves Saint Laurent Marrakech, a museum devoted to his life and work, located just steps from his beloved sanctuary.

1970s

"I like the idea of shocking people, but I don't do it for the sake of it. I do it because I think it's right"

Yves Saint Laurent

Throughout the 1970s, both YSL's pret-a-porter and haute couture lines became vessels for his radical experimentation and social commentary. His Spring/Summer 1971 collection, known as the 'Liberation Collection' the 'Forties Collection' and also the 'Scandal Collection', drew heavily on the wartime styles of Nazi-occupied France – specifically of those women who had became involved with the invaders. Padded shoulders, knee-length skirts, platform shoes, square-cut jackets, retro hairstyles with victory rolls, and heavy 1940s-style make-up, including red lipstick and pencilled eyebrows... The collection caused outrage. At the time, the world was still within living memory of World War II. In France, especially, the trauma of occupation and the moral wounds of collaboration were fresh. To reference that era in a celebratory fashion show - and with such overt sexuality - was seen as deeply insensitive, even obscene. Fashion critics condemned it, some denouncing it as *'ugly'* and *'vulgar'*. The French

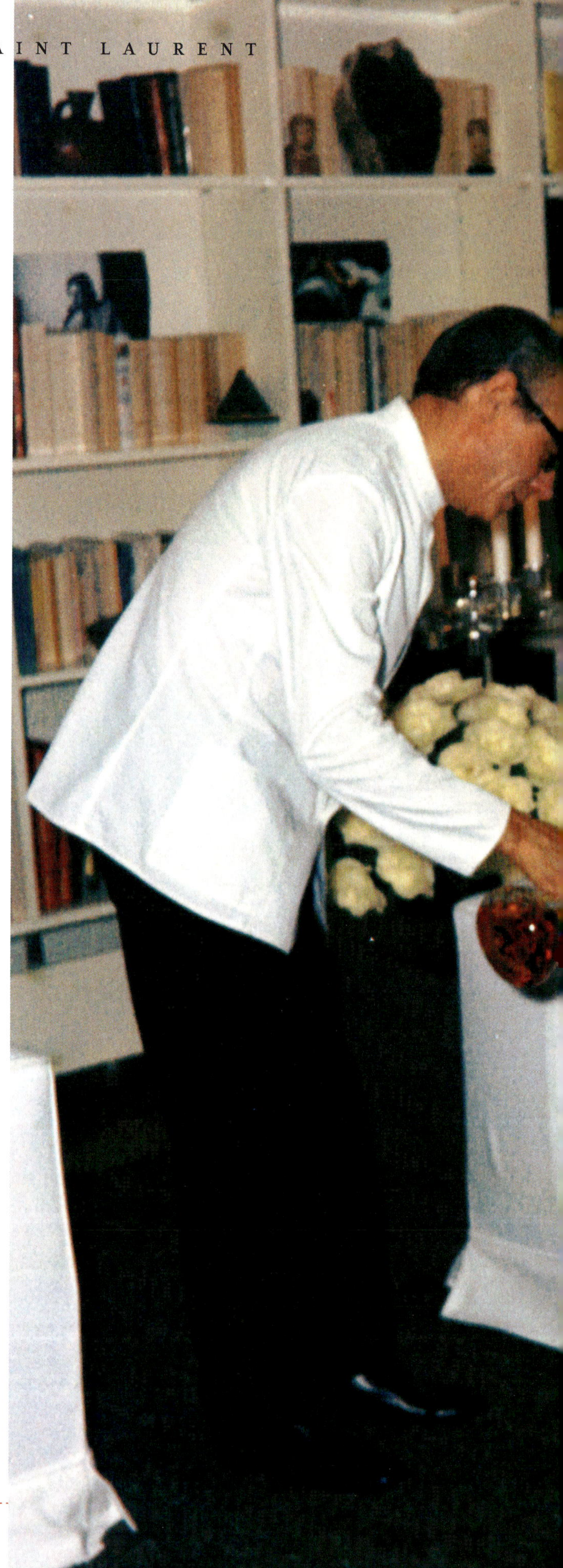

RIGHT: Yves Saint Laurent presents his Haute Couture Fall 1972 collection at his Paris residence

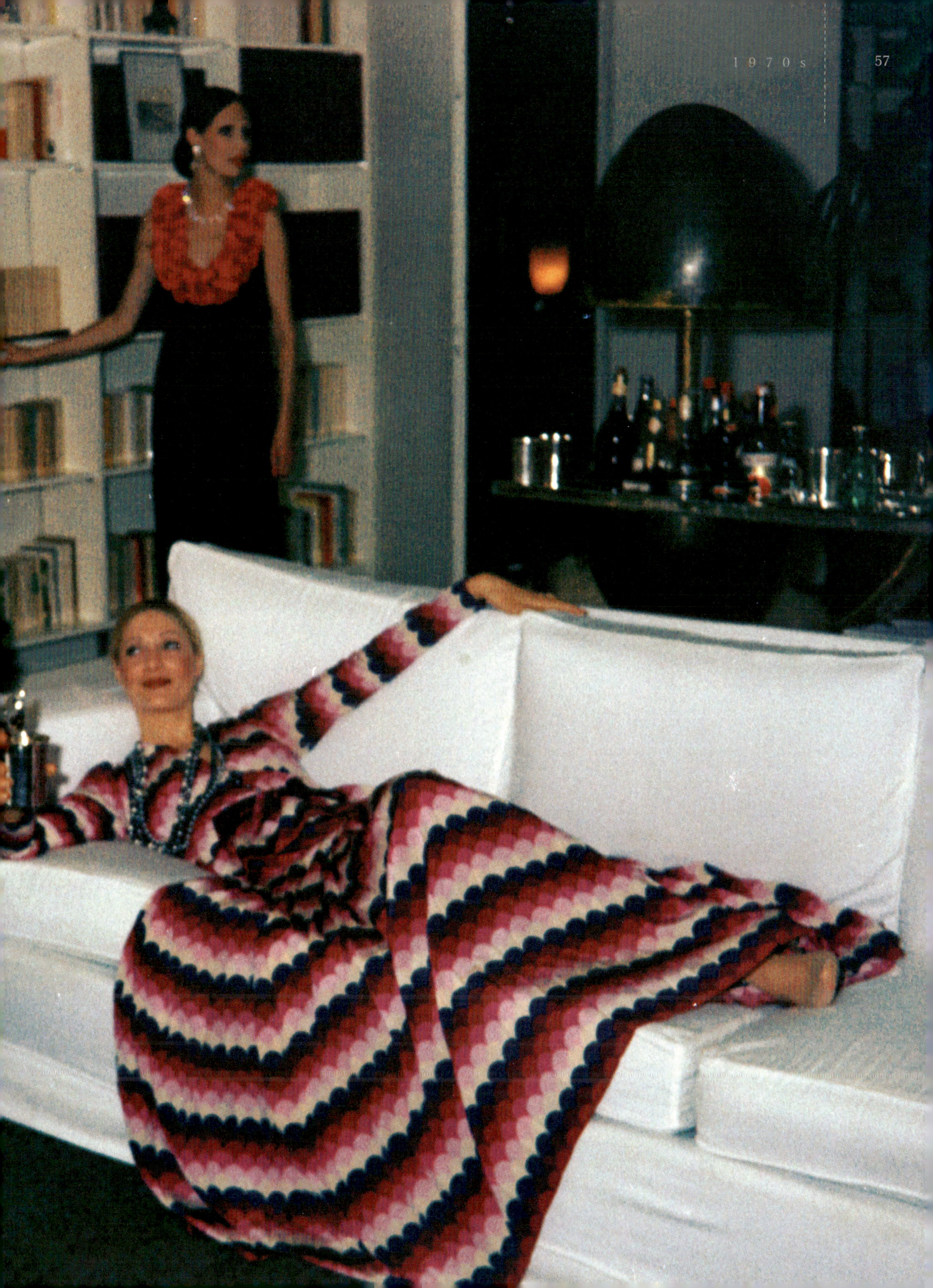

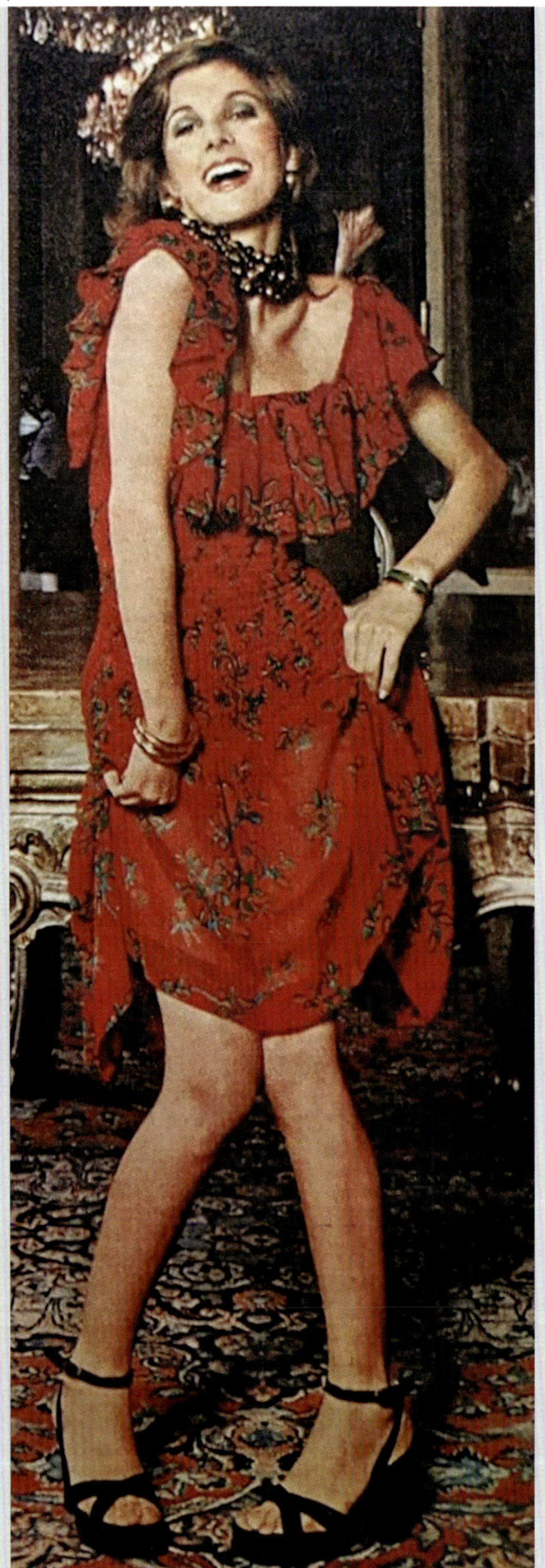

press described it as a *'tasteless flirtation with a shameful past'*. *American Vogue* initially refused to publish the images, and even fellow designers and clients were baffled. However, Saint Laurent himself was unapologetic. For him, the collection was about memory, resistance and bold femininity. He had lived through the war as a child in Algeria and had witnessed how women retained their dignity, even under extreme conditions, through style. He saw the 1940s look as powerful and a form of resistance rather than a nostalgia for fascism. While the collection was panned at the time, it would prove to be truly trendsetting. 1940s fashion and style were everywhere by the middle of the decade. Saint Laurent's decision to glorify an ugly moment in beautiful clothes — and to make people deeply uncomfortable in the process — established him as not just a designer but also provocateur. An artist who believed that fashion was not above history but an integral part of it.

The 1970s also marked a decade of global exploration for YSL. He drew inspiration from Moroccan kaftans, Russian folk dress, Chinese silk robes, Spanish national costume and African motifs. His 1976 Ballets Russes collection - a cacophony of colour, fur and embroidery - is often cited as one of the most opulent fashion shows in history. While lauded for their beauty and theatricality, these collections also sparked debate around cultural appropriation — a term not yet widely used but relevant in hindsight. Saint Laurent's interpretation of 'ethnic' elements was part admiration, part exoticism, and raised complex

ABOVE: Italian actress Stefania Casini poses in a Yves Saint Laurent dress, 19 July, 1973
OPP PAGE: Ballets Russes collection, Autumn 1976

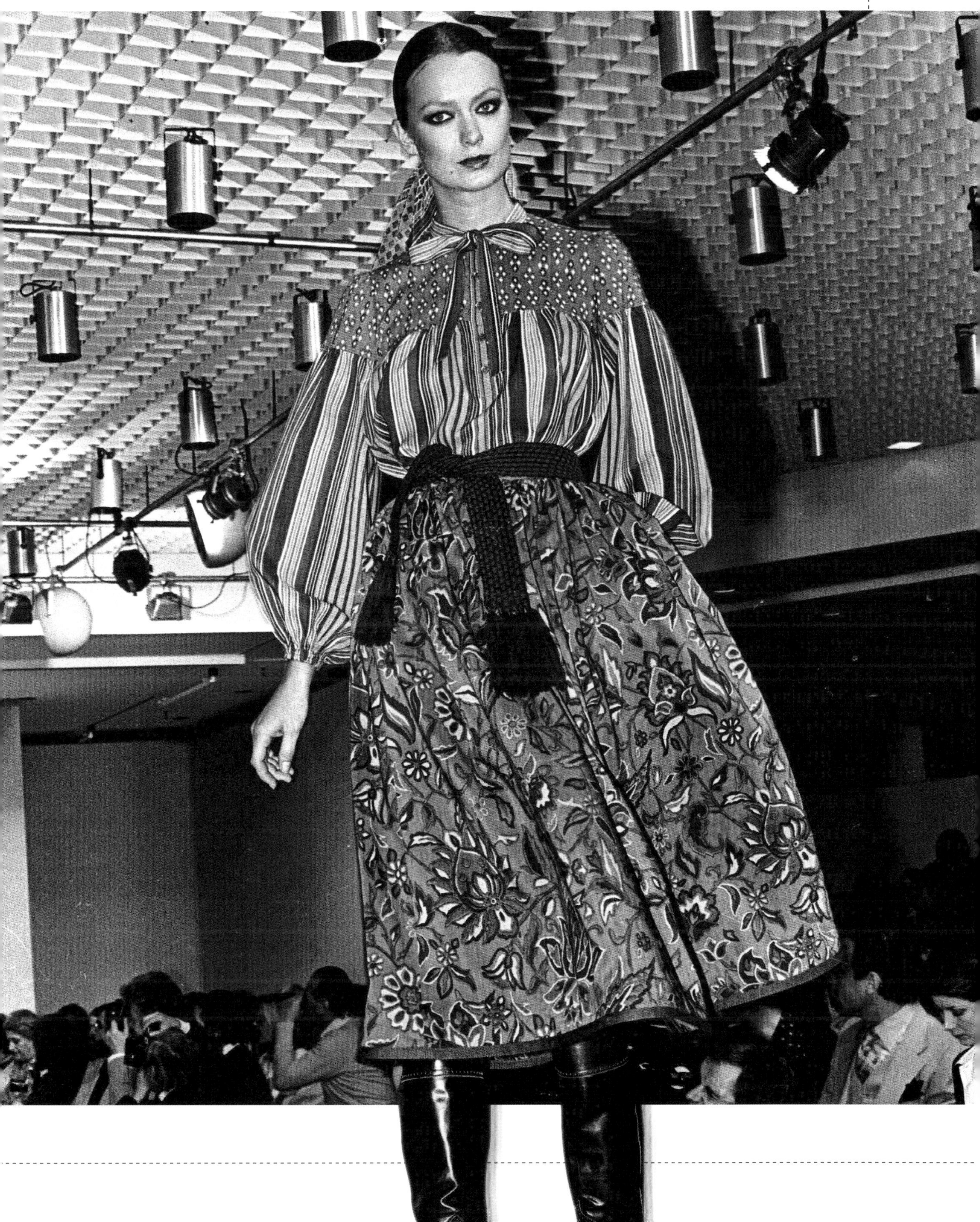

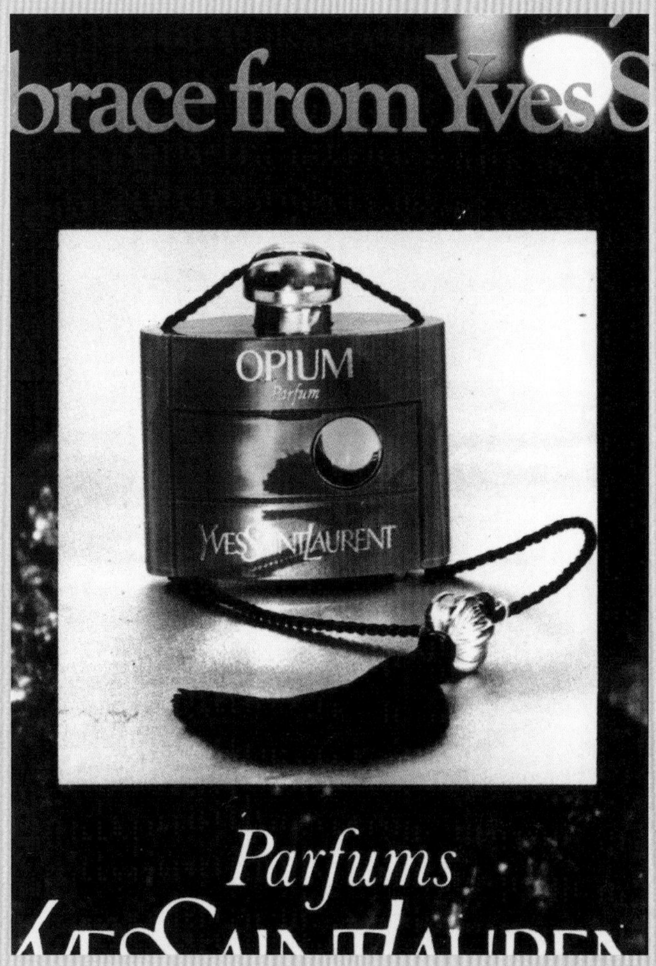

questions about fashion's use of non-Western cultures for aesthetic purposes.

There was further furore over the 1977 release of his Opium perfume - a sultry, spicy fragrance that courted controversy due to its name and also its advertising campaign. YSL muse Jerry Hall was pictured reclining on a luxurious sofa, surrounded by opulent accessories and decorations, while her head was thrown back, presumably in ecstasy from the high of sex, drugs ... or simply the scent. There

had been a similar scandal six years earlier when YSL himself opted to be photographed in the nude in order to promote his new cologne 'Poor Homme'.

'It was just a provocation on the part of Yves Saint Laurent,' Pierre Bergé was to later comment about his partner's decision to bare all.

The '70s saw Saint Laurent continue to rework traditionally masculine garments into symbols of female empowerment. The 'Le Smoking' tuxedo was reimagined for disco-era decadence — sleeker, sexier, more subversive. His safari jackets, peasant blouses, and sharply tailored blazers were worn by women who refused to be boxed into a single identity. YSL's designs in the 1970s were inseparable from the women who inspired him. His circle of muses included Loulou de La Falaise, the bohemian aristocrat whose eclectic style influenced his jewellery and accessory design, and Paloma Picasso, whose dramatic aesthetic helped shape YSL's flirtation with theatricality. Perhaps most iconically, Betty Catroux, the androgynous blonde who was often seen by his side at New York's Studio 54, embodied the blurring of gender that YSL celebrated in his work. Through these women, Saint Laurent created a new female archetype - worldly, sensual, strong, and unpredictable.

By the end of the decade, YSL had become more than a designer - he was a global symbol of avant-garde elegance and cultural boundary-pushing. His

ABOVE: 1978 *Vogue Australia* magazine advertisement for Yves Saint Laurent's 'Opium'
OPP PAGE: A preview of the Yves Saint Laurent Fall 1977 ready-to-wear collection, in Paris, France

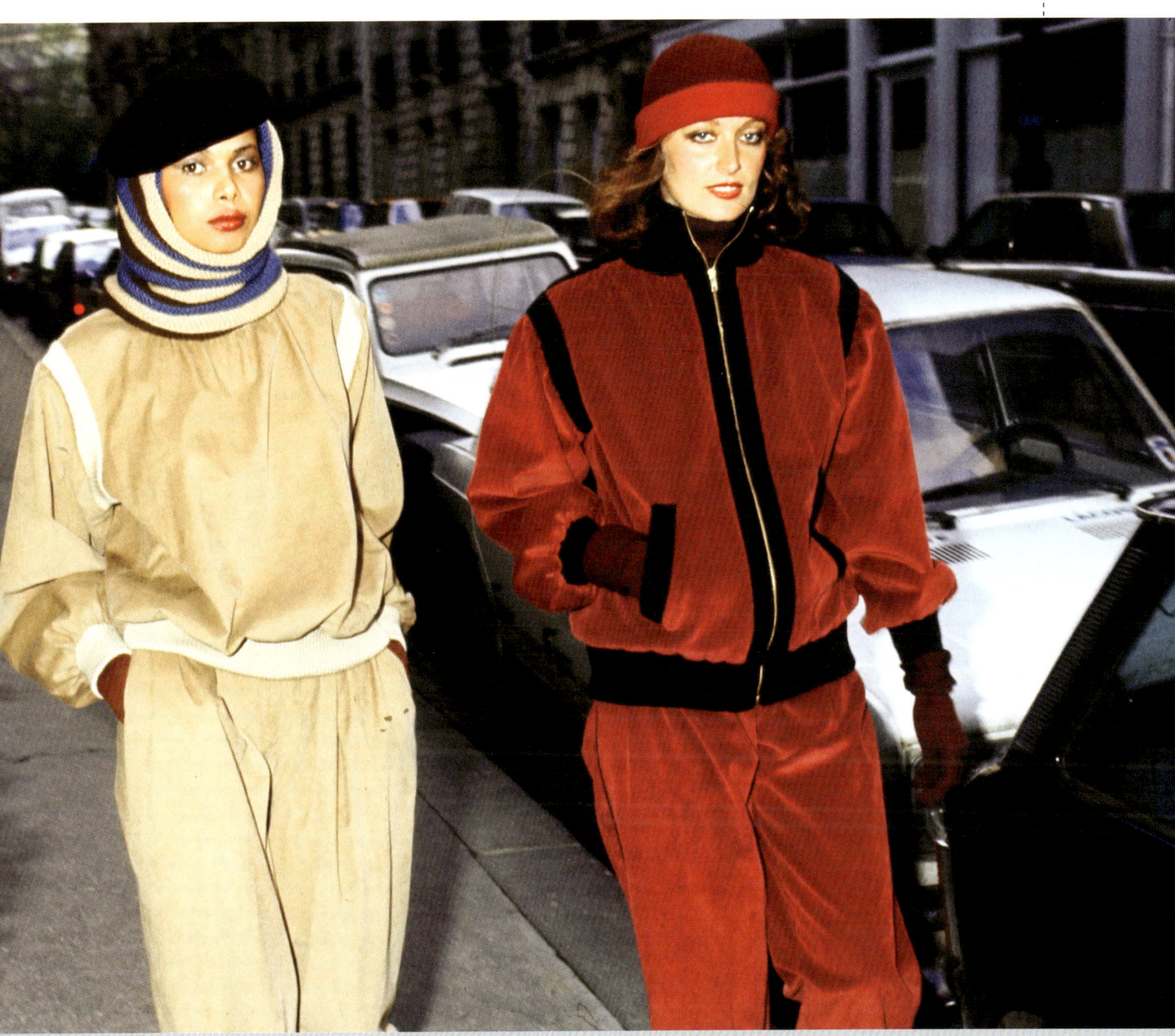

ability to inject sensuality into tailoring, to elevate everyday garments to objects of desire, and to turn women into icons rather than mannequins left a permanent imprint on fashion. The 1970s were not his most commercially stable years — addiction and emotional instability would take their toll — but creatively, they were unmatched. Saint Laurent's work in this period laid the foundation for many of the trends that dominate contemporary fashion today - gender fluidity, street-to-runway crossover and the politicisation of style.

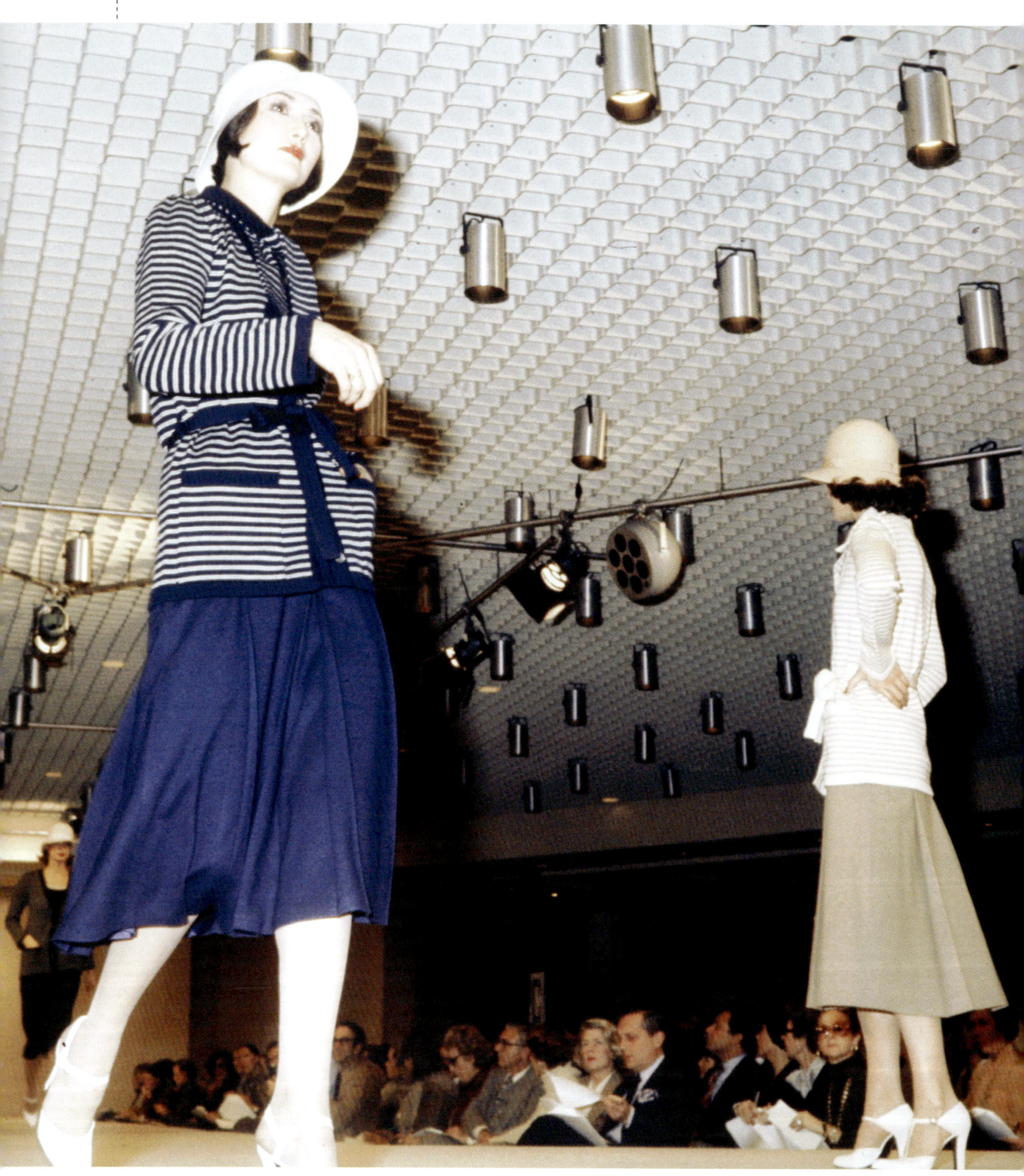

ABOVE: Yves Saint Laurent Spring 1976 ready-to-wear
runway show
OPP PAGE: Model Sayoko Yamaguchi during the Yves
Saint Laurent Spring 1979 ready-to-wear runway show

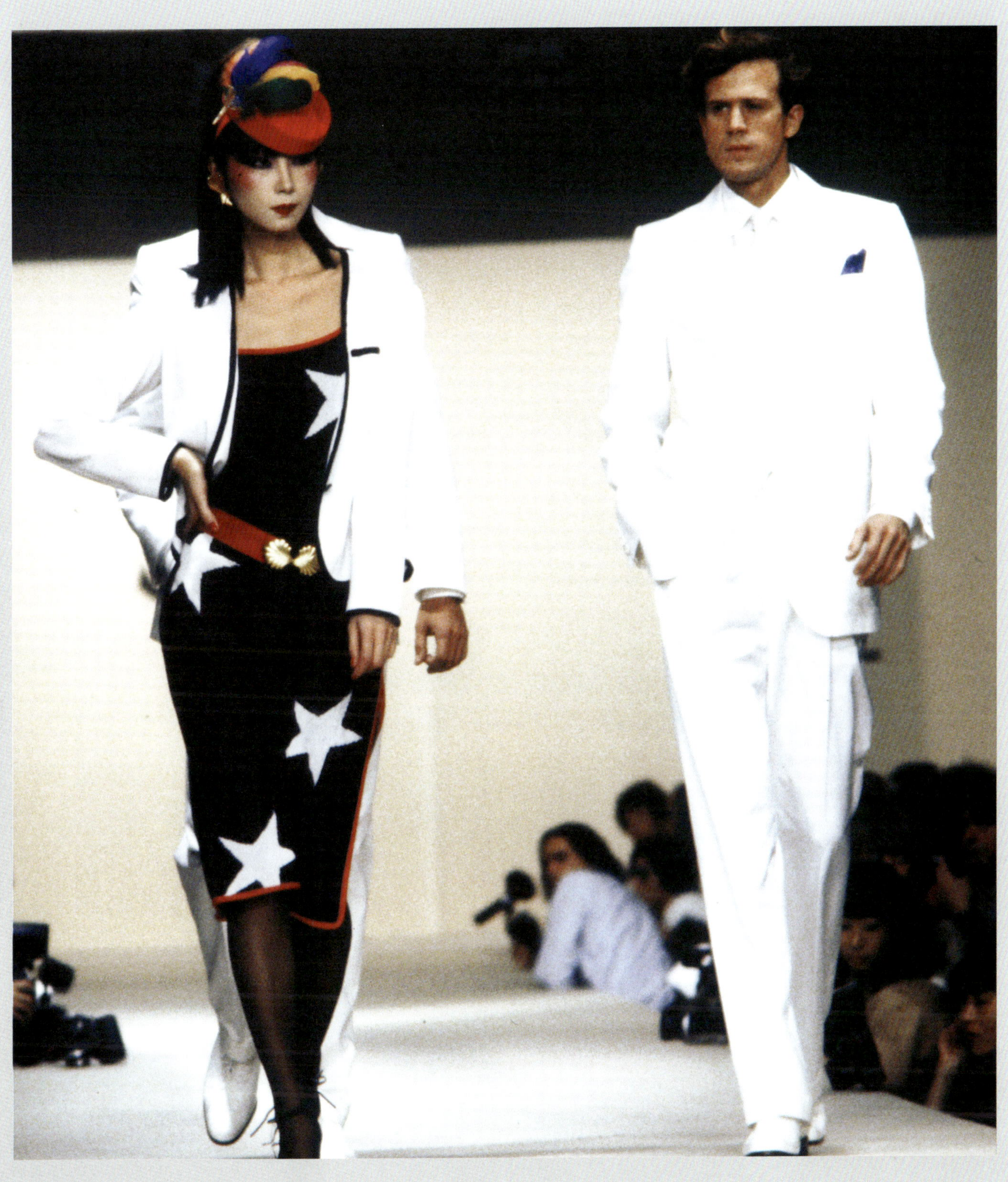

MENSWEAR

"I find men's clothing fascinating because sometime between, say, 1930 and 1936, a handful of basic shapes were created and still prevail as a sort of scale of expression, with which every man can project his own personality and his own dignity"
Yves Saint Laurent

While Yves Saint Laurent is most often celebrated for his revolutionary impact on women's fashion, his influence on menswear is equally significant — though more subtly woven into the fabric of modern style. It is no exaggeration to say that Saint Laurent didn't just design menswear - he redefined it. He modernised men's wardrobes by bringing the spirit of youth, sensuality and relaxed sophistication into what was traditionally rigid, formal clothing. As much as he empowered women by giving them suits and trousers, he also liberated men — softening strict sartorial codes without sacrificing a sense of power and mystery.

'I think fashion should evolve, not revolutionize,' Saint Laurent said.

His menswear did exactly that. It was steady evolution - radical yet refined.

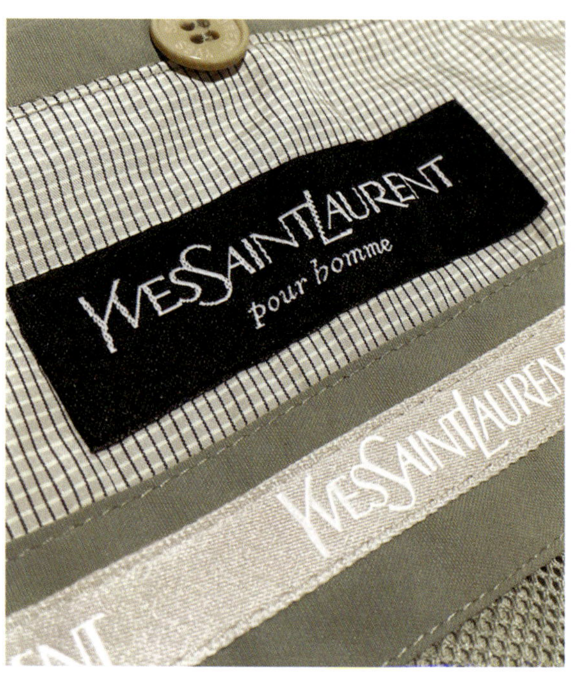

Yves Saint Laurent officially launched his first menswear line, Rive Gauche Homme, in 1969, building on the success of his Rive Gauche ready-to-wear line for women. This new collection brought the ethos of Saint Laurent's womenswear — modernity, luxury, accessibility — into a male context. Key elements

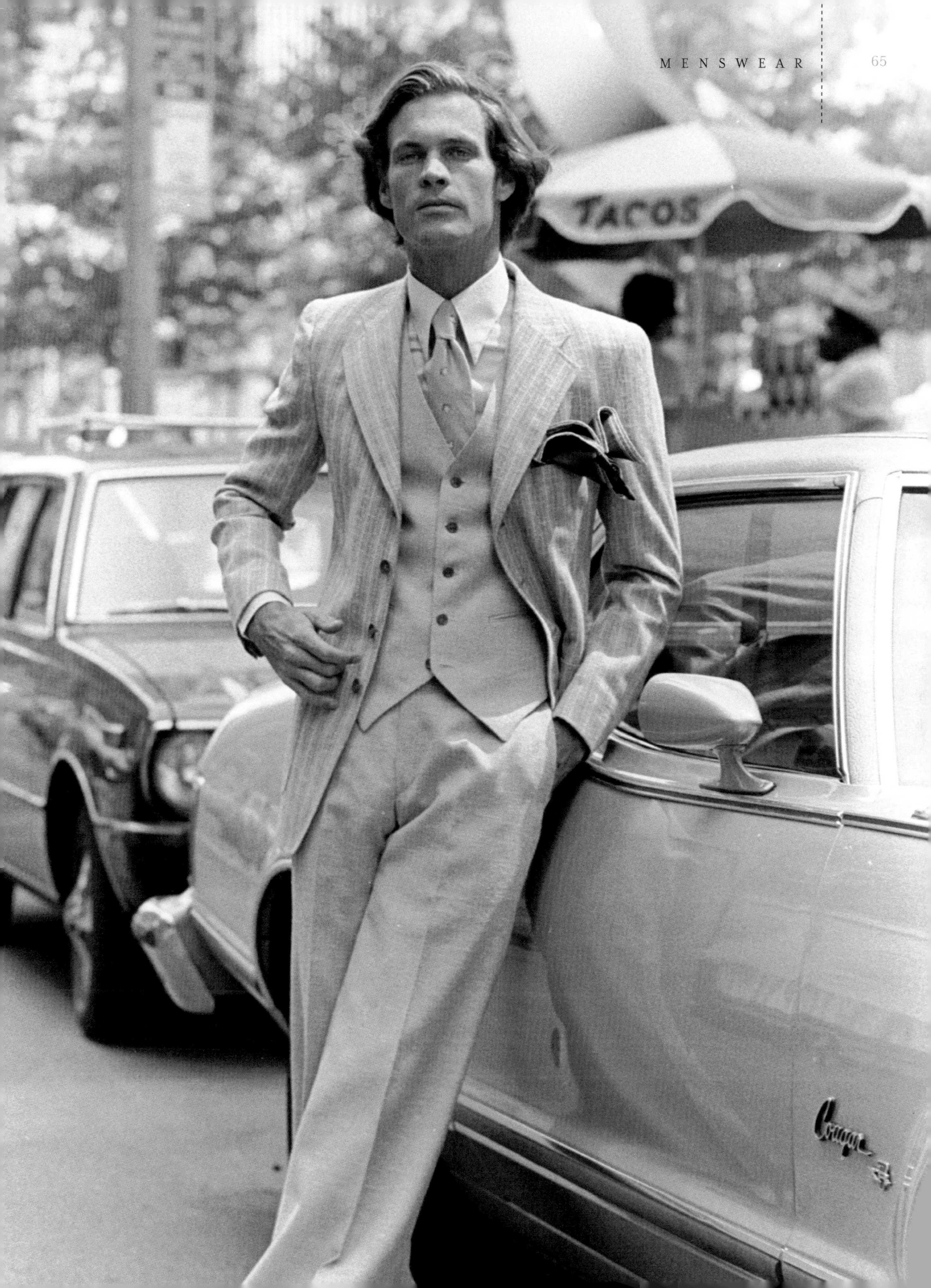

TACOS

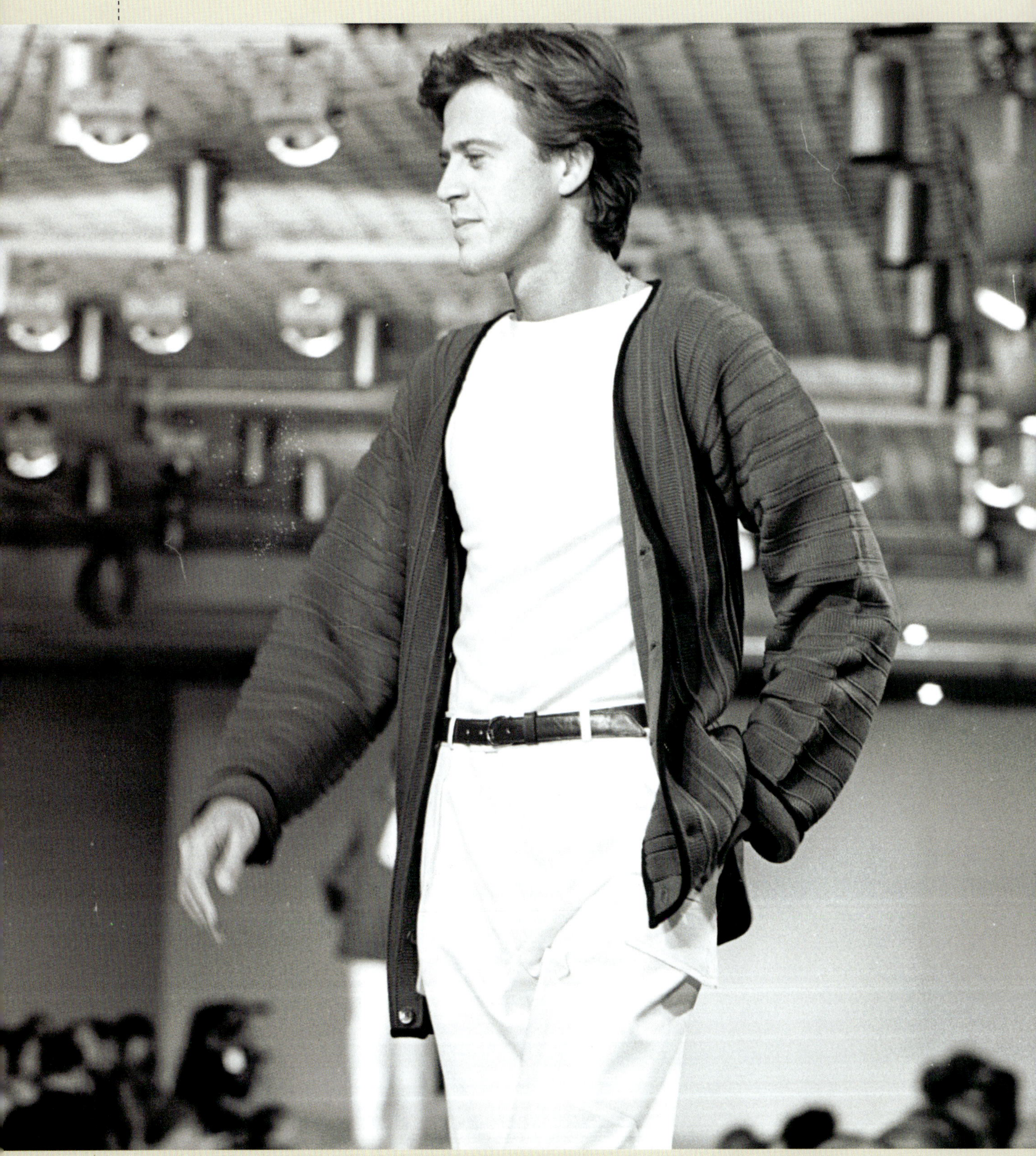

ABOVE: Yves Saint Laurent Spring/Summer Menswear
collection runway show, 1977
OPP PAGE: Yves Saint Laurent Menswear show, Spring/
Summer, 1992

of YSL Rive Gauche Homme included slim, almost languid tailoring, favouring soft shoulders and fluid lines over stiff structure. Saint Laurent rejected the boxy, aggressive suits that dominated mid-20th-century menswear.

Instead, he proposed a softer, more romantic silhouette - narrower jackets, slim trousers and delicate shirts often unbuttoned lower than the norm. This wasn't about emasculating men — it was about giving them access to sensuality and elegance. Saint Laurent was among the first to present menswear that carried an erotic charge. He adapted his beloved safari jackets and utility styles for men, giving them an adventurous, worldly edge – this casual sophistication became part of the DNA of modern luxury menswear. While Saint Laurent's colour palette for menswear featured greys, navy and olive shades, YSL's favourite hue for his male clothing line was black. For him it was the ultimate colour for stylish menswear – sleek, rebellious and elegant. Black suits, black leather, black shirts... all became essential thanks to YSL's vision. YSL men were stylish, but never overdressed. Saint Laurent created a wardrobe that was understated, seductive and timeless.

It's not possible to look at YSL's menswear without mentioning the designer himself. Slim and angular, Yves Saint Laurent was his own favourite muse and was often photographed in his own designs. His personal style — understated, intellectual, slightly melancholic — became a blueprint for a new kind of

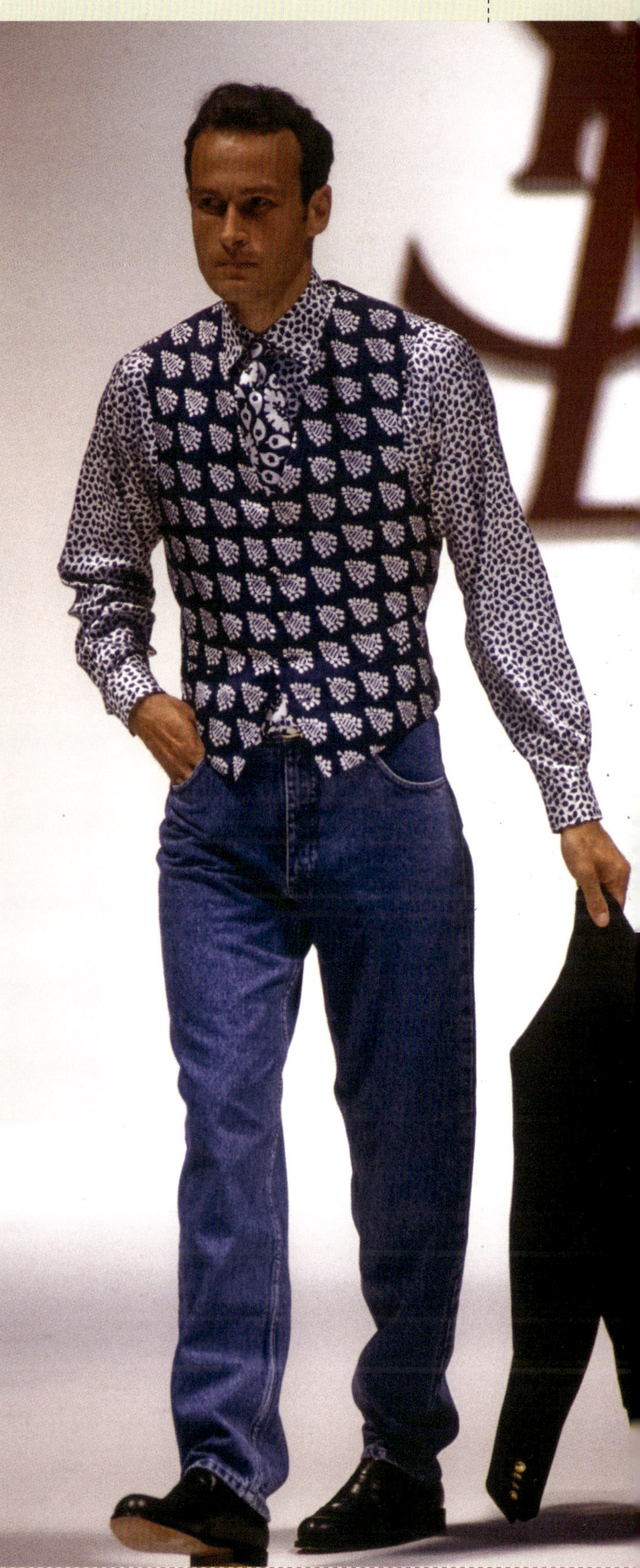

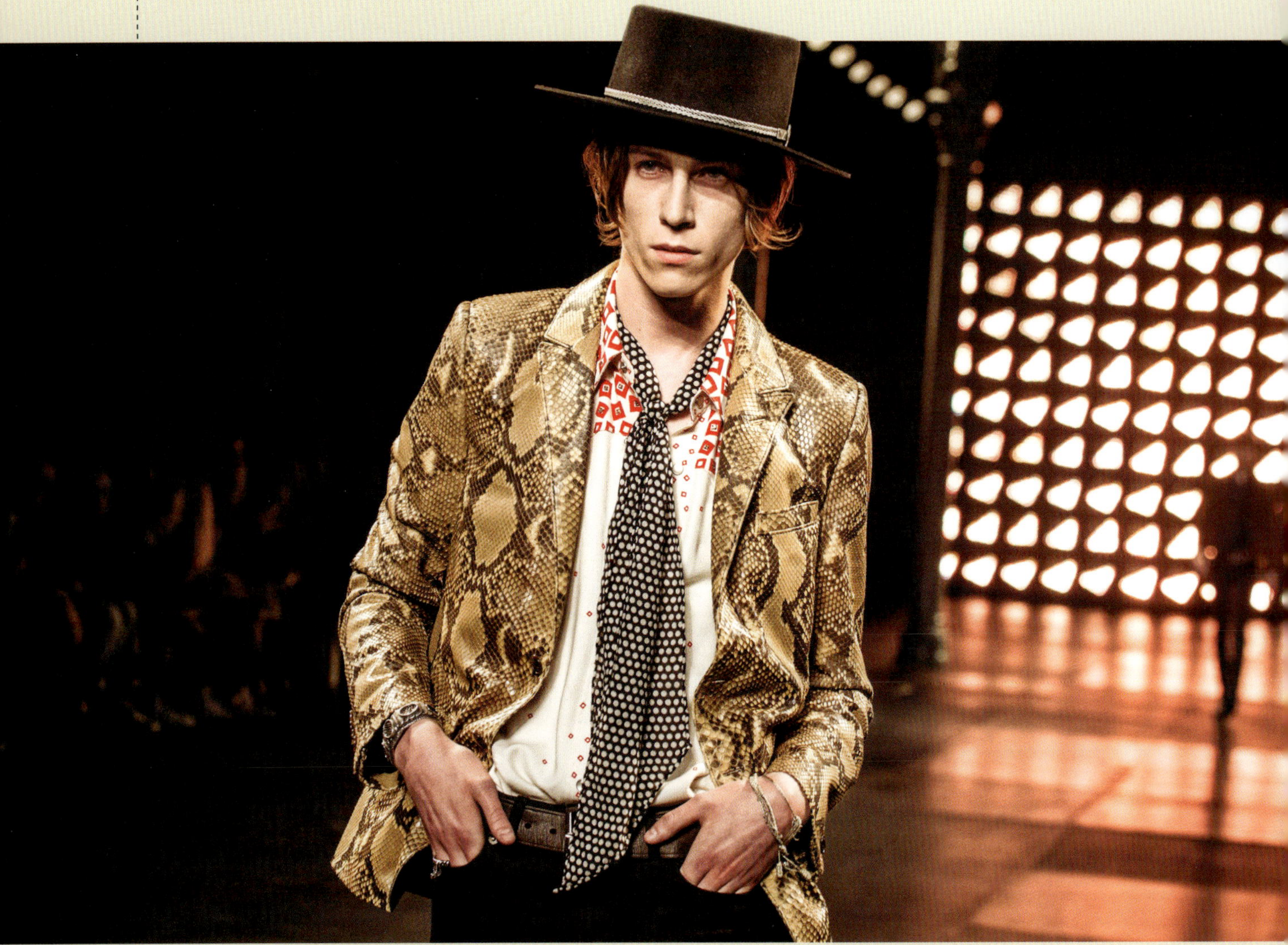

modern man. One who was cultured, sensitive, stylish and slightly aloof. Saint Laurent's image helped set a cultural tone - a man could be fashionable without being frivolous, elegant without losing his authenticity.

Saint Laurent's menswear has had a tremendous legacy, even though it's less loudly celebrated than his work for women. His influence can be seen directly in Hedi Slimane's Dior Homme collections (early 2000s) which featured ultra-skinny tailoring and rock-star energy; in Anthony Vaccarello's current Saint Laurent which continues the sharp, black, effortlessly sexy menswear codes, and in Tom Ford's sensual menswear collections during his Saint Laurent tenure - lush, sexy, but always tailored. Saint Laurent also inspired the rise of luxury casualwear such in the form of field jackets and pea coats. Today, when you see men in slim suits, silk shirts or understated black tailoring, you are seeing echoes of Yves Saint Laurent. Elegant yet rebellious. Strong yet sensitive. Timeless yet subversive.

ABOVE: Yves Saint Laurent 2015 Menswear collection, Spring/Summer 2015

OPP PAGE: Yves Saint Laurent Menswear Autumn/Winter 2025/2026 show as part of Paris Fashion Week

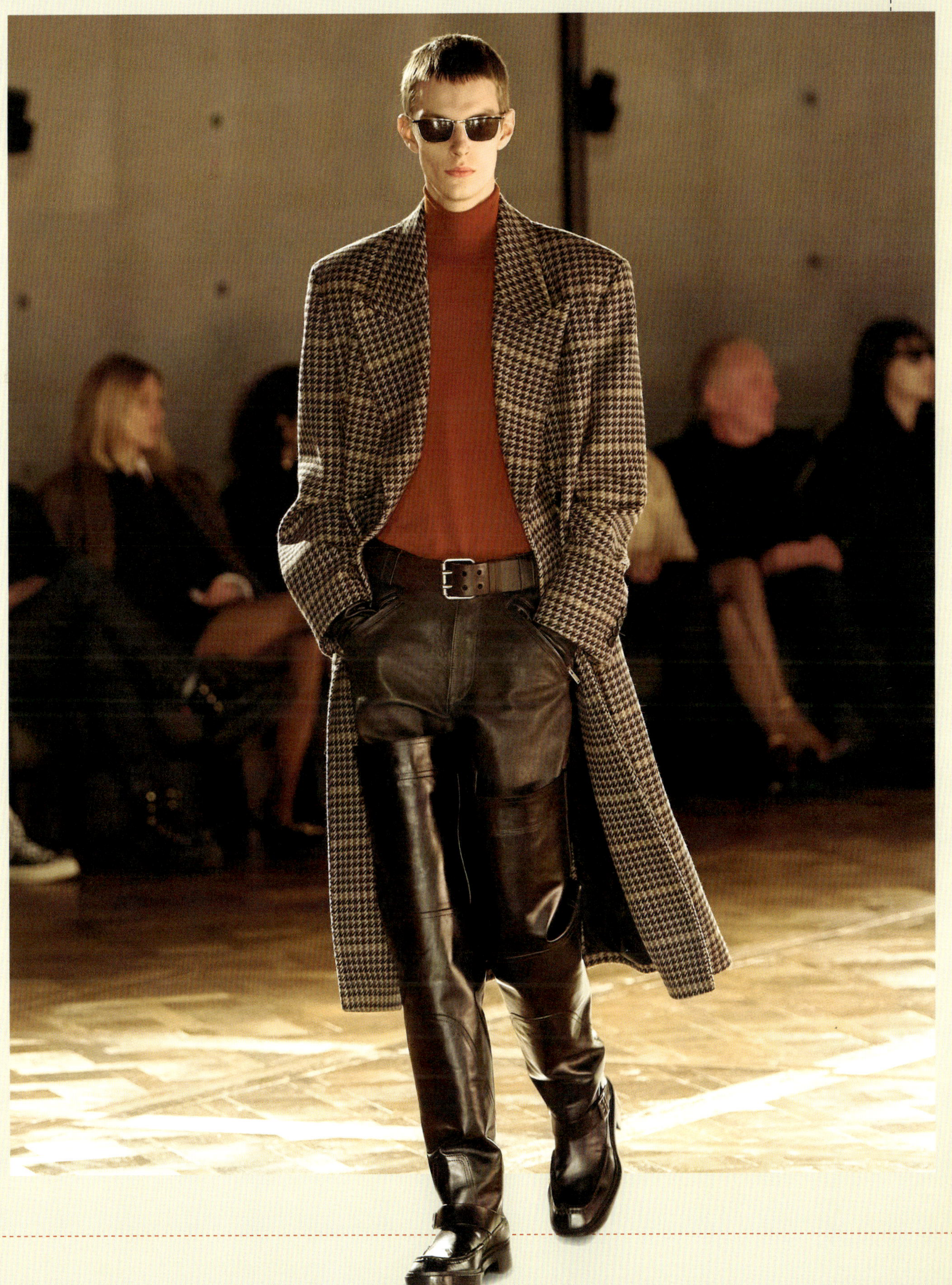

1980s

"I have always believed that fashion was not only to make women more beautiful but also to reassure them, give them confidence"
Yves Saint Laurent

The 1980s were a time of boldness and exuberance in fashion. The global economy was booming, the Reagan and Thatcher eras were ushering in a period of wealth and power dressing became the dominant trend. Within this environment, Yves Saint Laurent continued to define himself as a designer who was always forward-thinking yet also rooted in a sense of timeless elegance. For Saint Laurent, the 1980s were an era of empowered femininity — when the modern woman was beginning to demand a more assertive and independent role in society. Saint Laurent's designs mirrored this by incorporating strong silhouettes, structured lines and a sense of confidence that made his work resonate deeply with the changing times.

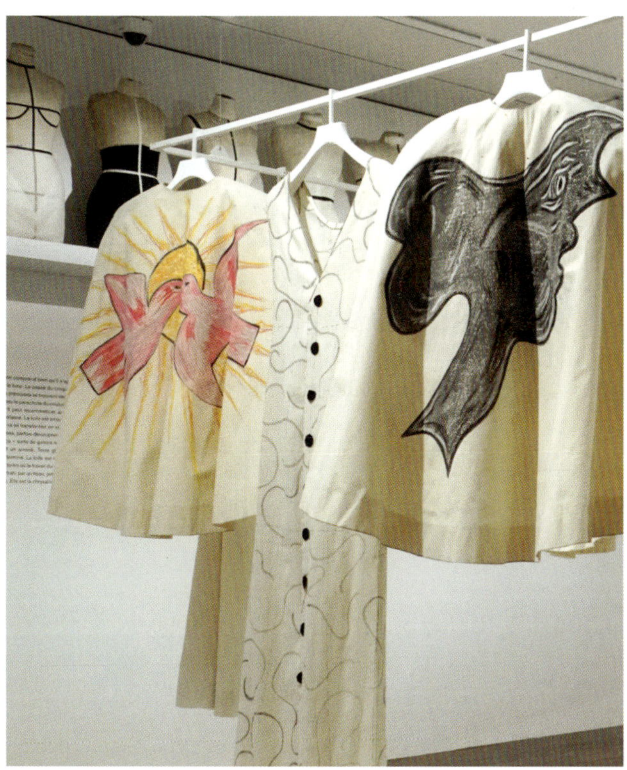

The power suit was one of the defining trends of the 1980s, and Yves Saint Laurent played a critical role in shaping its emergence. His take on it was unique because it combined his signature elements of elegance and comfort with the bold, masculine-inspired tailoring of the time. Saint Laurent had already been a trailblazer with the Le Smoking in the 1960s but 20 years on, he reinterpreted it with his tuxedos becoming symbols of the empowered woman in the workplace. His couture tuxedo jackets with satin lapels combined with slim trousers were as chic as they were revolutionary, providing women with a sense of both authority and sensuality. The sharp, structured lines of the tuxedo became the

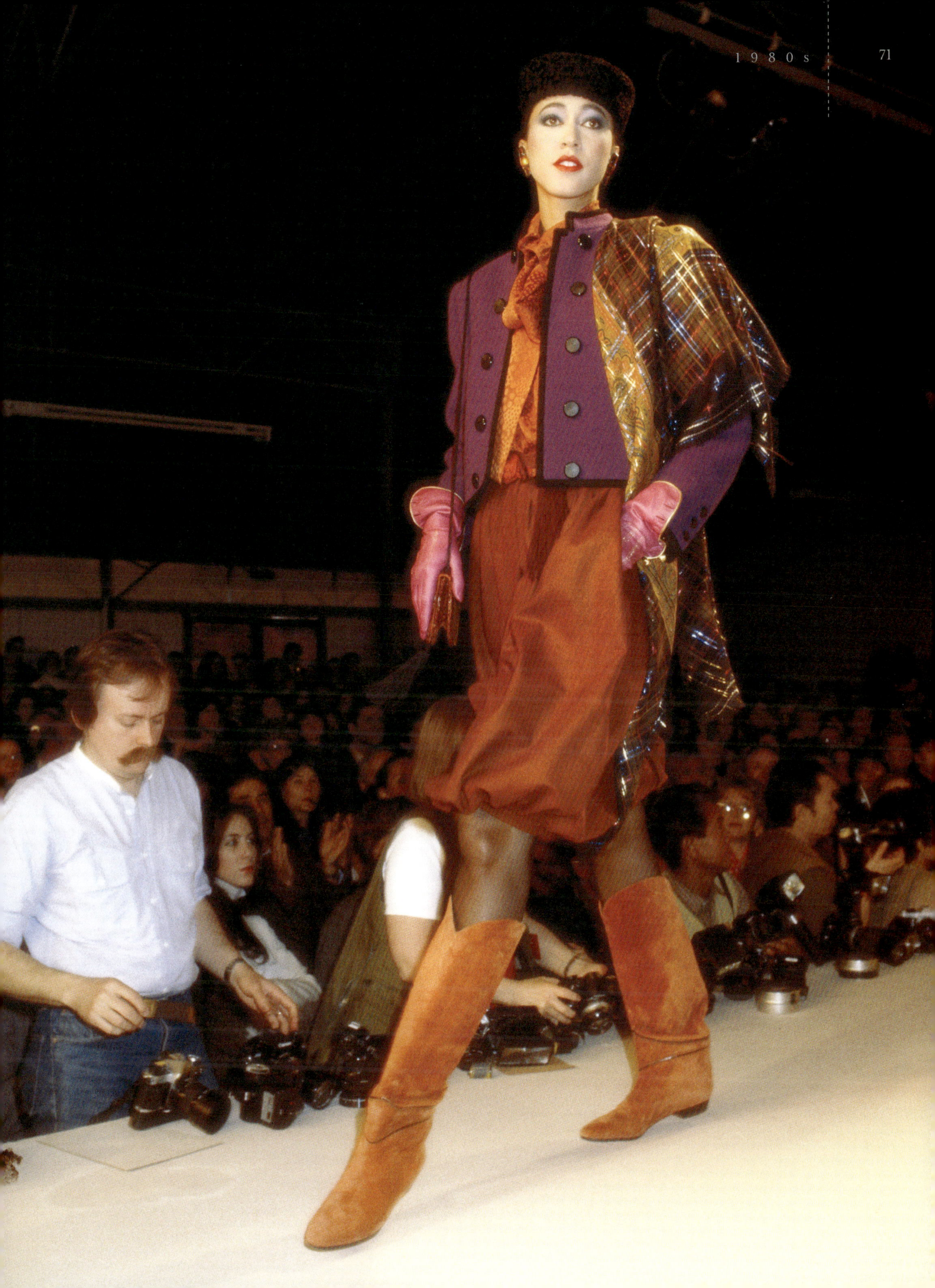

foundation for the power suit — a look designed to exude confidence, authority, and strength.

Also synonymous with the power dressing trend were Saint Laurent's tailored pieces - sharp, masculine-inspired shoulder pads, double-breasted jackets and high-waisted trousers. Yet YSL maintained a sense of chic femininity even within the structured, androgynous power dressing movement. His tailoring was always immaculate, with a focus on luxurious fabrics, rich details and perfect proportions. His designs gave women a way to assert themselves without losing their sense of femininity. The 1980s were defined by social and economic change and Yves Saint Laurent's designs reflected these shifts. As women continued to enter the workforce in greater numbers, they were demanding clothing that was both powerful and elegant. YSL's designs were an answer to that demand, offering a way for women to present themselves as confident, assertive, and successful without sacrificing style.

Yves Saint Laurent's collections throughout the 1980s were bold, opulent, and influential - cementing his legacy as a master of couture and ready-to-wear. In 1980, he paid tribute to the poets he admired. References to Louis Aragon, Guillaume Apollinaire, and Jean Cocteau appeared in his designs. The 'Shakespeare' bridal gown he designed for

RIGHT: 1980 Yves Saint Laurent Rive Gauche black satin pantsuit with gold guipure lace trim

OPP PAGE: A model wears an outfit from the haute couture collection from Yves Saint Laurent, Spring/Summer, 1983

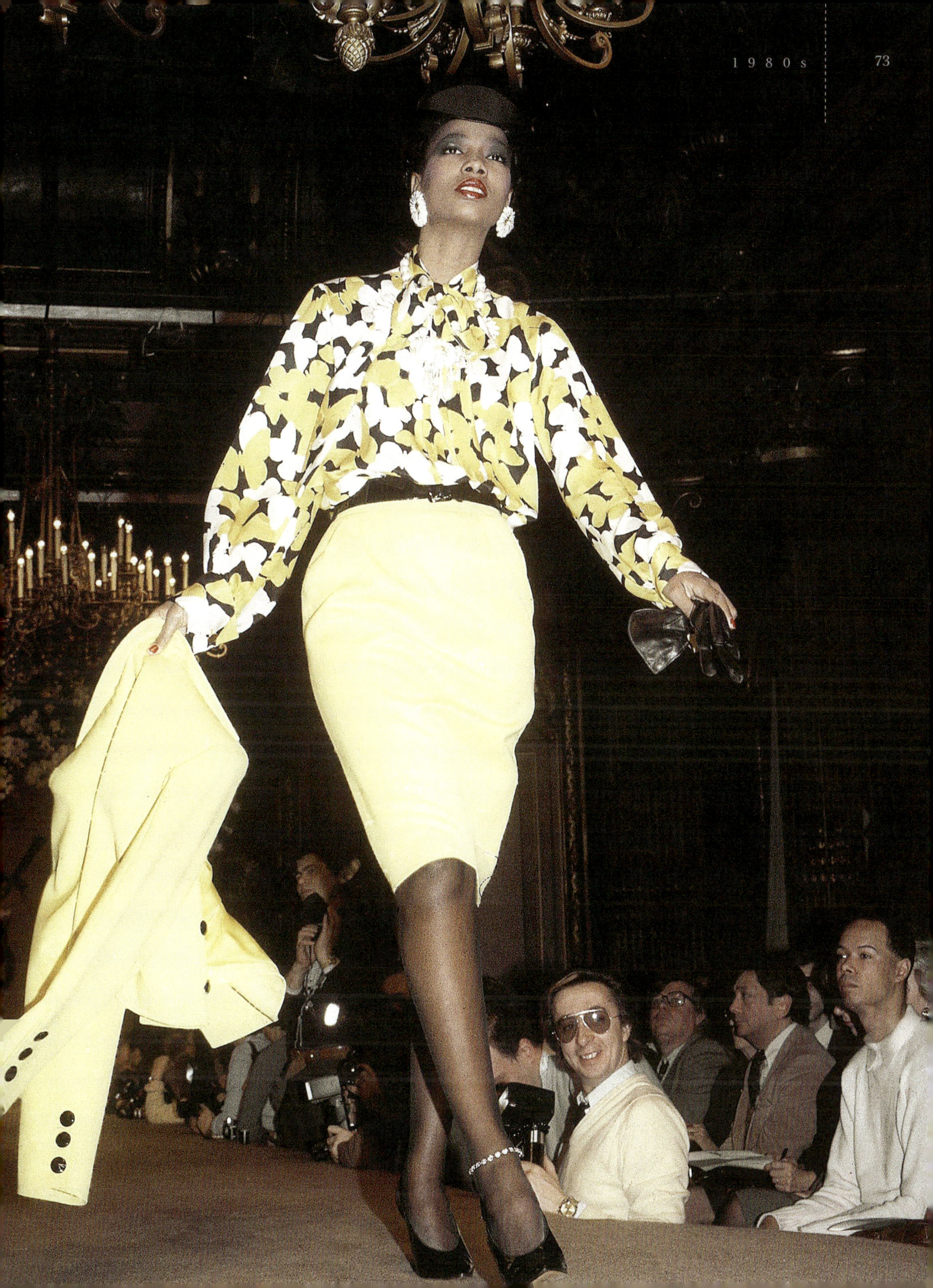

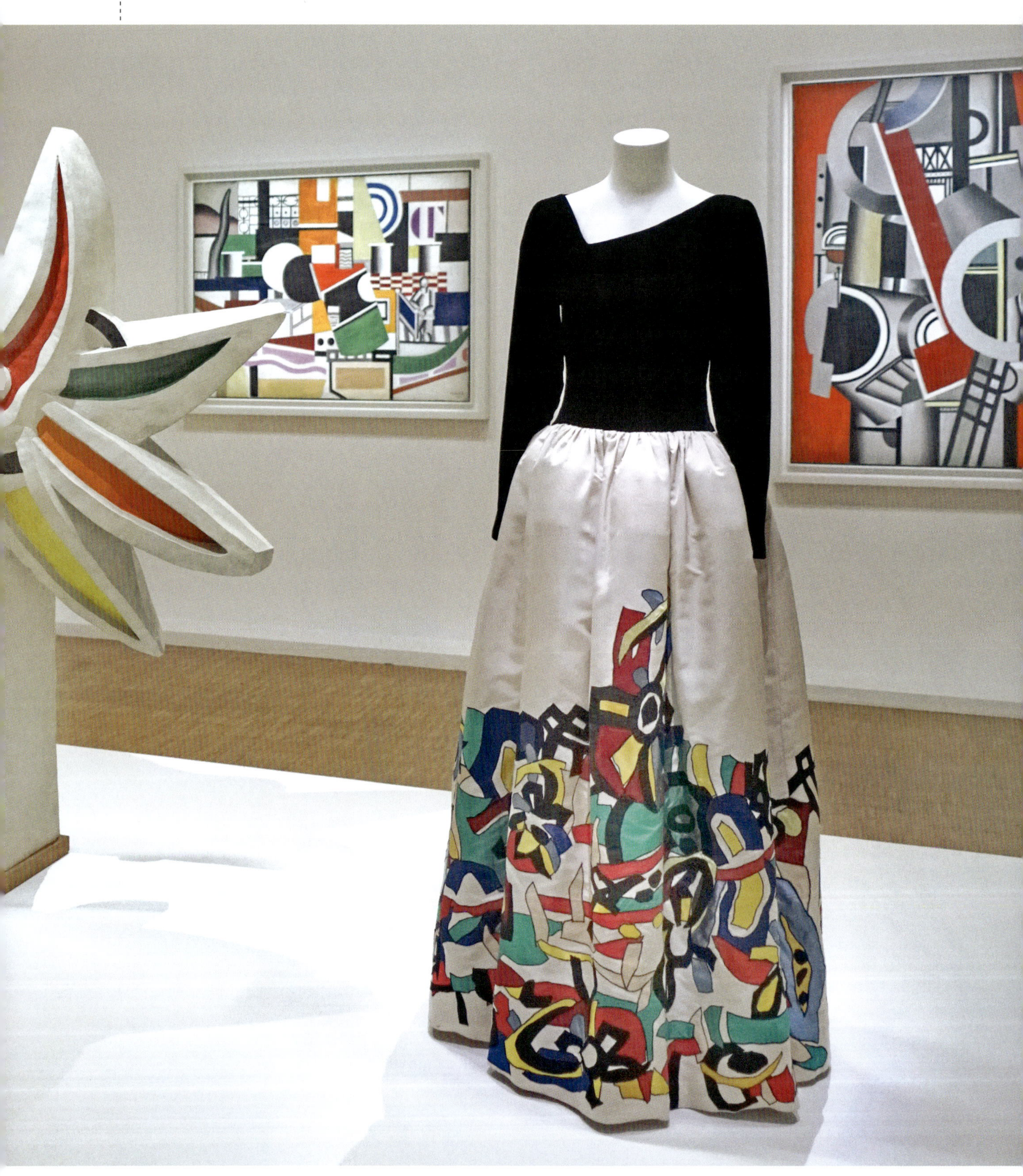

ABOVE: 'Homage to Fernand Léger' dress by Yves
Saint Laurent, Autumn/Winter 1981
OPP PAGE: 1988 Yves Saint Laurent Jacket, 'Homage to
Vincent van Gogh'

this collection was a lavish dress decorated with jewels.

'I did a whole collection paying homage to Shakespeare. A blouse evoked Hamlet's shirt and red silk gown, that of Lady Macbeth; it was reminiscent of the Middle Ages but still completely modern. I also thought about Emma Bovary a lot. This character is extremely contemporary. Madame Bovary expressed women's disarray, which is the same today as it was a century ago,' he was to recall.

Other notable collections from this decade include his 25th Anniversary Collection in 1984. Celebrating a quarter-century of design, he paid homage to his most influential creations. The runway featured reimagined versions of the Mondrian dress, safari jackets, and Le Smoking tuxedo where he blended nostalgia with contemporary flair. This collection reaffirmed YSL's status as a visionary in the fashion world. The year later, he delved into lavish evening attire, characterized by rich fabrics, intricate embroidery, and dramatic silhouettes. The Fall/ Winter 1985 collection showcased velvet gowns, gold embellishments, and bold accessories - capturing the extravagance of the era. These designs emphasized glamour and sophistication, solidifying YSL's reputation for luxurious couture. In 1988, in another fusion of fashion and art, YSL's haute couture collection drew inspiration from Vincent van Gogh's masterpieces. The standout pieces included jackets adorned with intricate beadwork replicating Van Gogh's 'Sunflowers' and 'Irises'. It was also during

the 80s that Saint Laurent's immersion in Moroccan culture inspired him to incorporate elements such as the djellaba, kaftan, and burnoose into his haute couture and ready-to-wear lines. These traditional garments were reimagined with luxurious fabrics, intricate embroidery and bold colours - reflecting the designer's unique blend of Parisian sophistication and North African artistry.

The 1980s solidified Yves Saint Laurent as a visionary designer who was able to navigate the ever-changing fashion landscape while staying true to his artistic roots. The decade saw the continued evolution of his signature style, while also experimenting with new ideas, concepts and cultural references. As the fashion industry entered a new era of excess, boldness, and glamour, Yves Saint Laurent found ways to remain at the forefront, constantly challenging the boundaries of what fashion could represent.

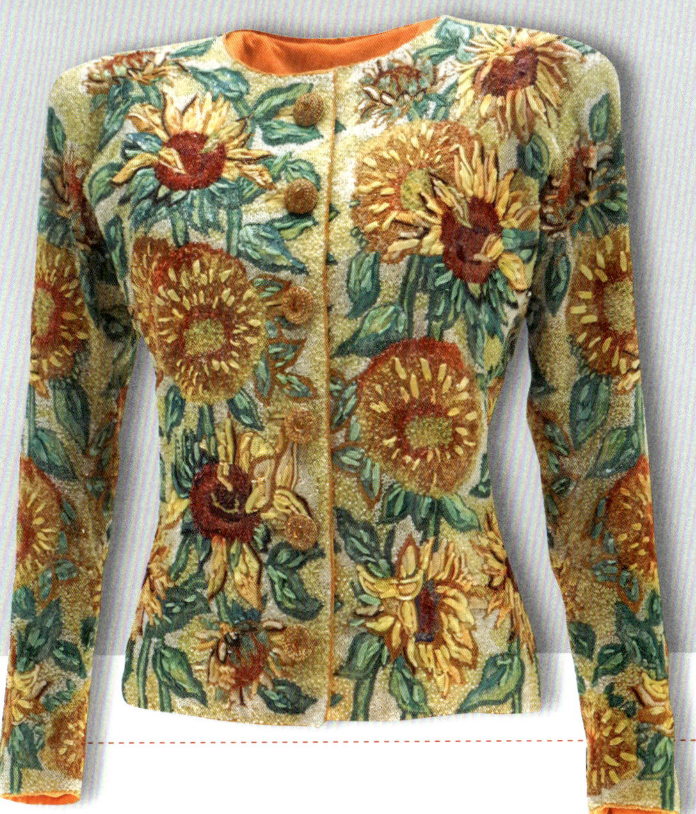

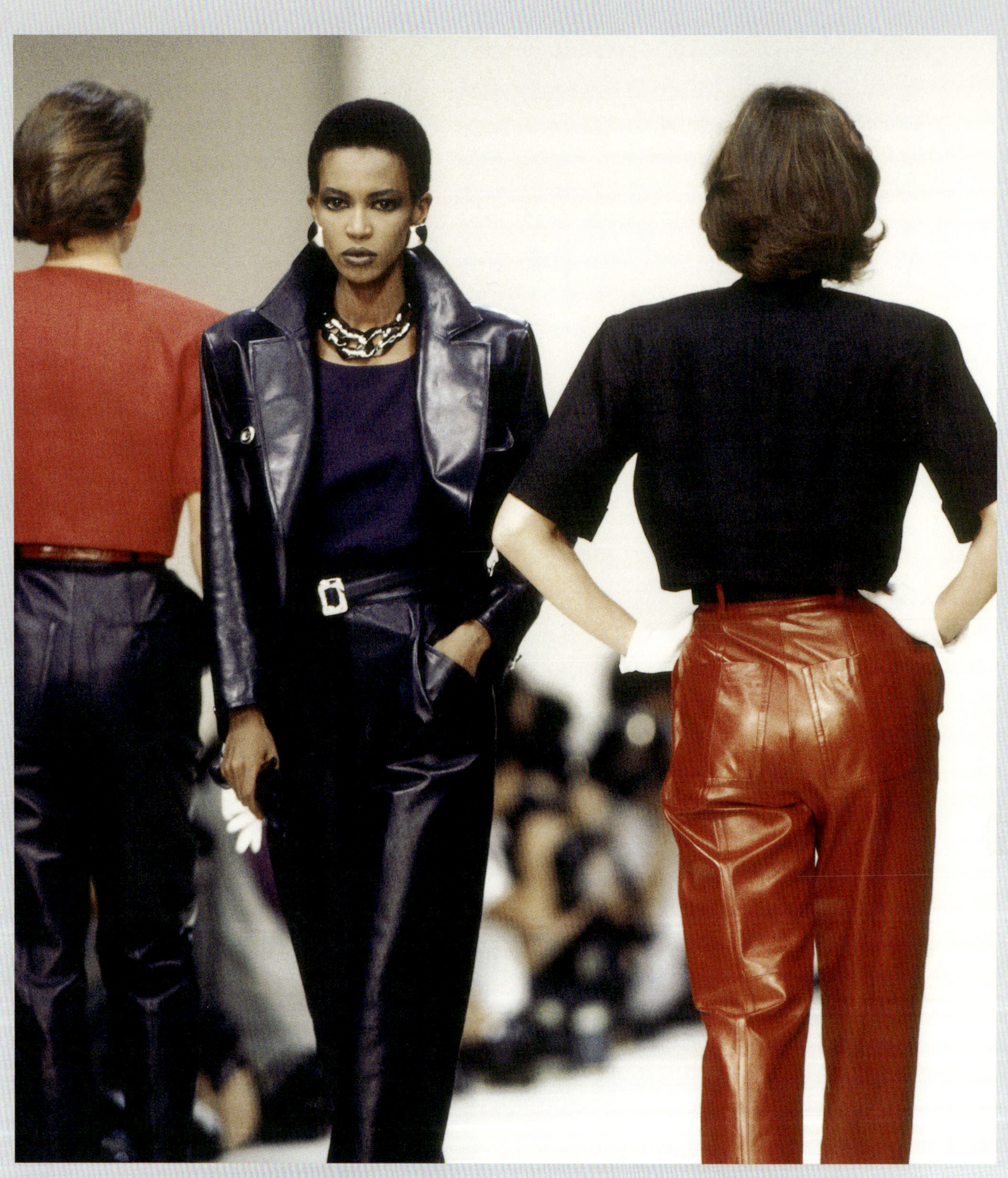

ABOVE: Yves Saint Laurent Summer Collection, Prêt-à-Porter fashion show, Paris, 1986
OPP PAGE: Yves Saint Laurent is congratulated by his models after his ready-to-wear Spring fashion collection for 1988

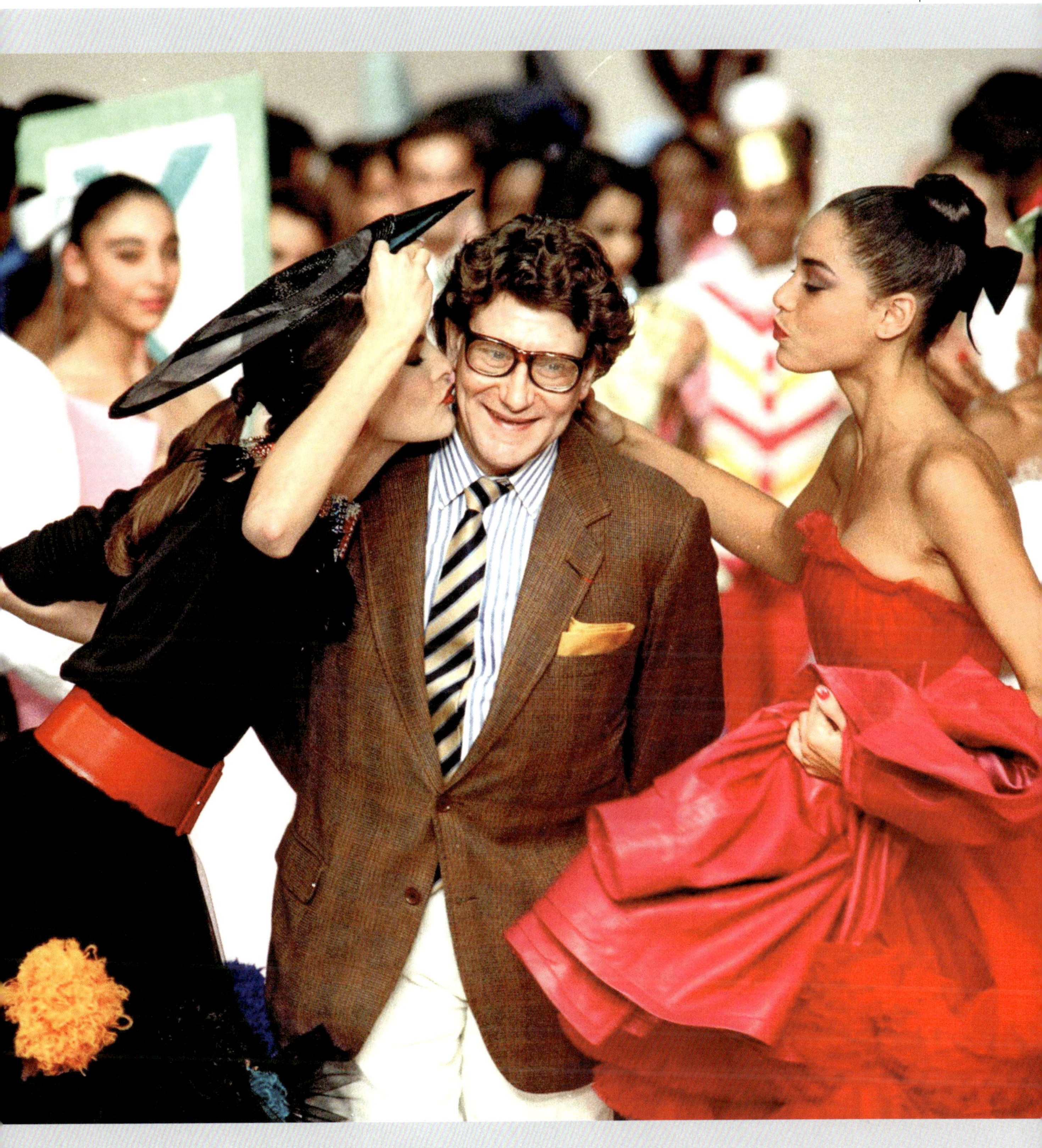

ACCESSORIES

"Accessories are essential to completing the look. They are not just extras, they are part of the whole picture"
Yves Saint Laurent

It was part of his genius that Yves Saint Laurent designed accessories to elevate his sartorial creations. For Saint Laurent, accessories weren't just add-ons but essential elements of a woman or man's identity - each one perfectly designed to amplify the individuality, personality, mood and lifestyle of the wearer. From the perfect handbag to statement shoes, belts, scarves, and jewellery, Saint Laurent knew that details had the power to transform an outfit — and, by extension, the person wearing it. Yves Saint Laurent's accessories were always integral to his brand's identity. They were as meticulously crafted and daring as his clothes. Today Saint Laurent accessories remain just as relevant and just as highly coveted as they continue to define high fashion luxury for new generations.

HANDBAGS

Saint Laurent's accessories line began with his innovative approach to handbags. With designs that were at once functional and visually stunning, he transformed the

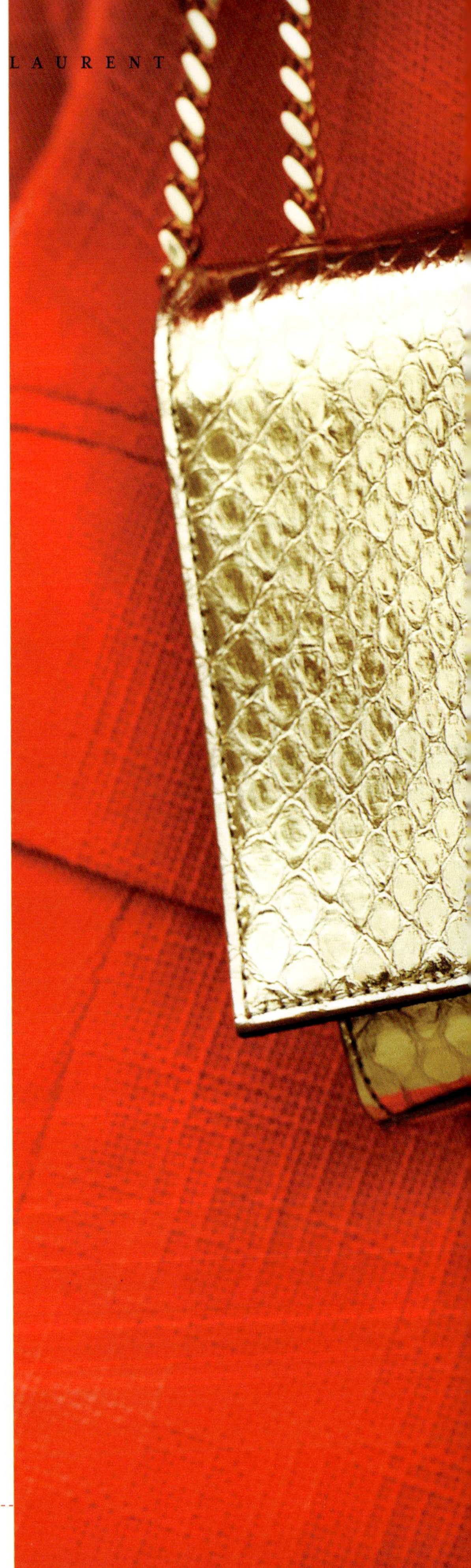

RIGHT: Kate Monogram shoulder bag in gold python-embossed leather

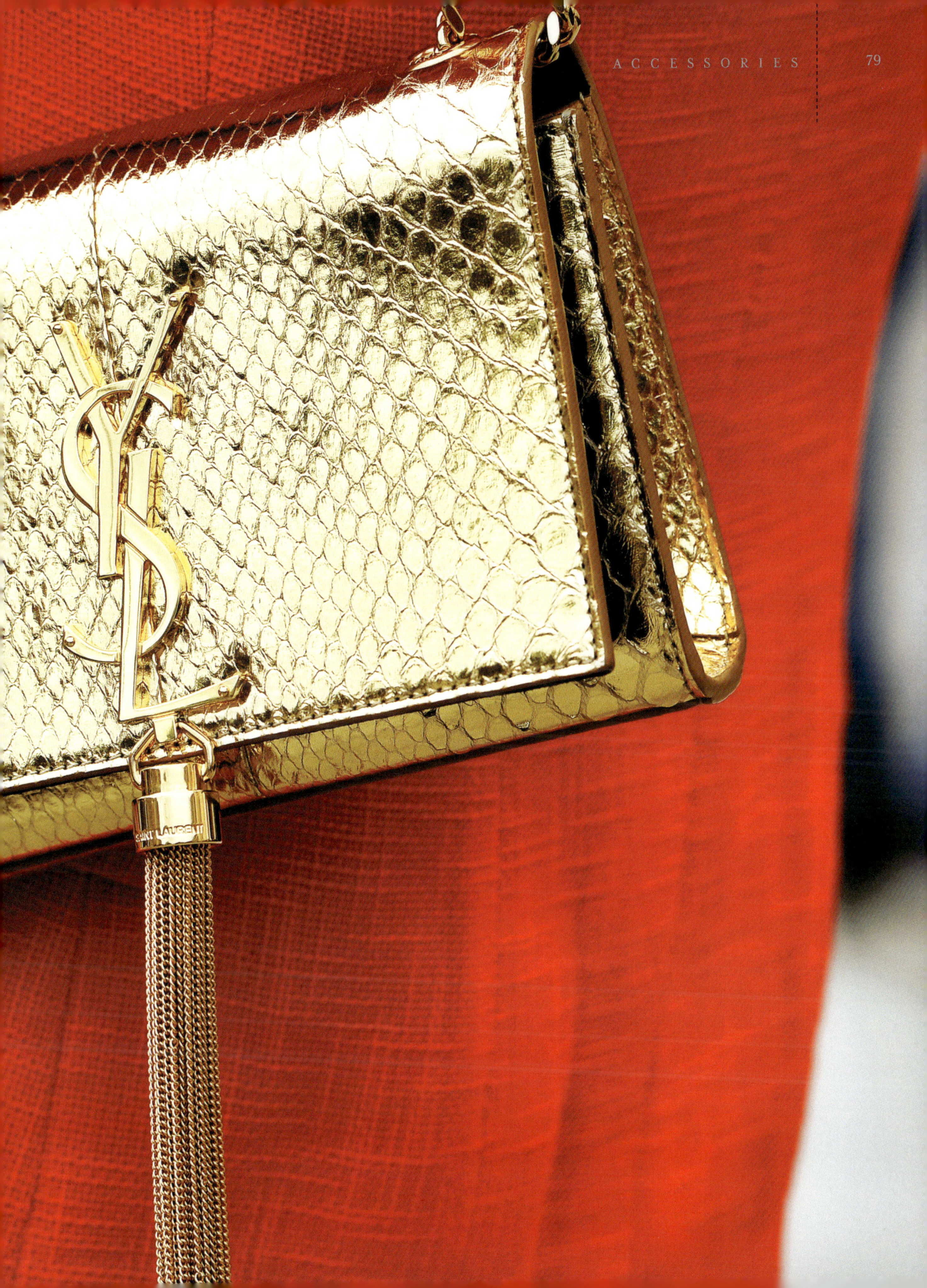

humble purse into a symbol of luxury and sophistication. Iconic YSL handbag designs include...

THE 'SAINT LAURENT'

In the early years, YSL handbags took on a minimalist yet luxurious approach. Using fine leathers and structured silhouettes, the Saint Laurent bag – launched in the 1960s - epitomized Parisian chic. Featuring clean lines, gold hardware and typically available in classic shades like black, brown and deep red – the Saint Laurent continues to define luxury today.

THE 'SAC DE JOUR'

Decades after first designing handbags, Saint Laurent's Sac de Jour or 'day bag' was introduced as part of the Rive Gauche collection in 2013. This bag quickly became synonymous with high-end luxury. Its boxy structure evokes elegance and its soft, supple leather makes it practical for everyday wear. An ideal balance between functional sophistication and iconic design.

THE 'LOULOU'

The Loulou bag was introduced in 2017 by creative director Anthony Vaccarello. It's named after Loulou de la Falaise, Yves Saint Laurent's iconic muse. With its chic 'chevron' design and hewn from soft, quilted leather, the Loulou has become a brand staple.

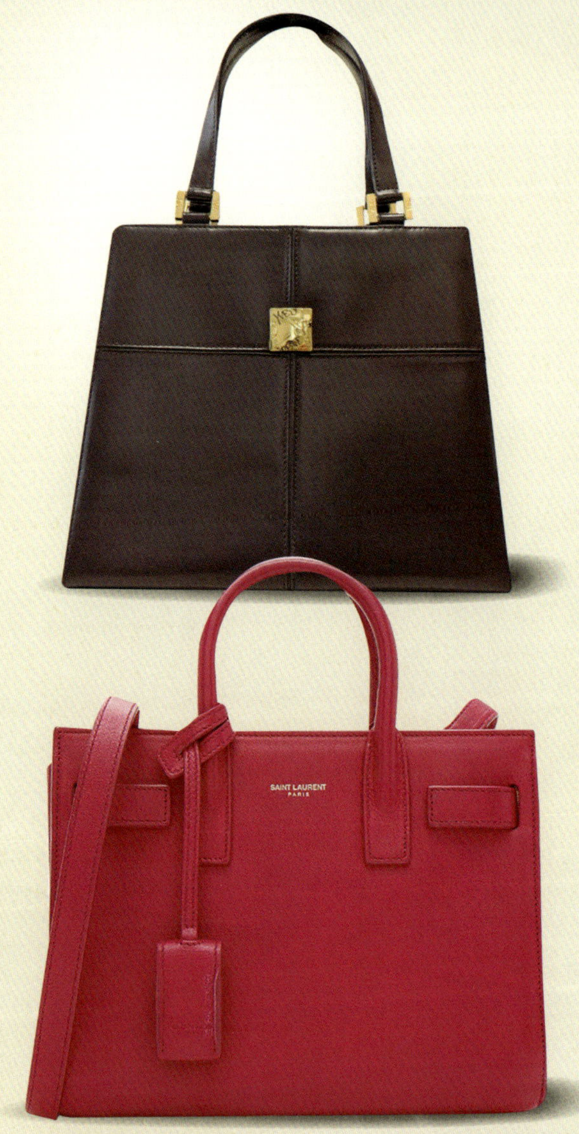

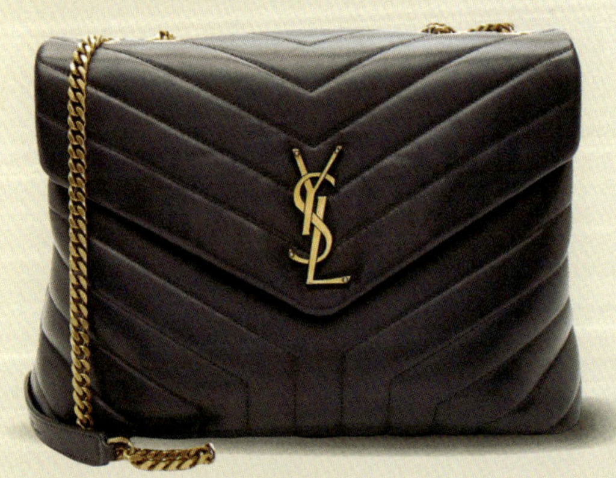

OPP PAGE: (TOP) Leather tote in burgundy leather (BOTTOM) Luxury handbag from the 2022 collection

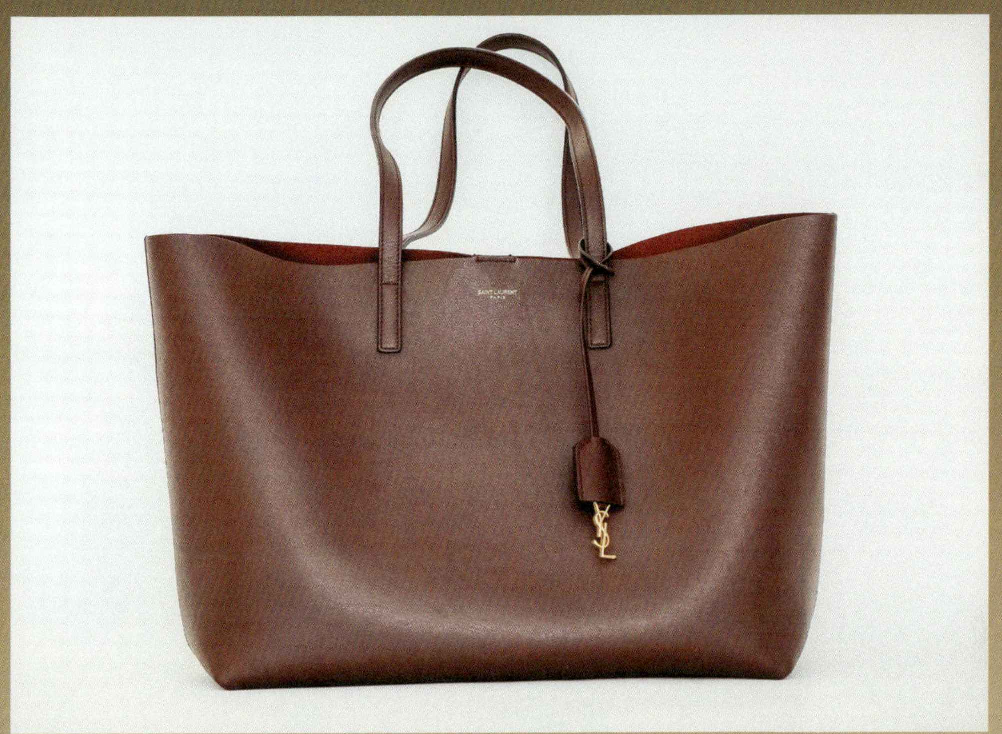

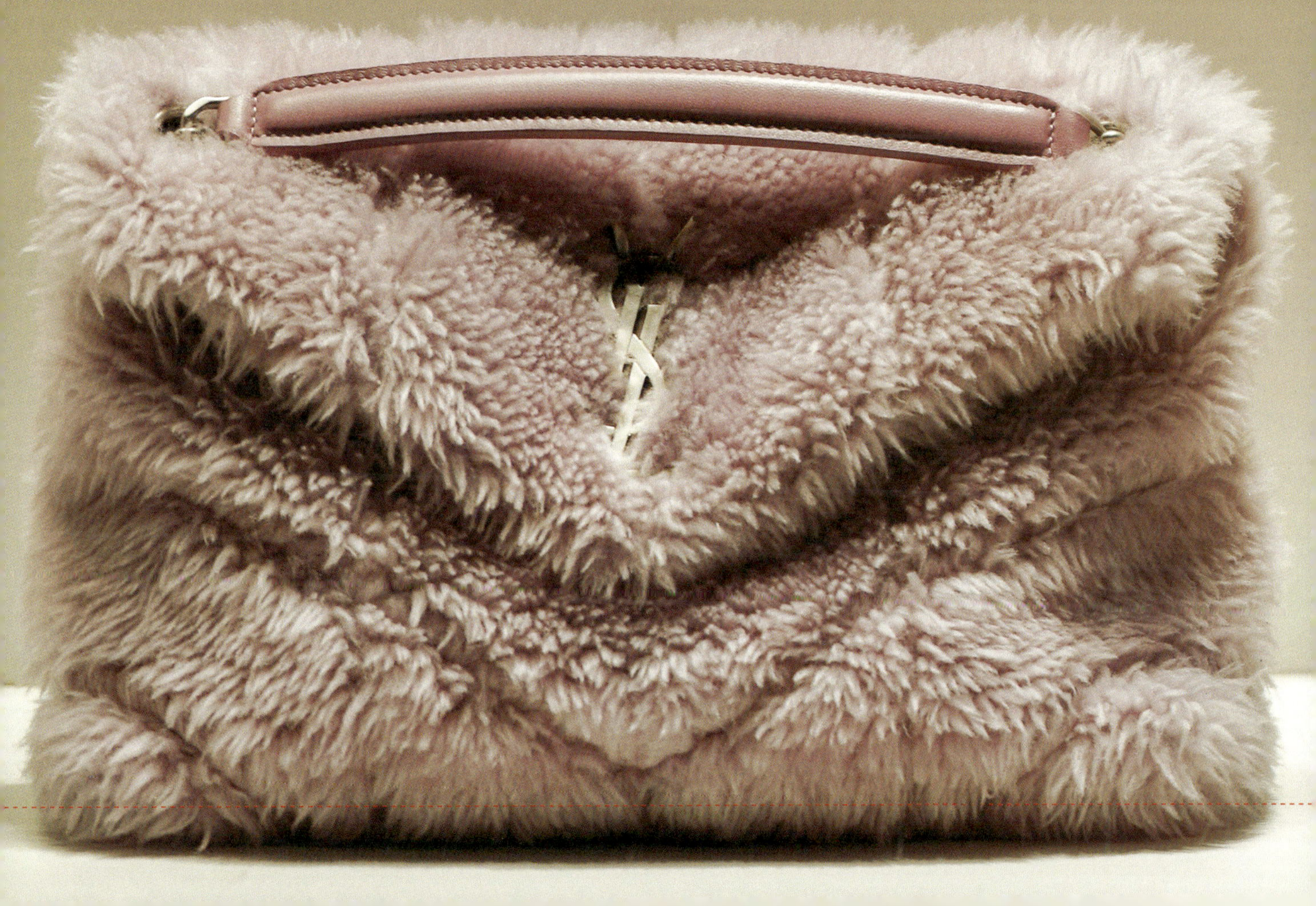

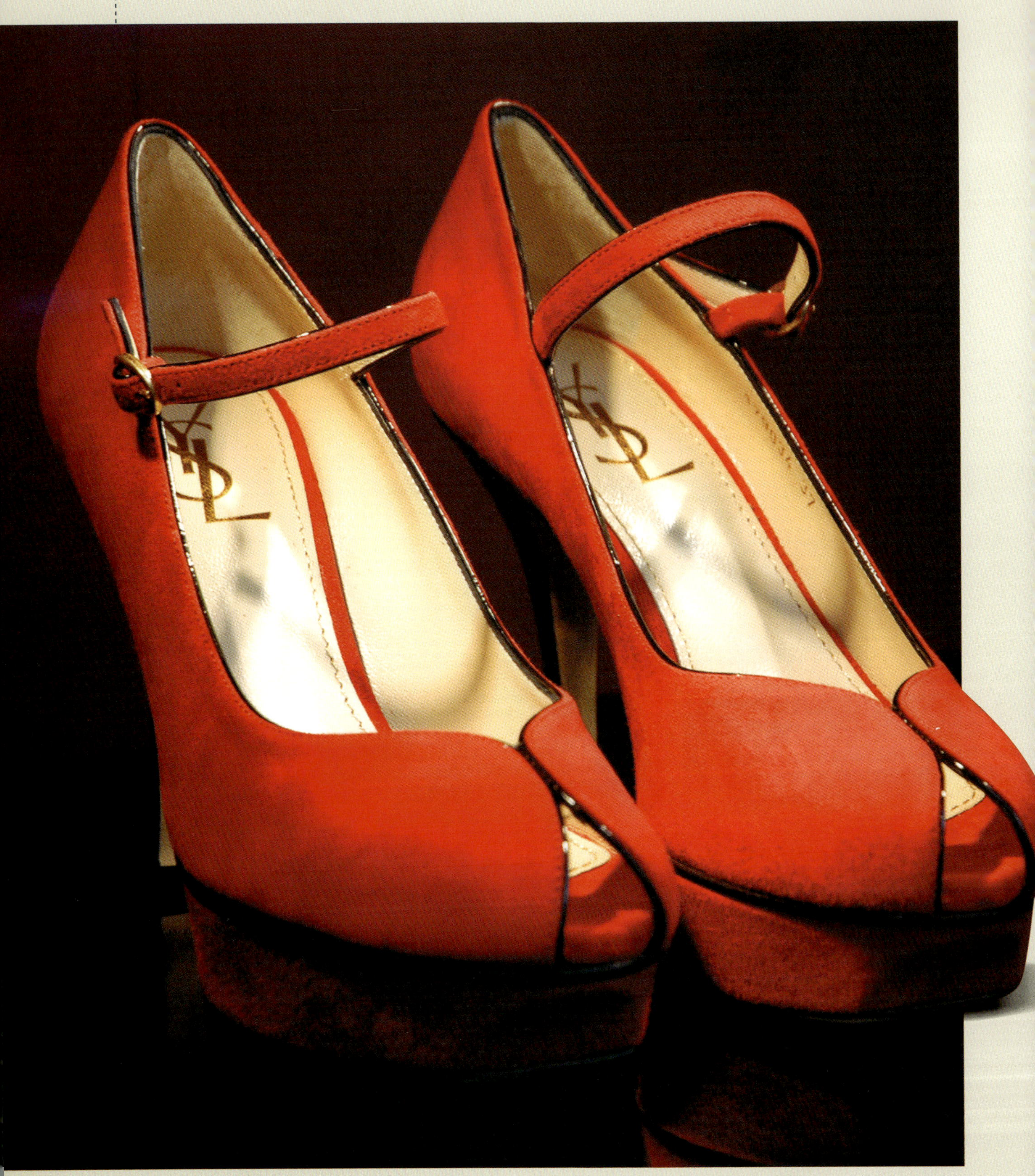

ABOVE: Tribute Mary-Jane platform heels in red suede with peep-toe design
OPP PAGE: Yves Saint Laurent logo-embossed leather espadrilles

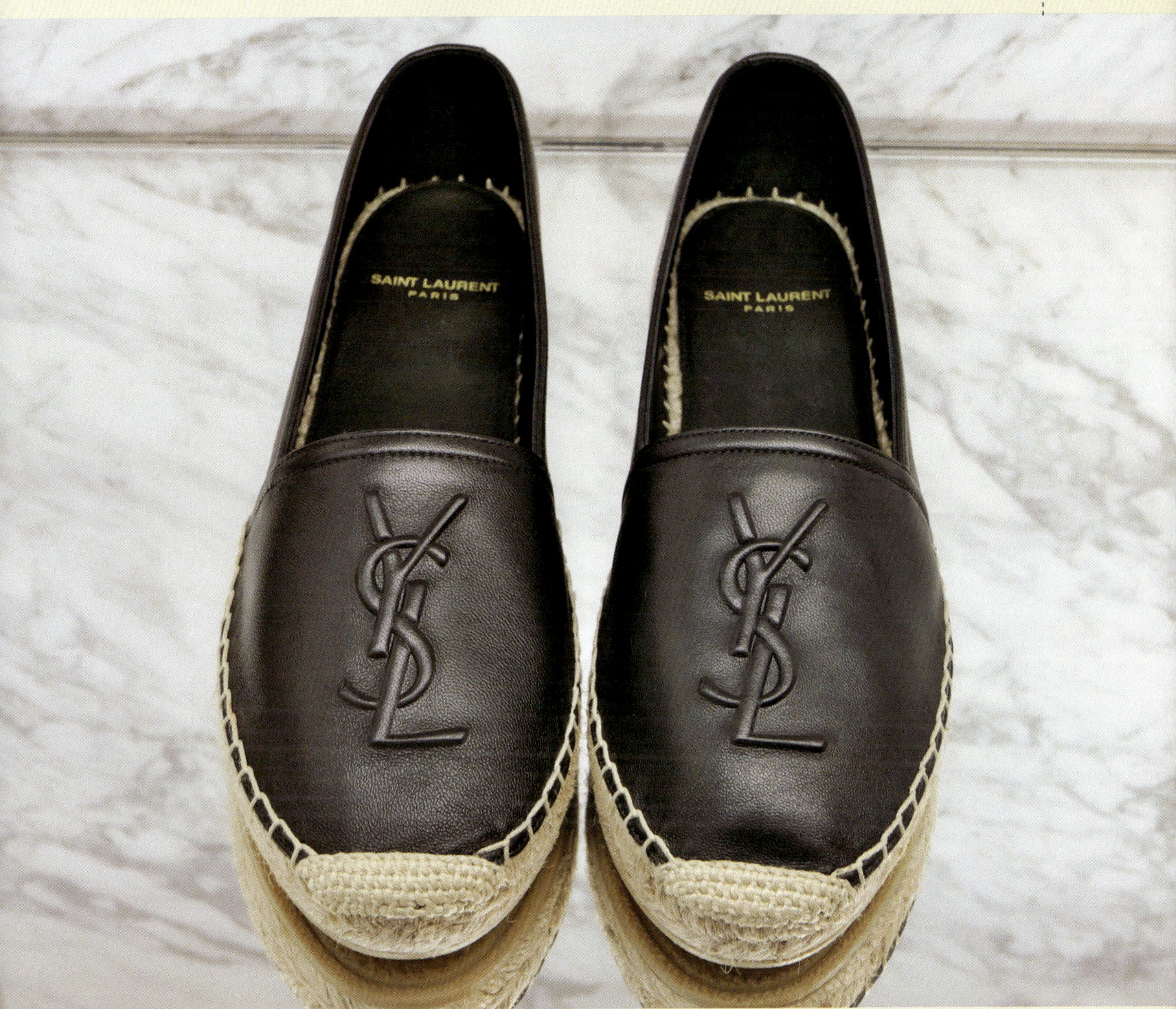

SHOES

Yves Saint Laurent's approach to footwear has always combined practicality, style and an aura of seduction. Whether creating low-heeled pumps or stiletto boots, each pair is crafted with the intention of elongating the leg, flattering the foot, and turning the ordinary into the extraordinary. YSL's influence on boots and sandals is undeniable, especially during the 1970s when the master created thigh-high boots and chunky sandals – often in metallic leathers – which defined the era's bohemian vibe. Other classic Saint Laurent footwear designs include...

THE BELLE VIVIER PUMP

Co-designed with Roger Vivier, this low-block heeled, square-toed shoe typically in black patent leather and featuring a large, chrome-plated buckle on the vamp, were first showcased at YSL's iconic 'Mondrian' fashion show in 1965. Worn by Catherine Deneuve in the 1967 film 'Belle du Jour'.

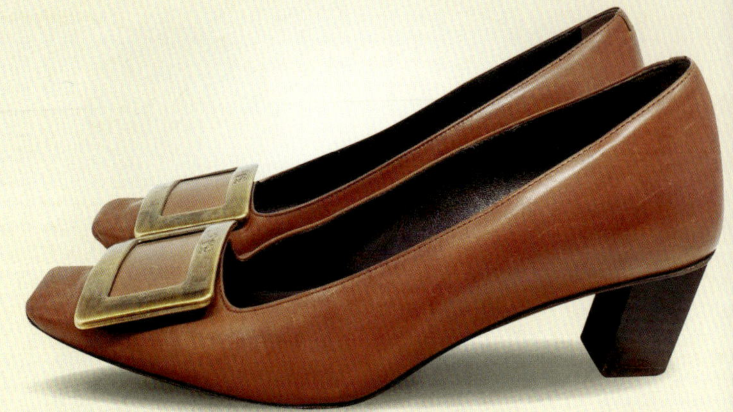

THE BALLET FLAT

Yves Saint Laurent introduced its first official line of ballet flats in November 2013 under the creative direction of Hedi Slimane. This collection, named 'Saint Laurent Dance' featured twelve styles crafted from soft leathers, including designs with silver-toned micro-studs, animal prints and bold primary colours. Prior to this, YSL had produced various flat shoe styles but the 2013 collection marked a significant moment in establishing ballet flats as a staple in the brand's offerings.

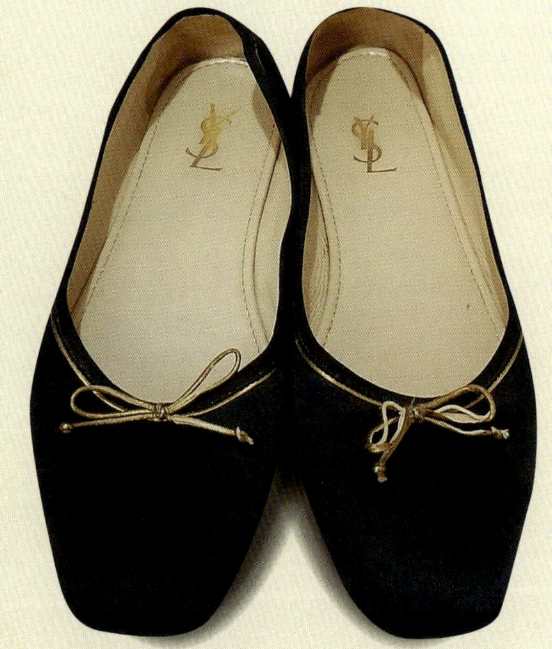

THE TRIB TOO PUMP

Saint Laurent's Trib Too pump is one of the designer's most iconic creations. First introduced during Tom Ford's tenure at YSL in 2006, the pump quickly became a symbol of luxury in the fashion world. Characterized by its platform sole and sharp stiletto heel, the Trib Too combines comfort with height, while maintaining a sleek and sculptural silhouette.

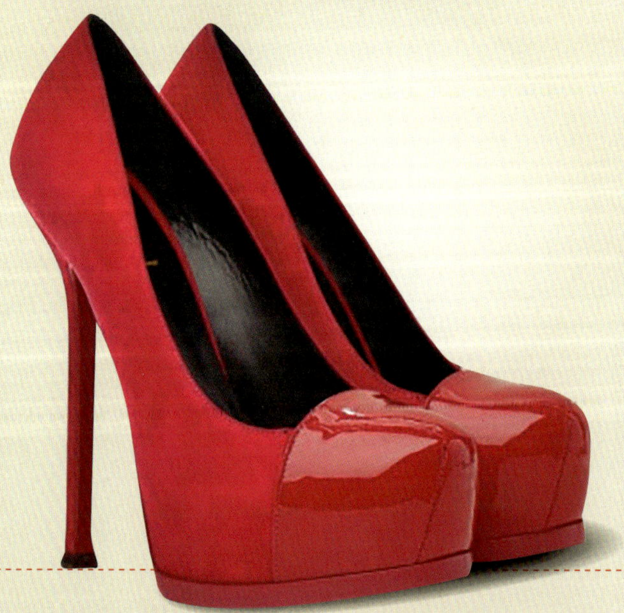

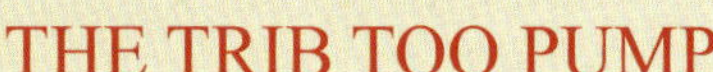

OPP PAGE: Linda Evangelista in burgundy Yves Saint Laurent shawl, Autumn/Winter haute couture, Paris, July 1996

BELTS

Never simply utilitarian, Saint Laurent belts are an essential accessory that define the silhouette and elevate an entire outfit. The label's statement belts often feature gold or silver buckles, adding a touch of glamour. When paired with high-waisted trousers, blazers, and dresses, SL belts create a classic Saint Laurent look that remains fashionable today.

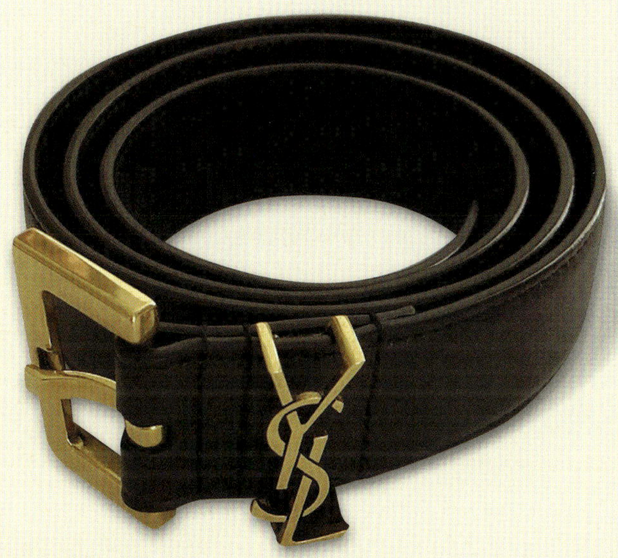

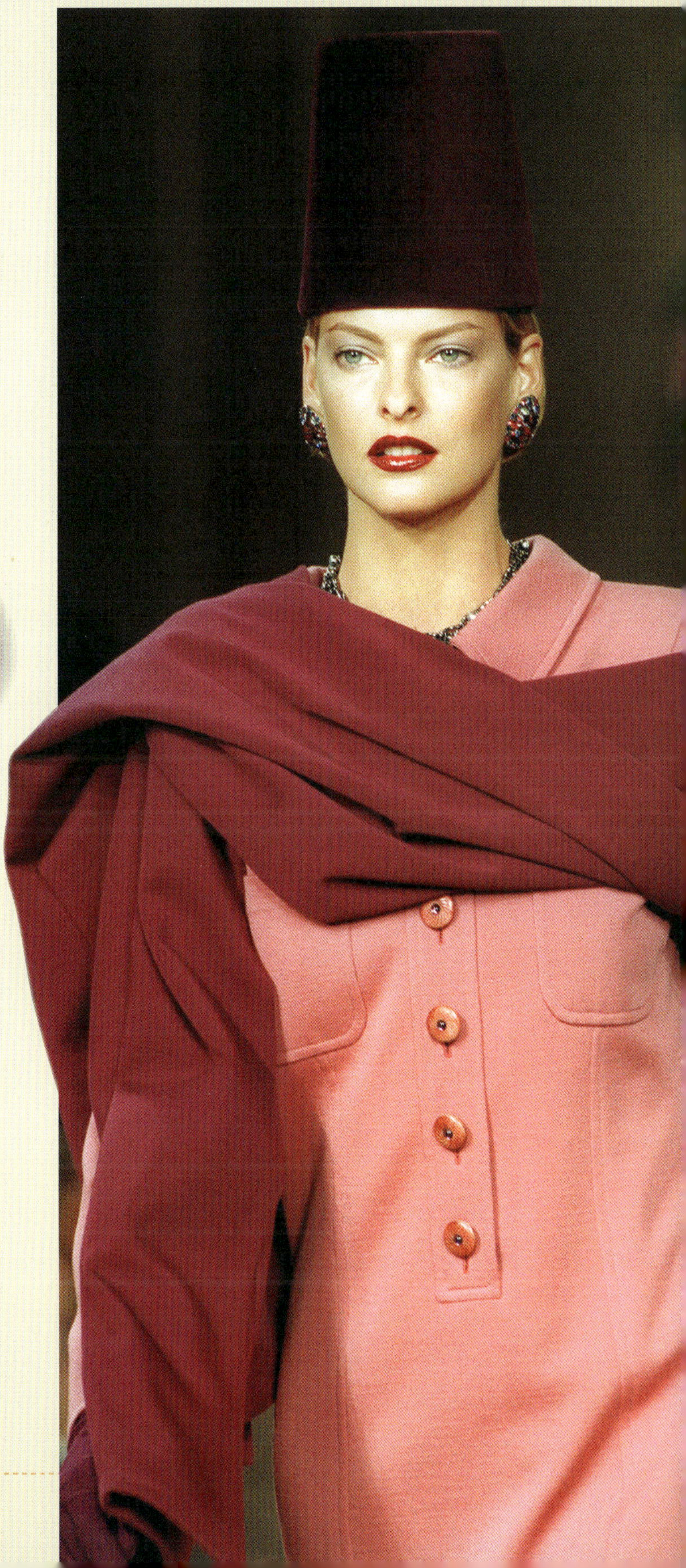

SCARVES AND SHAWLS

Yves Saint Laurent's scarves and shawls are some of the most elegant and versatile accessories in fashion history. Saint Laurent often used scarves as a way to soften a look, add an element of romantic femininity or bring a pop of colour to an otherwise neutral palette.

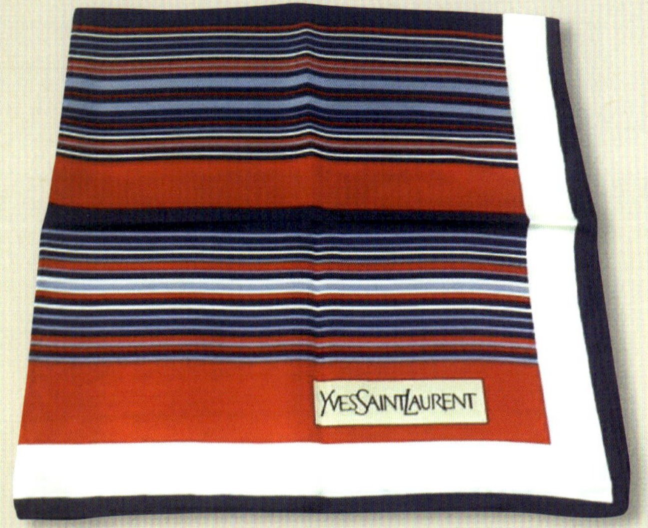

THE SQUARE SILK SCARF

Yves Saint Laurent began incorporating the square silk scarf into his collections during the 1960s, particularly as part of his Rive Gauche ready-to-wear line which launched in 1966. These scarves became iconic accessories, featuring bold colours, classic paisley patterns, graphic prints, and sometimes his signature or artistic collaborations. Worn as a necktie, headscarf or even a belt, the YSL silk scarf has become a timeless accessory.

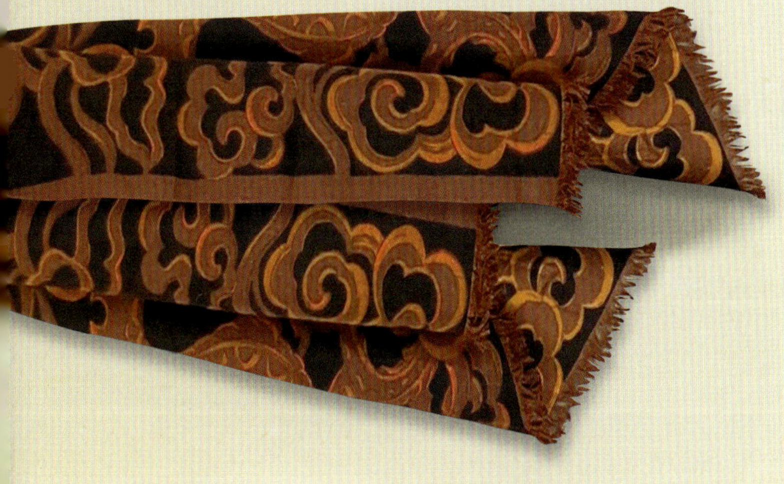

THE EVENING SHAWL

Typically made of cashmere, silk, or fur, Saint Laurent's evening shawls and wraps added a touch of luxury to eveningwear collections. Draped over a sleek dress or Le Smoking tuxedo, these items signalled elegance, class and sophistication — all hallmarks of the Saint Laurent ethos.

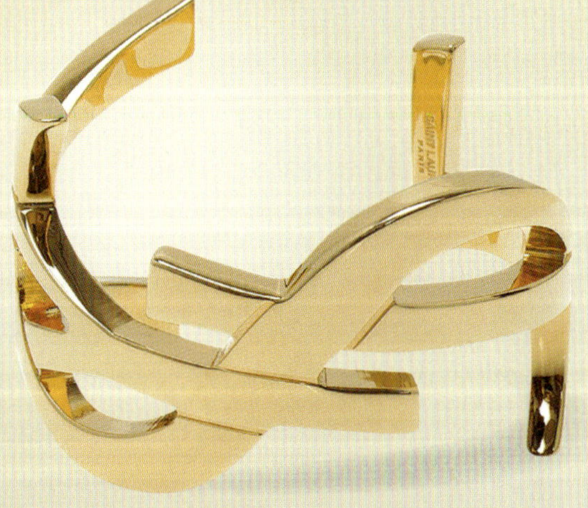

JEWELLERY

Saint Laurent's approach to jewellery was another facet of his desire to create powerful yet elegant statements. He believed bold, statement-making jewellery could add the finishing touch to a look, drawing attention to a woman's face and personality.

OPP PAGE: Singer Kelly Clarkson wearing Yves Saint Laurent earrings at the 54th Academy Of Country Music Awards, 2019

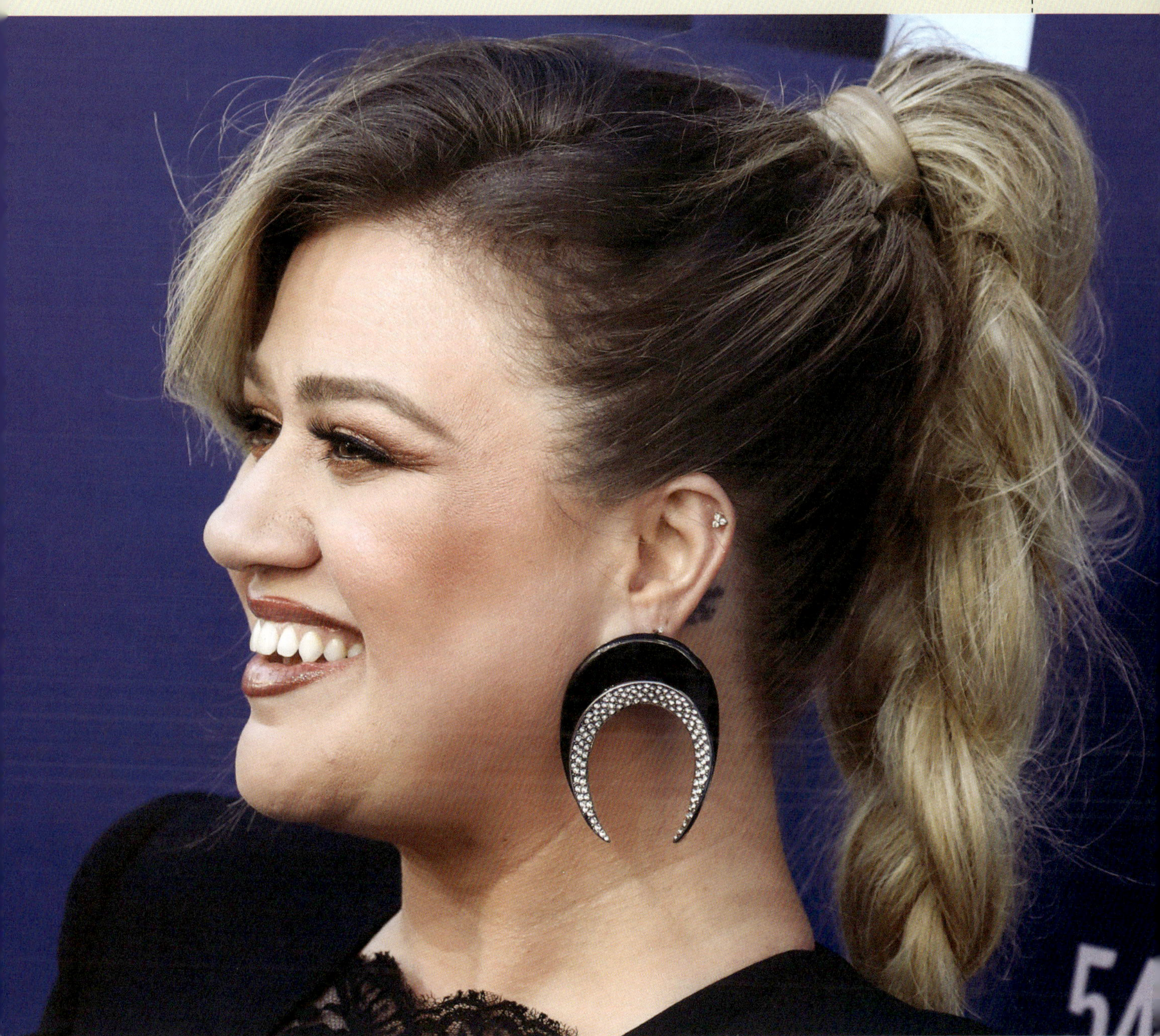

BIG EARRINGS

YSL's signature oversized earrings — hoops, geometric shapes, and dazzling stones — became a symbol of the designer's love for drama and luxury. These bold pieces, often in gold or silver, signalled confidence, power and sensuality.

CHOKERS AND NECKLACES

YSL's neck pieces were often statement items of jewellery that framed the face and accentuated the décolletage. From chunky gold chains to delicate diamond chokers, Saint Laurent knew that the right necklace could transform an entire outfit. His jewellery was always a reflection of refined glamour.

SUNGLASSES

Perhaps one of Saint Laurent's most enduring accessory contributions are his sunglasses. From the late 1960s onwards, Saint Laurent created a signature angular silhouette for his sun eyewear. Cat-eye shapes, oversized round frames, and bold, geometric styles – often featuring the iconic YSL logo - became an instant hit. These sunglasses became a symbol of the mysterious, cool YSL woman, making her look both timeless and contemporary. This remains as true today as it's always been.

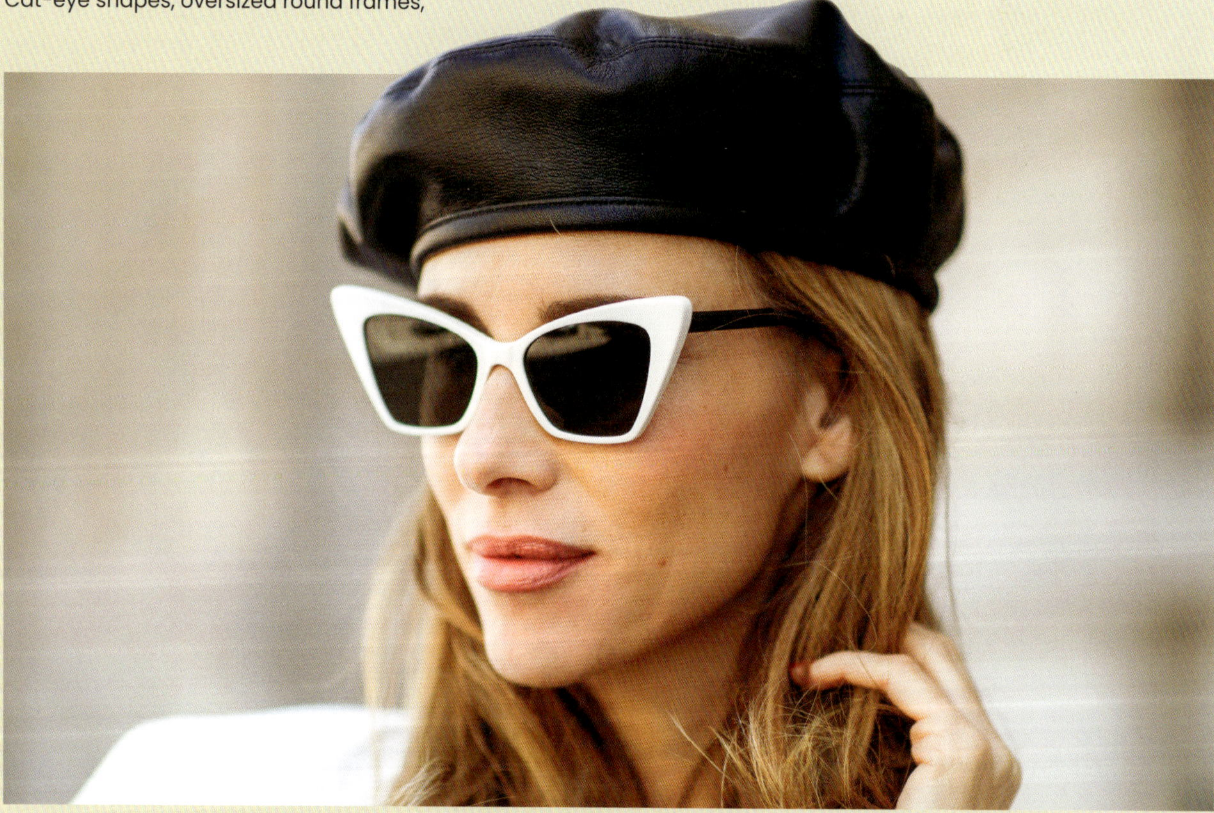

ABOVE: Alexandra Lapp wears white Victoire sunglasses by Yves Saint Laurent
OPP PAGE: Yves Saint Laurent accessories on display

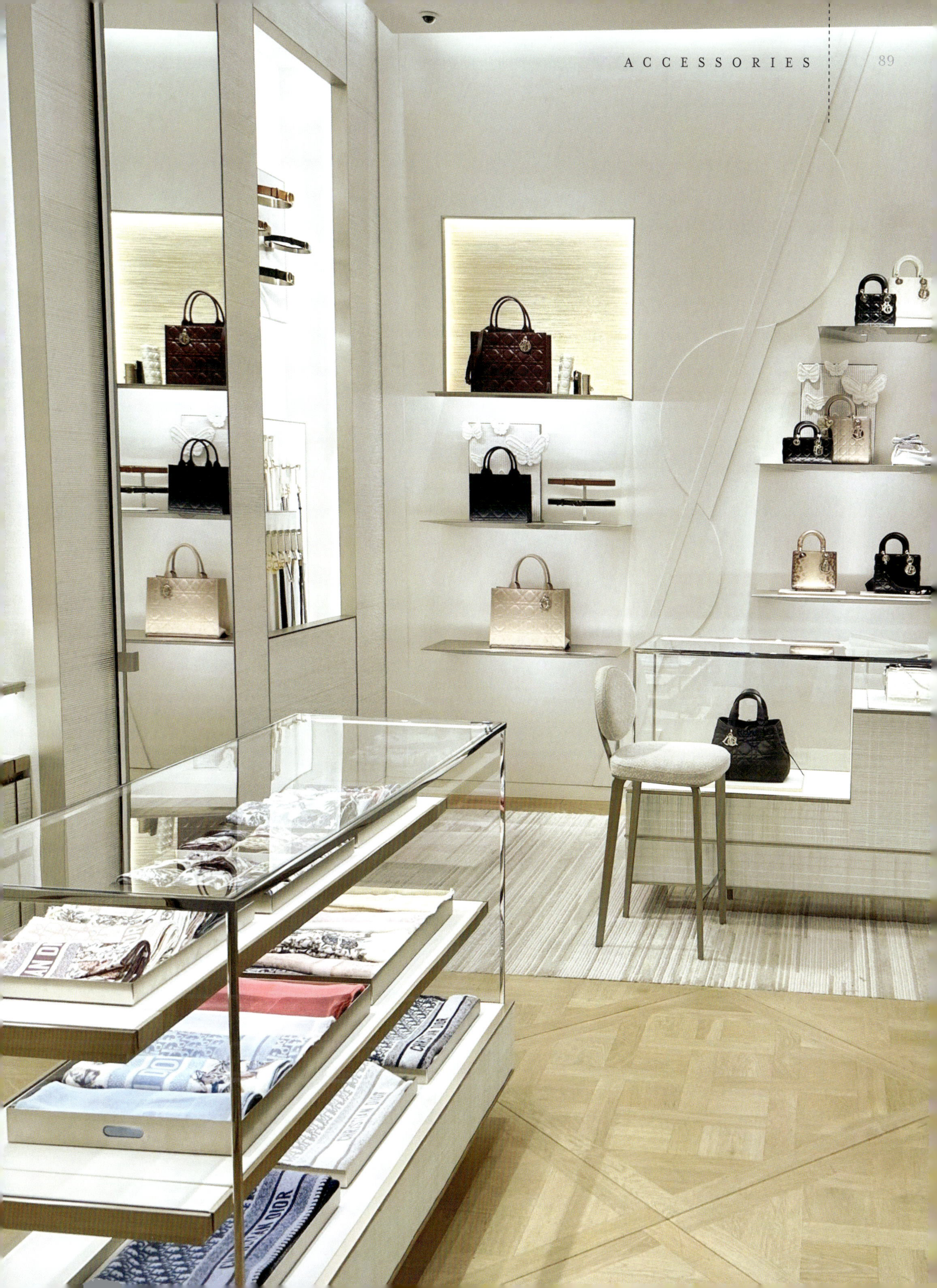

1990s

"Without elegance of the heart, there is no elegance"
Yves Saint Laurent

The 1990s were a transformative decade for Yves Saint Laurent - a time of continued success and creative evolution but also a period of reflection on his legacy. Saint Laurent continued to push boundaries with his designs while also embracing the minimalist trends, cultural dynamics and evolving technologies that were beginning to dominate the global fashion landscape. Yet, he also maintained his classic signature styles — opulent tailoring, romanticism and his celebrated understanding of femininity. The power dressing phenomenon continued to dominate at the beginning of the 1990s with tailored suits, sharp shoulders and structured silhouettes remaining a significant part of his output. However, YSL shifted toward a more refined version of these ideas, blending them with a more casual form of femininity.

In his first collection of the decade - Spring/Summer 1990 and entitled 'The Homages' - Saint Laurent honoured certain individuals who had inspired him. Luminaries such as Marilyn Monroe, Catherine Deneuve, Zizi Jeanmaire, Marcel Proust, Bernard Buffet and Christian Dior. The runway was transformed into the 'Jardin de Guermantes', a nod to Proust's literary world. Notable pieces included the 'Homage to Zizi Jeanmaire' embroidered sweater and the 'Homage to My House' jacket, reflecting his deep appreciation for his muses and mentors. For 'Feathered Elegance', the Fall/Winter 1990 collection, the highlight was a striking brown organza coat adorned with hundreds of pheasant and multi-coloured rhea feathers, crafted in collaboration with feather artisan, Lemairé. The garment resembled a lion's mane, showcasing Saint Laurent's flair for dramatic and luxurious designs.

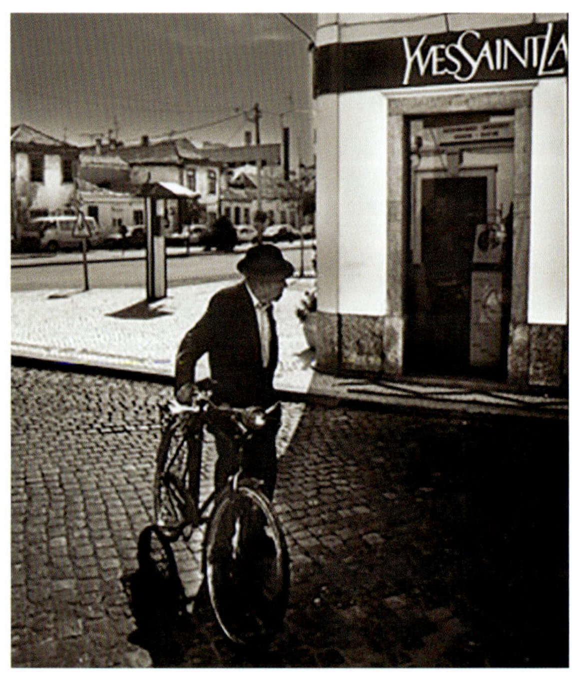

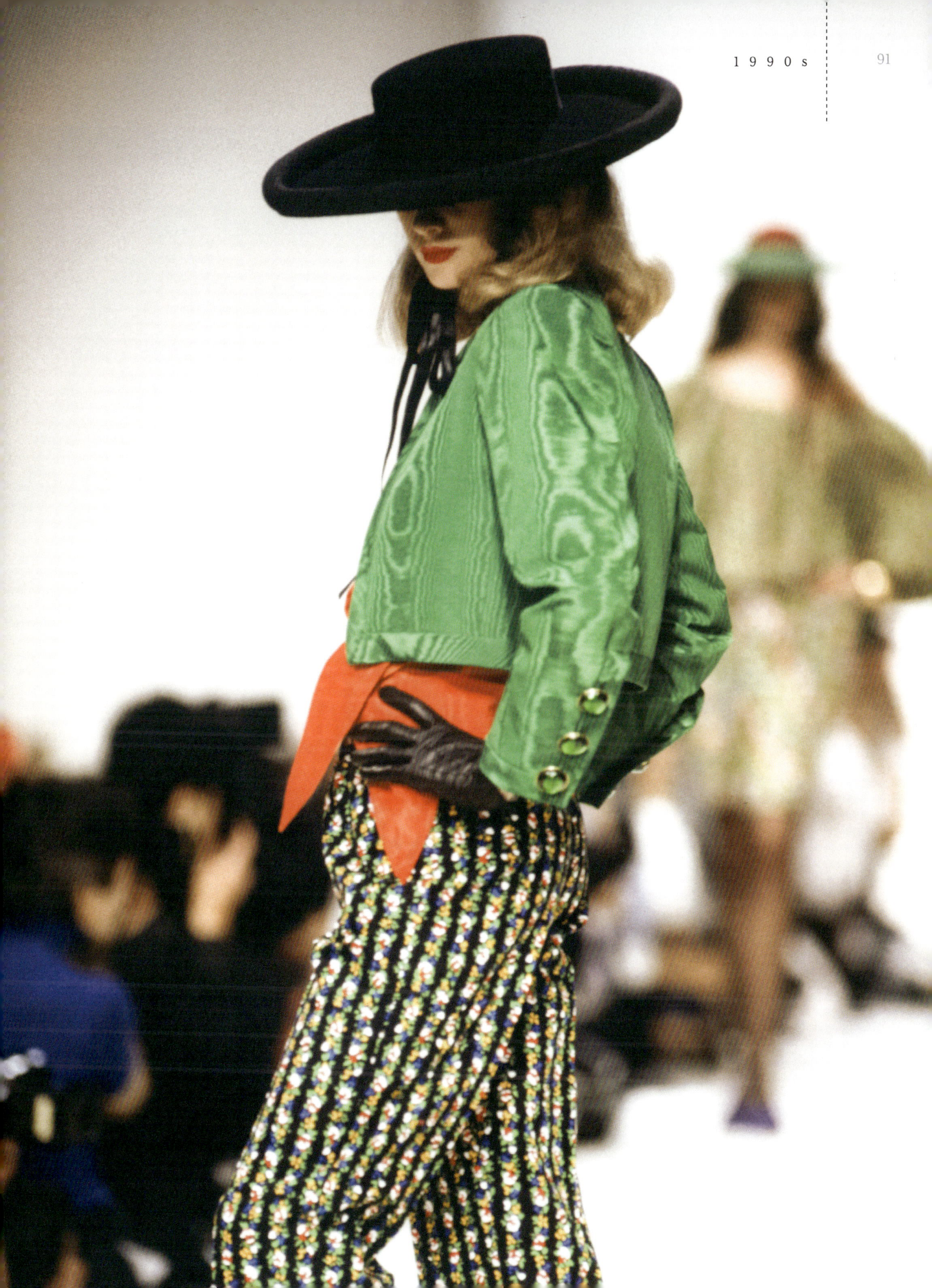

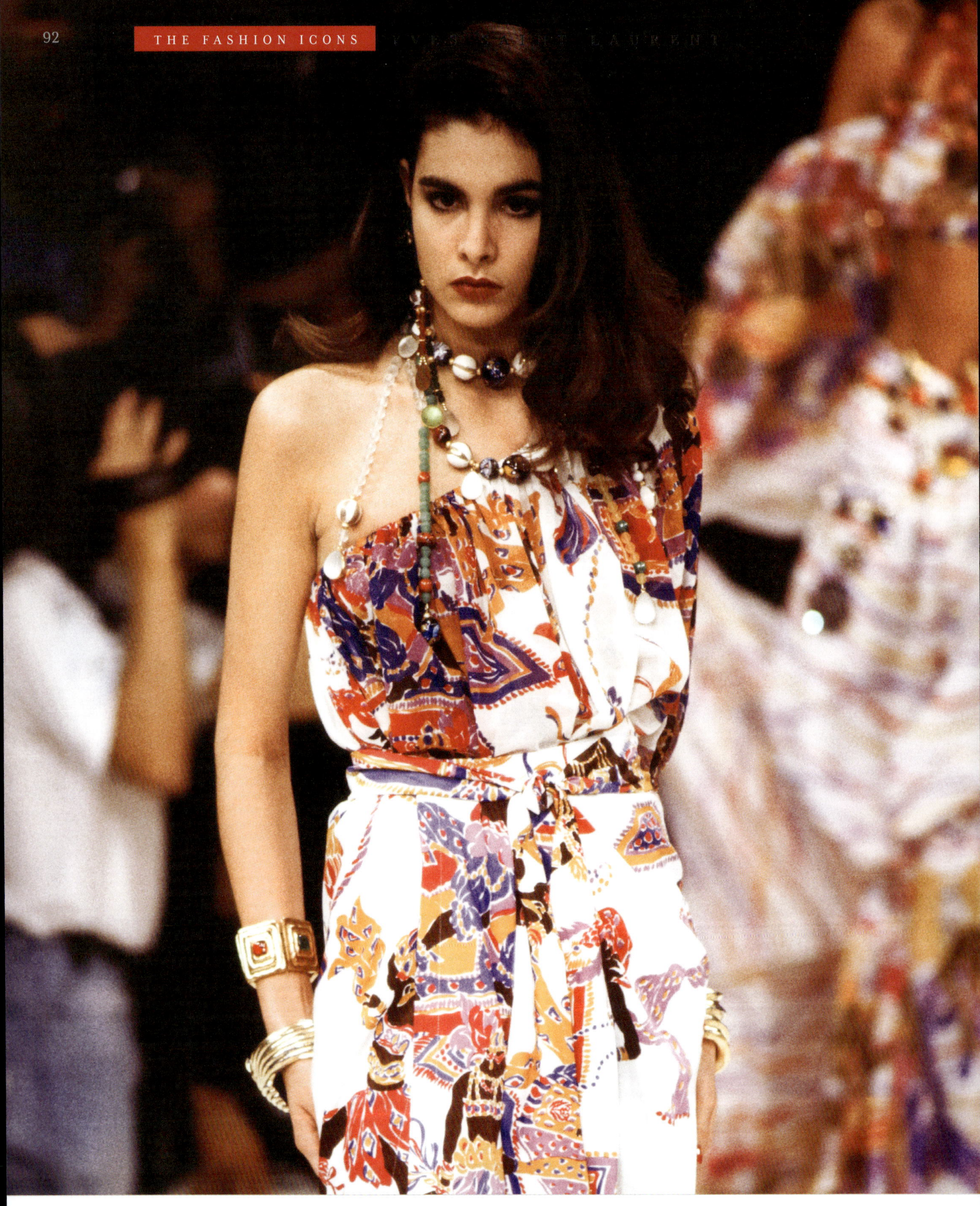

ABOVE: Ready-to-wear Spring/Summer 1991
OPP PAGE: A model walks the runway during the Yves
Saint Laurent Haute Couture Spring/Summer 1995 show

His 1991 spring/summer collection was a nod to both the avant-garde and classic elegance that characterized the YSL aesthetic. With elements of grunge and bohemian chic, the collection showed a new take on the powerful woman — one that was more contemplative, liberated and less reliant on the hard-edge tailoring of the past decade. The 1980s power suit remained but it was softened with flowing fabrics and more fluid lines.

With the grunge movement in full swing, the mid-1990s were defined by a wave of bohemian and hippie influences. Yves Saint Laurent responded to these cultural shifts by integrating more relaxed and romantic styles into his collections. This was evident in his 1995 Spring/Summer collection, where he showcased a boho-chic aesthetic - featuring loose, billowing silhouettes, ethereal fabrics and floral prints that harked back to the carefree spirit of the 1960s and 1970s. Saint Laurent's bohemian-inflected designs were modern, yet deeply rooted in the romanticism and opulence that had defined his early work. His maxi skirts, vividly patterned dresses and tunic-style tops reflected a more easy-going yet still elegant approach to dressing.

Throughout the mid-90s, Saint Laurent continued to draw inspiration from art and culture. His collections often featured bold colours, intricate embroidery and references to various artistic movements, maintaining his reputation as a designer who seamlessly blended fashion with art. One such collection was in 1996 when he showcased pieces

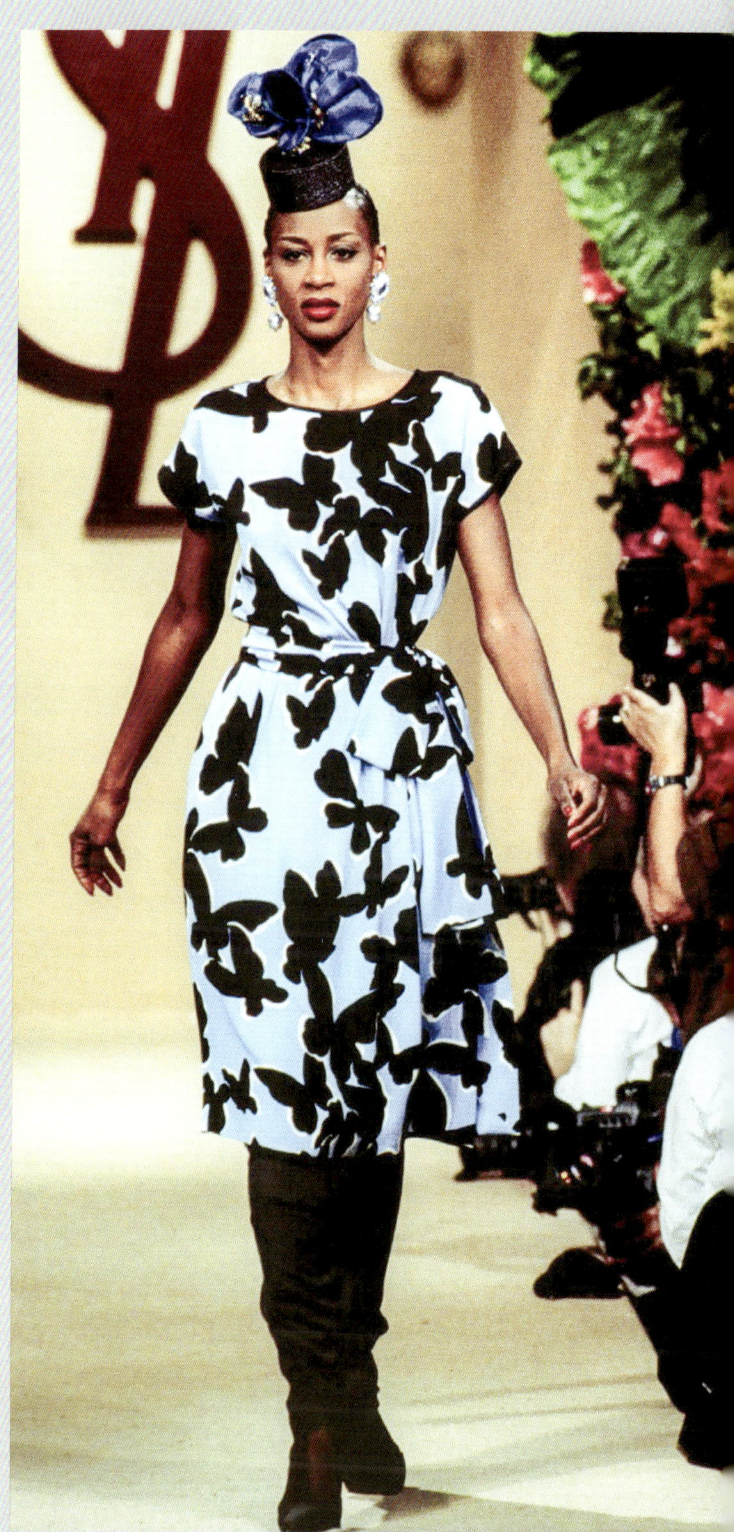

inspired by abstract art. It was also in '96 that the iconic 'Le Smoking' experienced a notable revival.

Yves Saint Laurent's retrospective collection for the YSL Rive Gauche line prominently featured updated versions of his revolutionary women's tuxedo. His reimagining of the garment in silk, velvet and brocade fabrics became synonymous with a modern, independent woman's wardrobe and reaffirmed its place as a house signature. Supermodels like Kate Moss and celebrities such as YSL long-time muse Catherine Deneuve and also Madonna helped bring it back into mainstream fashion culture, often wearing modernized versions in photoshoots or red-carpet appearances.

In the latter part of the decade, Saint Laurent's designs evolved to incorporate more minimalist and modern elements. While still rooted in his classic aesthetic, these collections reflected a shift towards sleeker silhouettes and contemporary styles, demonstrating his adaptability and forward-thinking approach to fashion. Saint Laurent, while known for his luxurious and dramatic aesthetic, was not immune to the minimalist trend. However, he took a different approach by maintaining his elegant craftsmanship and luxury while experimenting with simplicity and restraint in his designs. His 1997 fall collection, for instance, featured sleek, streamlined silhouettes in neutral tones like black, ivory and camel but still held onto his signature classic shapes and rich fabrics. His minimalist designs were always more opulent than the bare-bones looks seen in other houses.

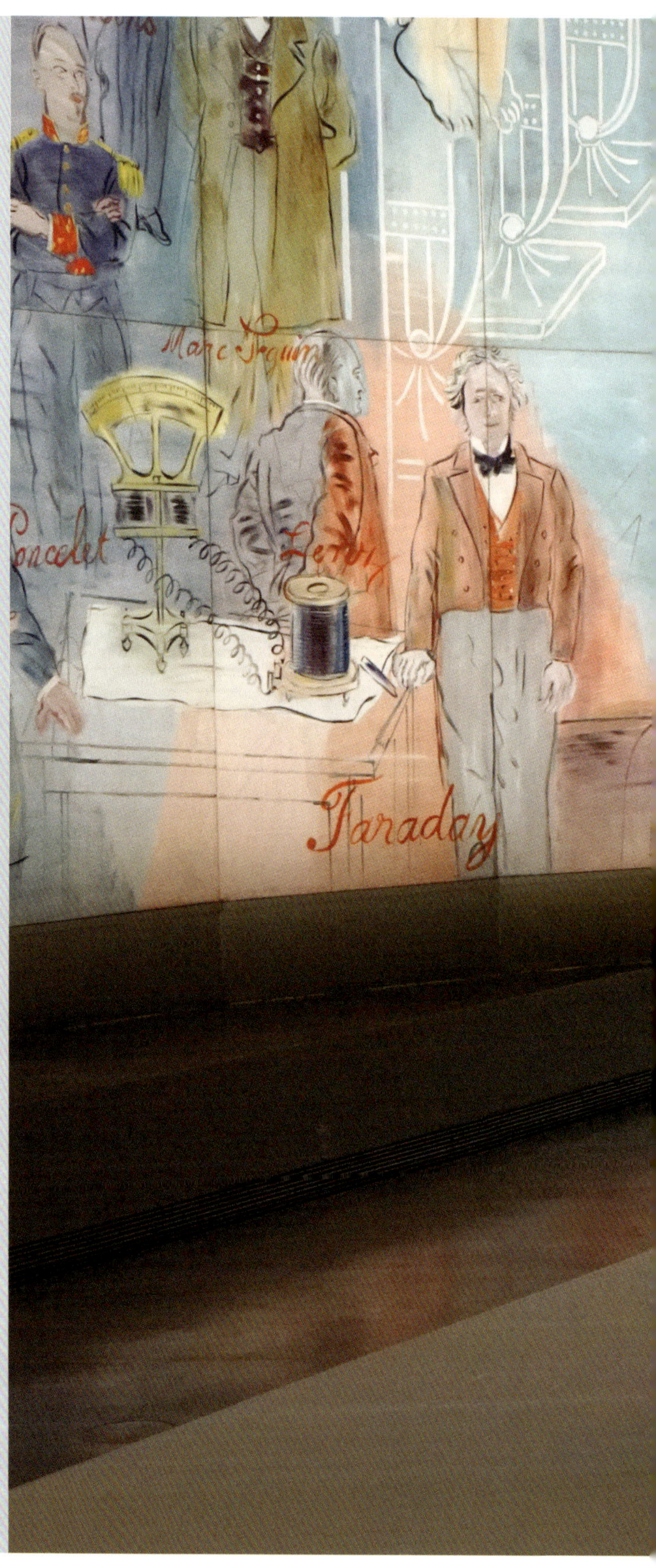

RIGHT: Yves Saint Laurent satin overcoats and dresses from the Autumn/Winter 1992 collection displayed at the Museum of Modern Art, Paris, with Raoul Dufy artwork in the background

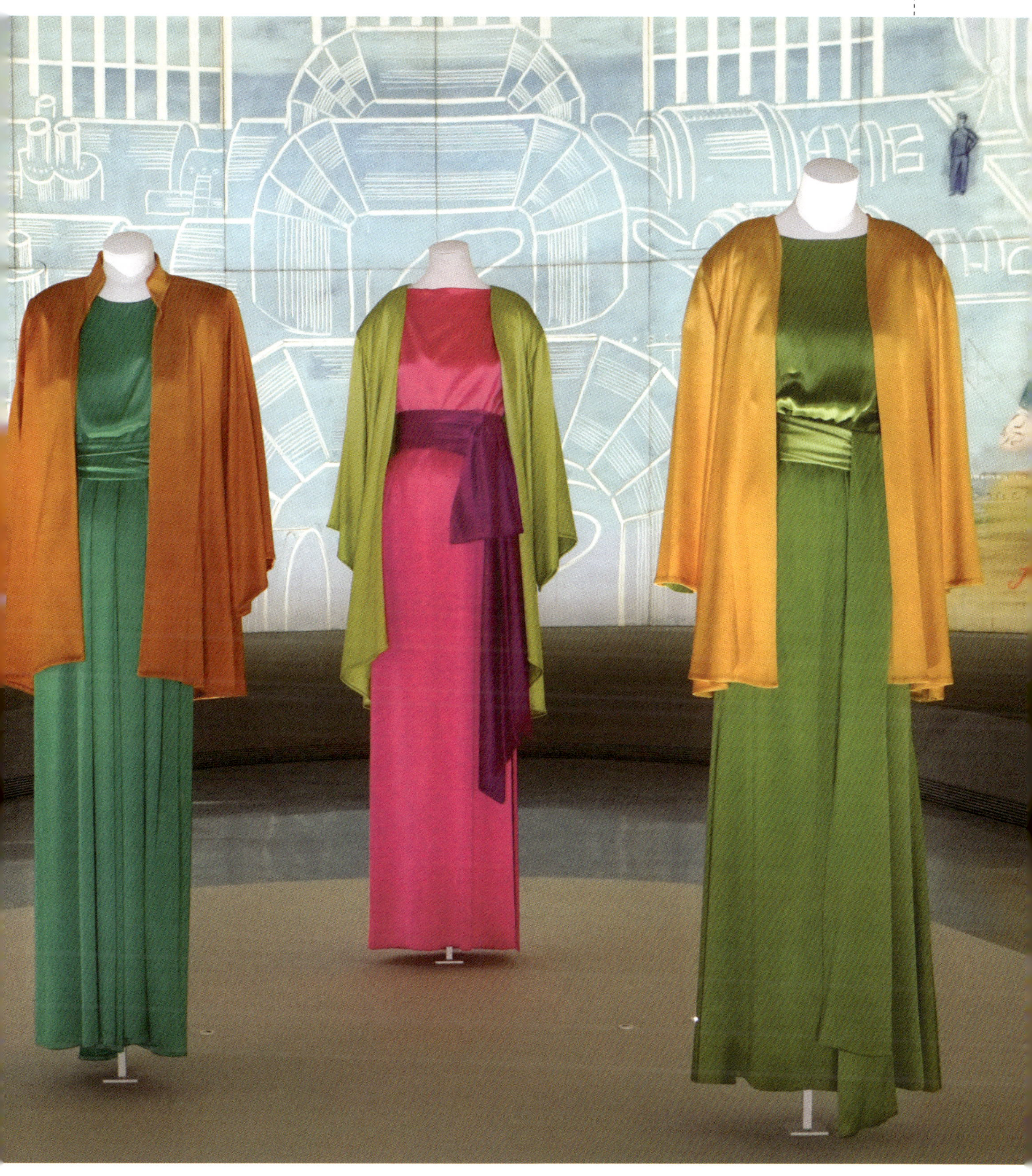

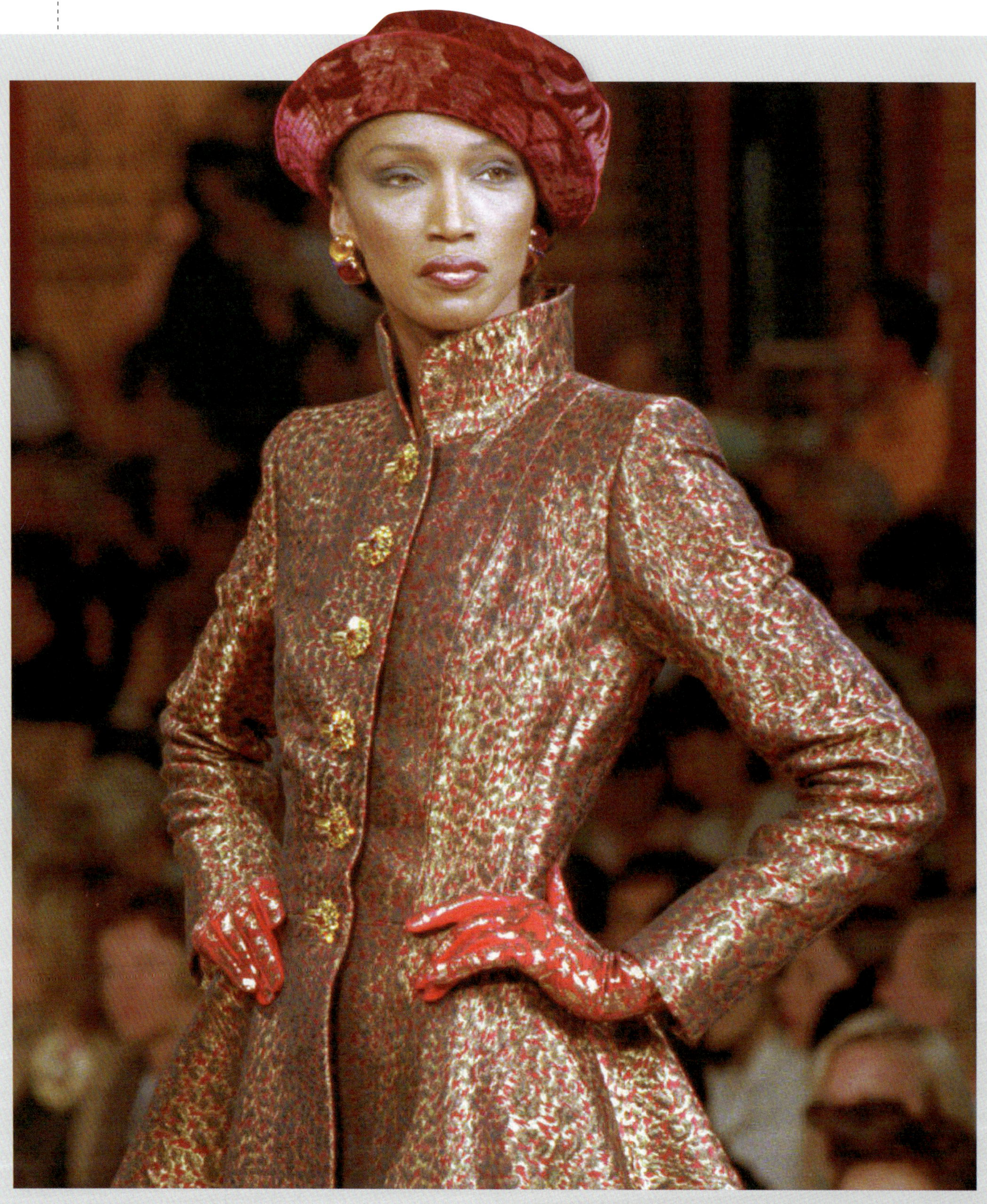

ABOVE: Model Katoucha Niane poses during the presentation of the 1997 Autumn/Winter collection
OPP PAGE: 1999 Autumn/Winter ready-to-wear runway show

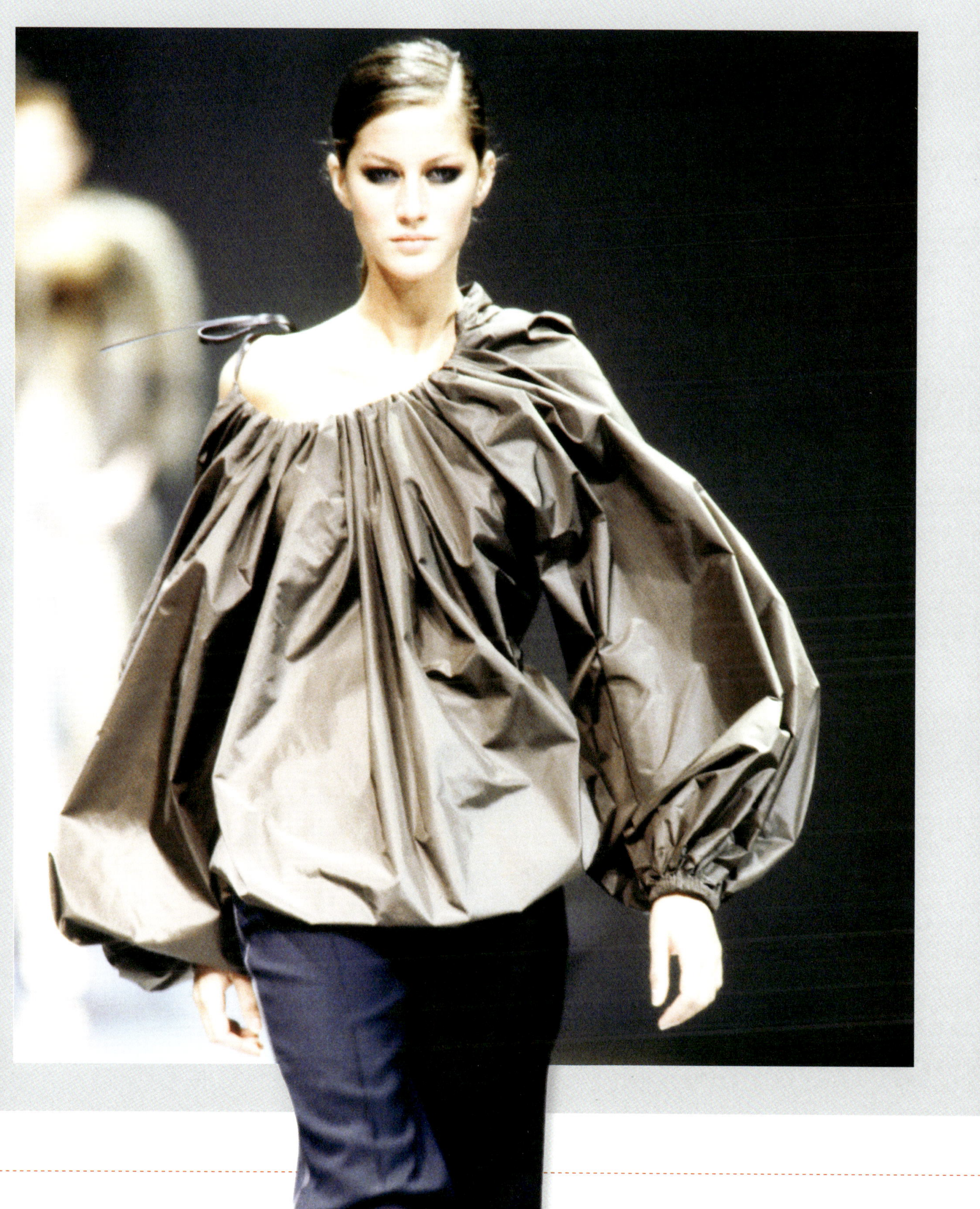

BEAUTY

"Makeup is not a mask, it's a way to express yourself"

Yves Saint Laurent

Launched in 1978, 'Yves Saint Laurent Beauté' revolutionized the beauty industry by introducing products that were not just about aesthetics but also embraced empowerment, individuality and luxury. The brand's bold approach to cosmetics paralleled Saint Laurent's fashion philosophy - sensual, avant-garde and unapologetically modern. Saint Laurent regarded beauty as an art form and wished his make-up line to reflect this.

Yves Saint Laurent's stellar career in fashion was not initially replicated by his foray into cosmetics. His Beauté brand failed to achieve the same standard of success and acclaim until YSL collaborated with the likes of L'Oreal. However, from the get-go, YSL Beauty was built upon the premise that makeup should be bold, expressive and luxurious — concepts that were inherently linked to the core of the YSL brand. Saint Laurent's vision was for his make-up products to not only enhance a woman's natural beauty but also encourage experimentation - giving consumers a way to create their own version of glamour.

Saint Laurent understood that beauty is more than skin deep, believing it to be a reflection of a person's mood, personality and desires. Through his beauty line, he enabled women (and men) to express themselves in a vibrant, individualistic and luxurious way. By combining the finest ingredients, ground-breaking formulas and the same avant-garde approach that defined his fashion collections, YSL Beauty has managed to remain a timeless symbol of luxury while also embracing modern concepts of beauty and inclusivity. The brand continues to be a pioneering force in the beauty industry. With products that combine both artistry and luxury, it remains one of the most sought-after labels in cosmetics and skincare. Its continued innovation and dedication to high-quality products ensure that the YSL beauty ethos — a holy trinity of elegance, modernity and boldness — lives on in every bottle, tube and compact.

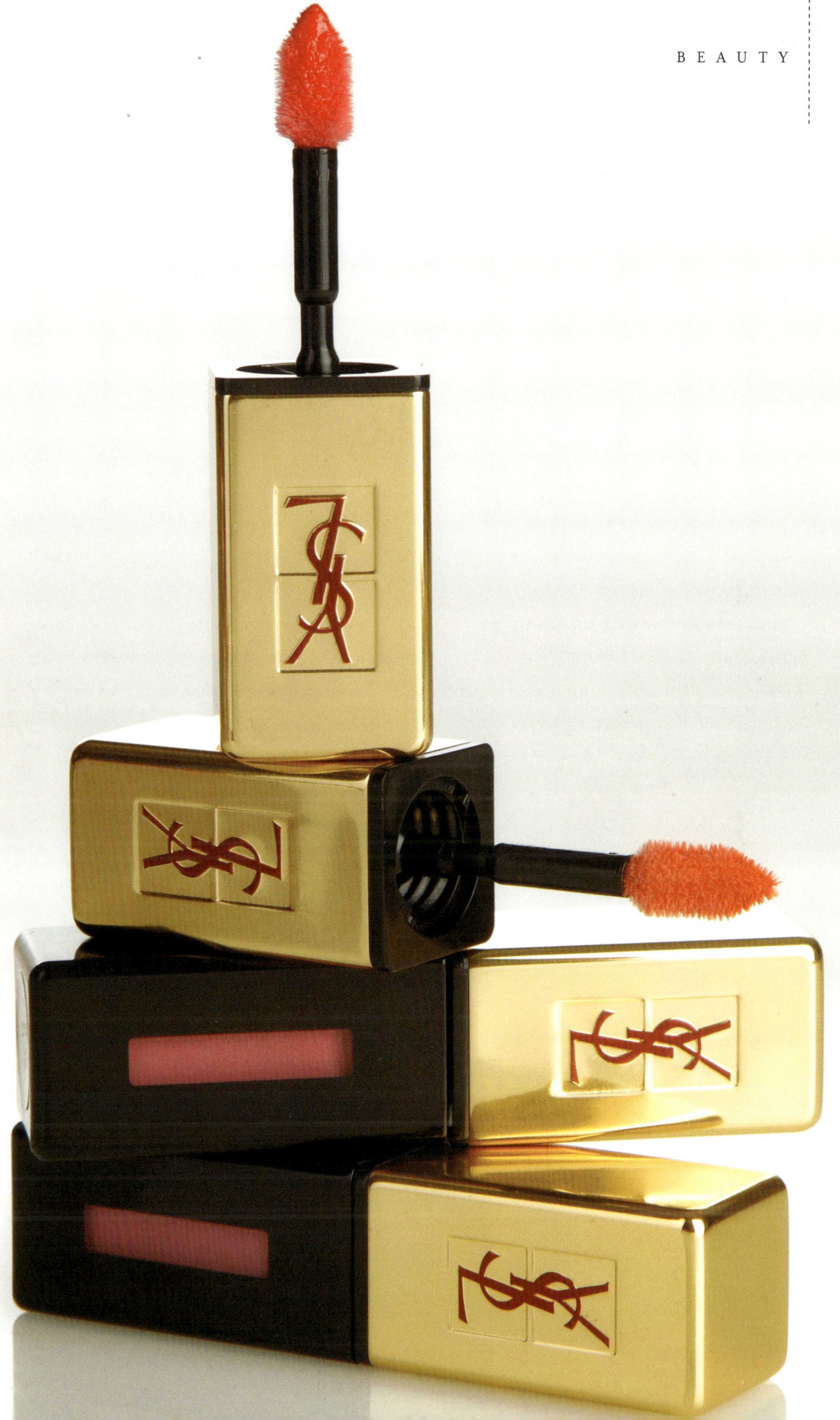

ICONIC YSL BEAUTY PRODUCTS

ROUGE PUR COUTURE LIPSTICK

The Rouge Pur Couture lipstick was introduced in 1978 – the year YSL Beauté was born. Saint Laurent's aim was to create lipsticks that not only offered intense colour payoff but also luxury and sophistication. These lipsticks came in a variety of rich, luxurious shades - ranging from bold reds to plum and nude tones. YSL was one of the first brands to create long-lasting, moisturising formulas without sacrificing depth or richness of colour - making Rouge Pur Couture an instant favourite. The luxurious gold packaging further elevated the Rouge Pur Couture experience. A classic product in makeup bags and on runway shows the world over.

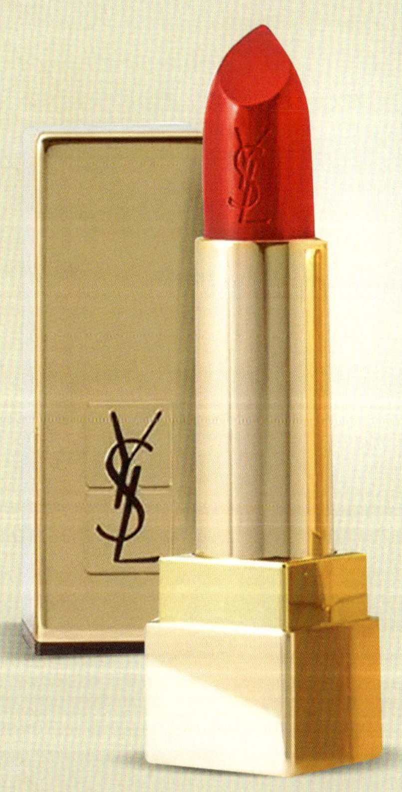

TOUCHE ÉCLAT

Arguably one of the most iconic beauty products in the world, Touche Éclat is synonymous with the YSL beauty brand. Launched in 1992, this radiance-boosting pen revolutionized the make-up world by offering a solution to dark circles, uneven skin tone and fatigue. It became the holy grail of highlighting and the first product of its kind to seamlessly blend make-up and skincare. What made Touche Éclat so unique was its ability to give a woman's complexion a refreshed, radiant and youthful appearance without caking on heavy concealer or foundation. Its lightweight, radiant formula was a game-changer for make-up artists and beauty enthusiasts alike. As YSL himself said, *'Touche Éclat is not a concealer, it is a highlighter — it doesn't hide, it reveals'*. Over the years, Touche Éclat has maintained its status as a make-up classic and remains one of the brand's best-selling products. La crème de la crème in complexion highlighting and brightening.

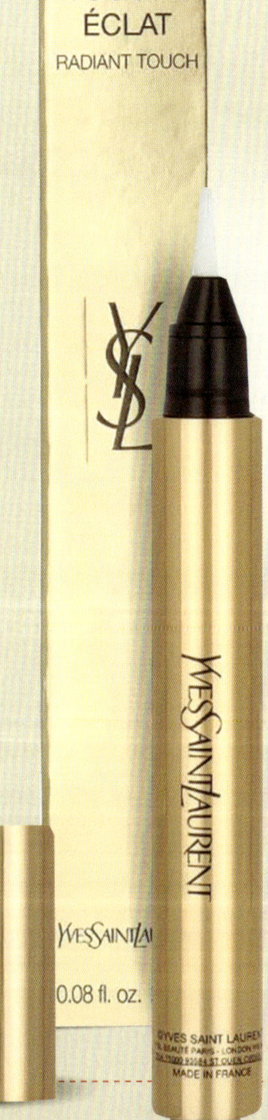

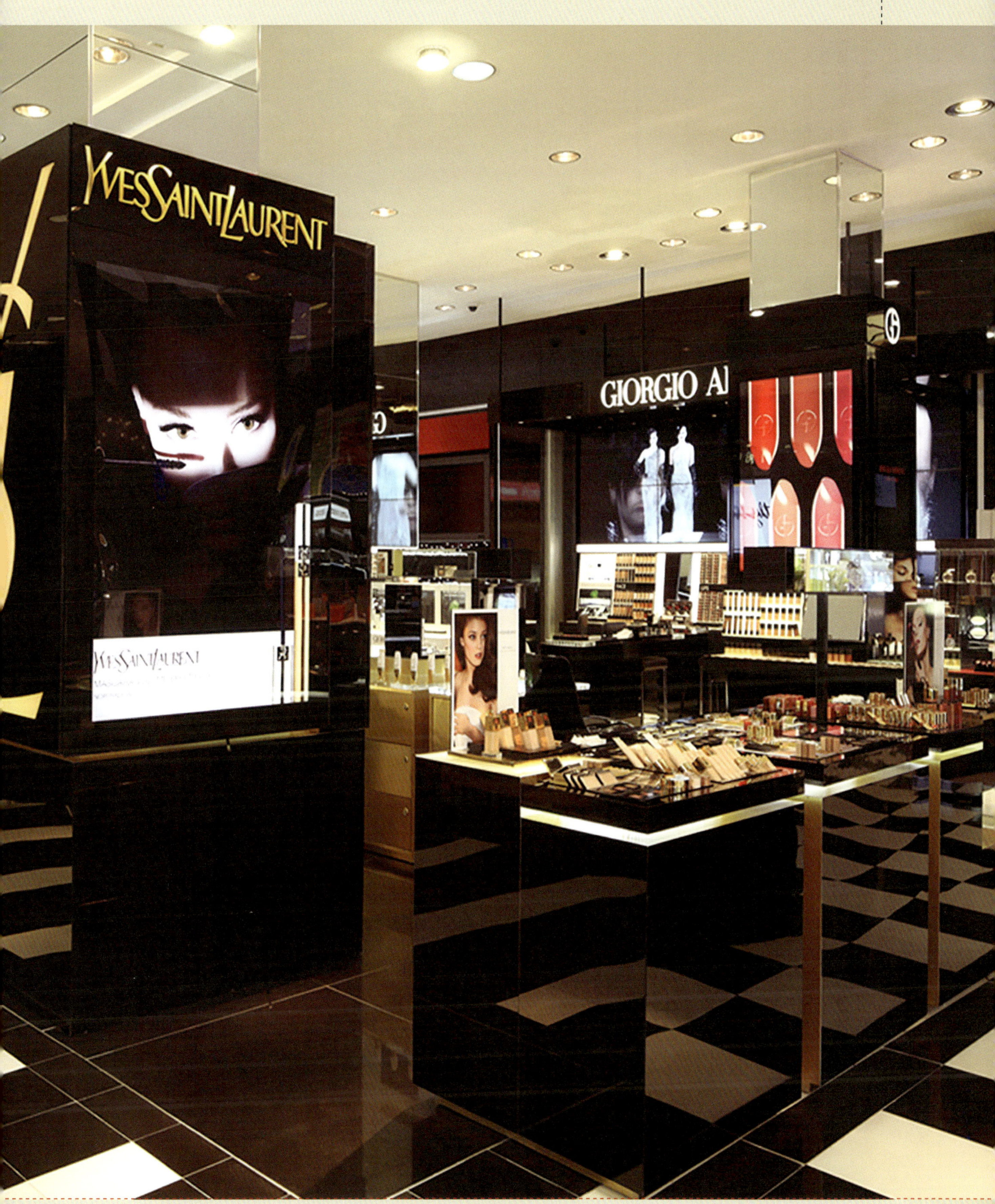

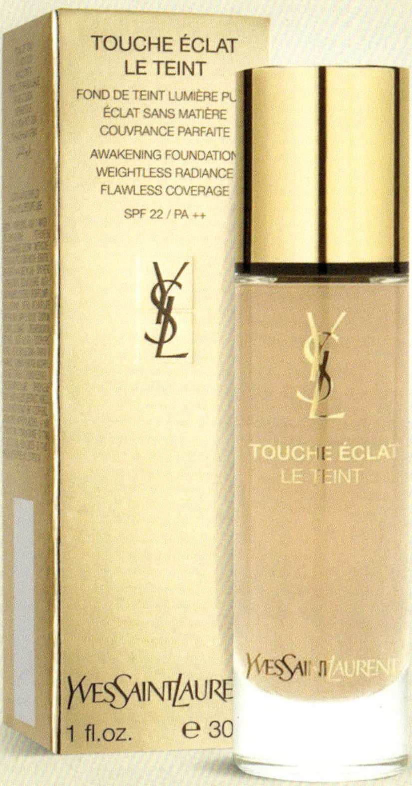

LE TEINT TOUCHE ÉCLAT FOUNDATION

Following the success of Touche Éclat, Yves Saint Laurent expanded the brand's range of foundations with the Le Teint Touche Éclat Foundation in 2012. True to YSL Beaute's philosophy of creating products which enhance natural beauty, this foundation provides a lightweight, buildable finish with an inherent glow. Combining skincare and makeup, the foundation offers hydration while providing flawless coverage. The result is a radiant, dewy finish that mimics the effortless beauty YSL always championed. The launch of Le Teint Touche Éclat was another milestone in YSL's ongoing commitment to radiant, youthful-looking skin combined with the highest standards of quality.

YSL BEAUTY CAMPAIGNS - GLAMOUR MEETS PROVOCATION

'Beauty is a tool of seduction, of rebellion, and of power' — Yves Saint Laurent.

Yves Saint Laurent Beauty advertising campaigns have always embodied the same boldness, provocation and artistry the brand stands for. The campaigns have often featured powerful, confident, unapologetically sensual women. Women like Kaia Gerber, Cara Delevingne and Zoë Kravitz – the faces of YSL's iconic 'Dress Your Lips' campaign for Rouge Pur Couture lipstick. Saint Laurent's beauty campaigns blur the lines between fashion photography, art and advertising. The imagery conjures up elements of mystery, intimacy and the concept of self-expression — values deeply embedded in the YSL fashion legacy.

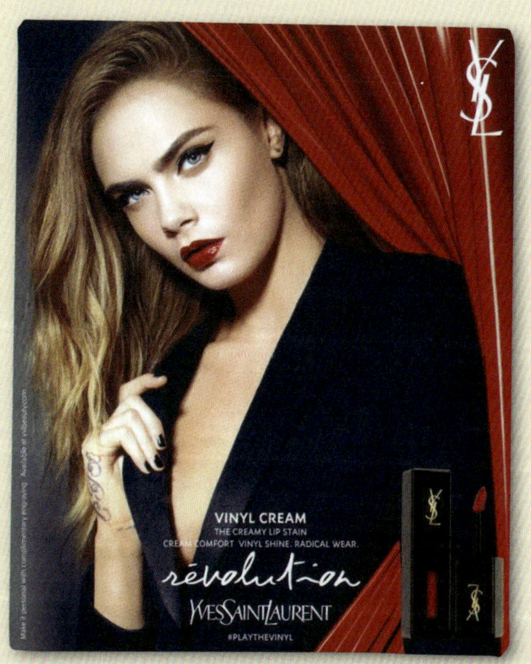

RIGHT: 2016 YSL Beauté magazine advertisement
OPP PAGE: Cara Delevingne attends the YSL Beauté: "YSL Loves Your Lips" party in London, England, January 2015

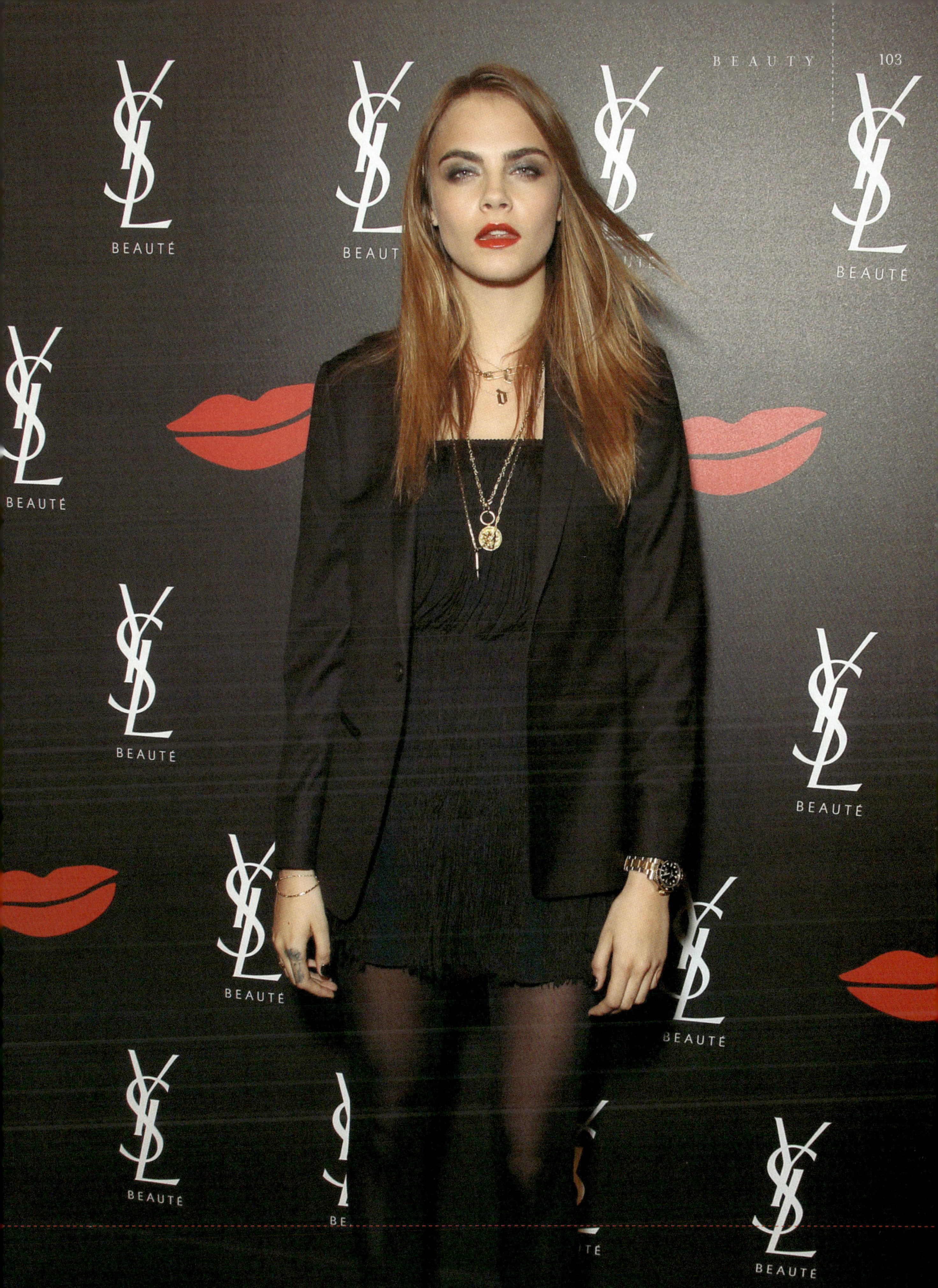

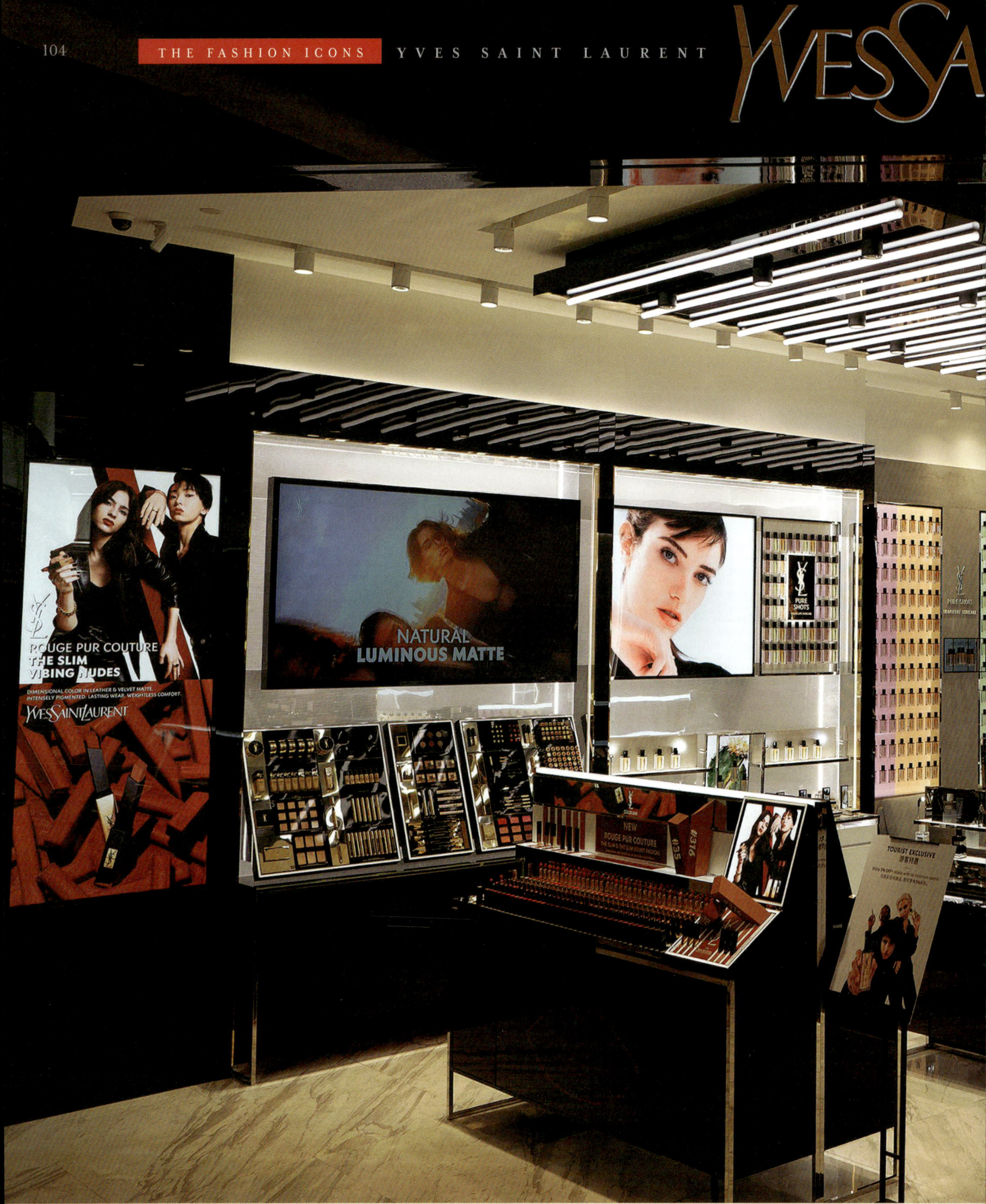

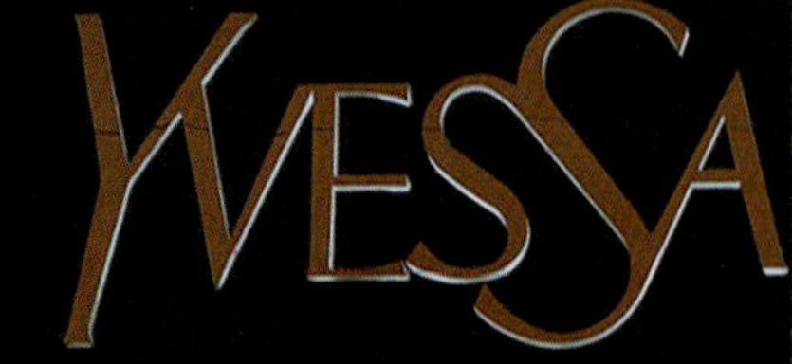

ABOVE: Beauty products on display at an Yves Saint Laurent store in Kuala Lumpur

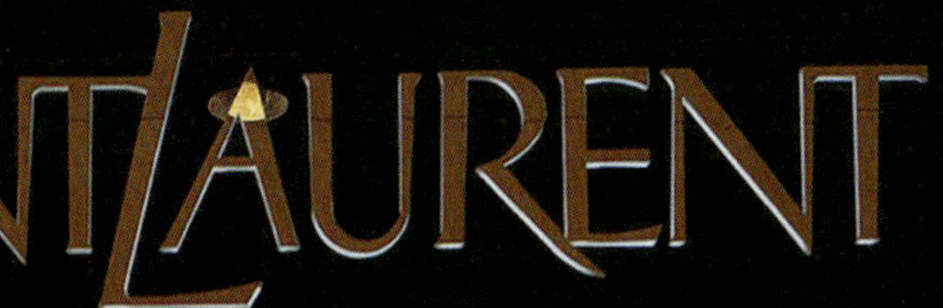

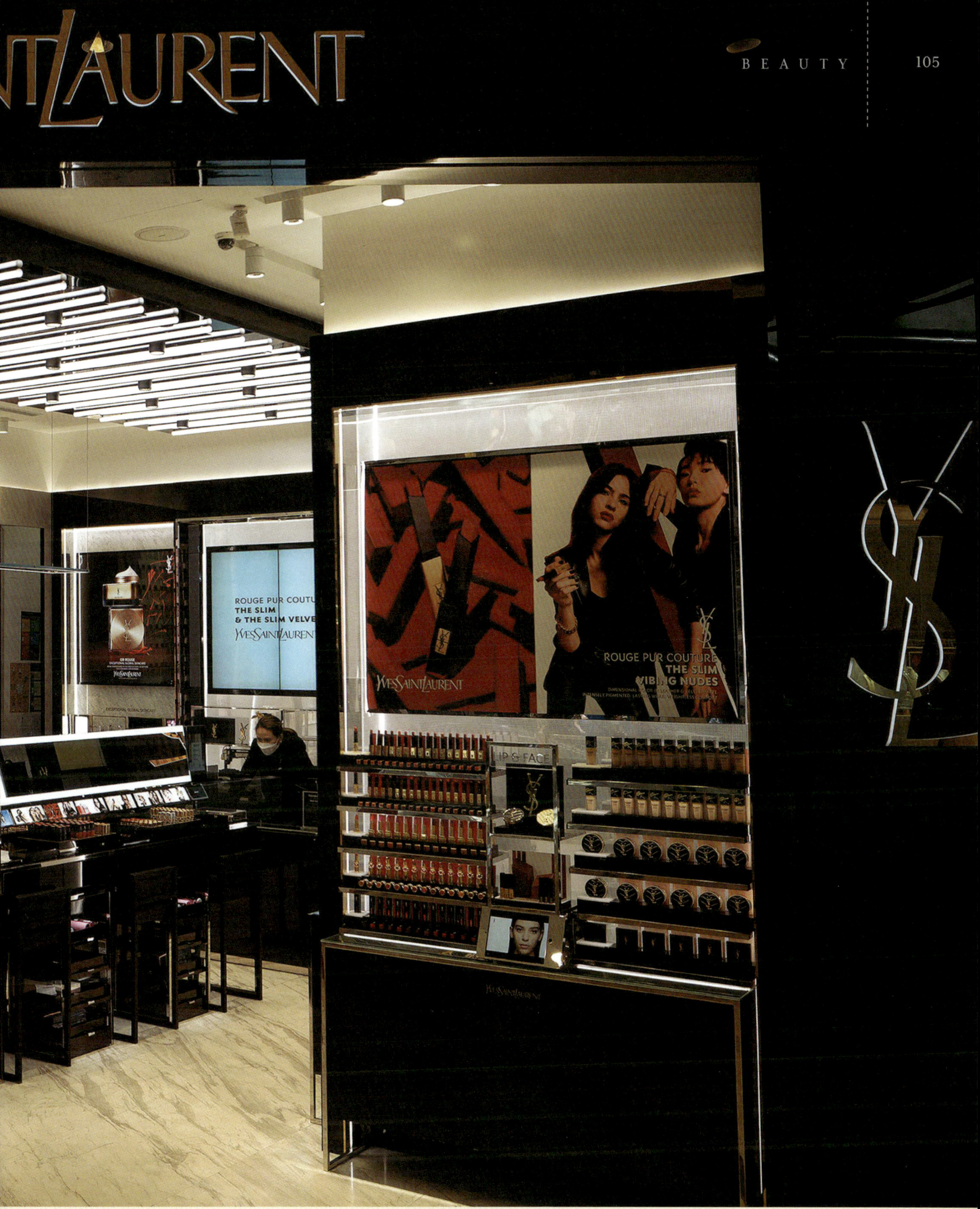

THE FINAL COLLECTION

"I have chosen today to bid farewell to this profession, which I have loved too much"

Yves Saint Laurent's retirement speech

It can surely be no coincidence that Yves Saint Laurent began to distance himself from his beloved label once it had been purchased by the PPR, now Kering, group which also owned Gucci, in 1999. PPR split YSL into two lines – Haute Couture which would remain under Yves Saint Laurent's creative control, while Ready-to-Wear (Rive Gauche) was handed to American designer Tom Ford, then creative director at Gucci. Saint Laurent was reportedly unhappy with Tom Ford's direction, feeling it strayed too far from his own elegant, refined aesthetic. He found Ford's designs overly provocative and commercial. Though Saint Laurent was still designing haute couture, he felt increasingly sidelined by his own brand. The corporate culture of PPR and the pressures of brand profitability clashed with Saint Laurent's more artistic, couture-focused vision. This contributed to his disillusionment and a sense that the fashion industry was no longer a space where he could create freely. On a personal level, he also knew something had to give. He had long

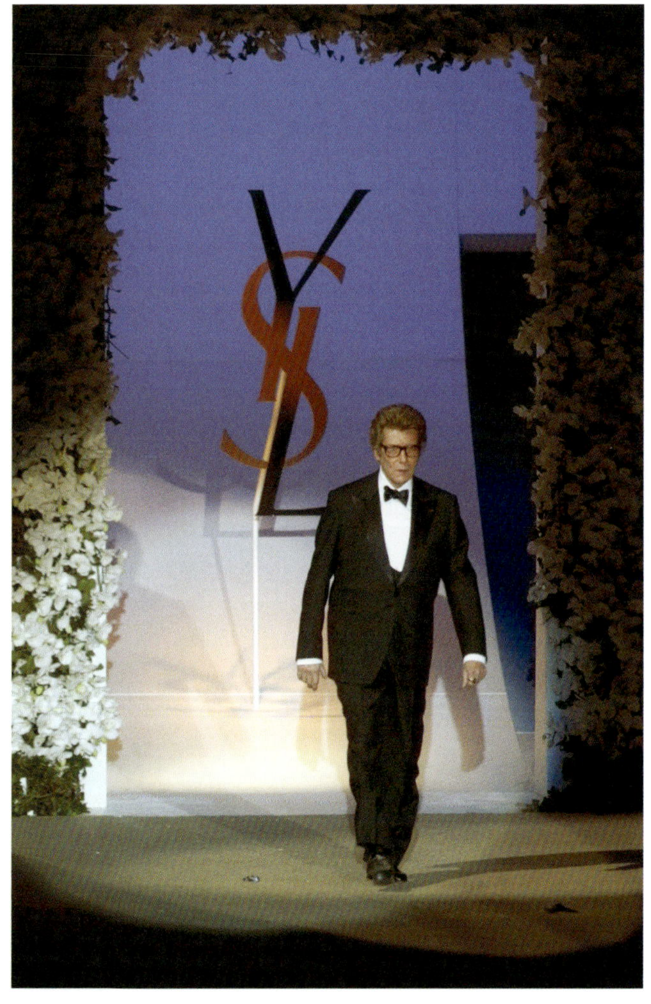

RIGHT: Yves Saint Laurent walks down the catwalk to salute the crowd before unveiling his last ever collection
OPP PAGE: Carla Bruni walks the runway during the same show, the final collection, 22 January 2002

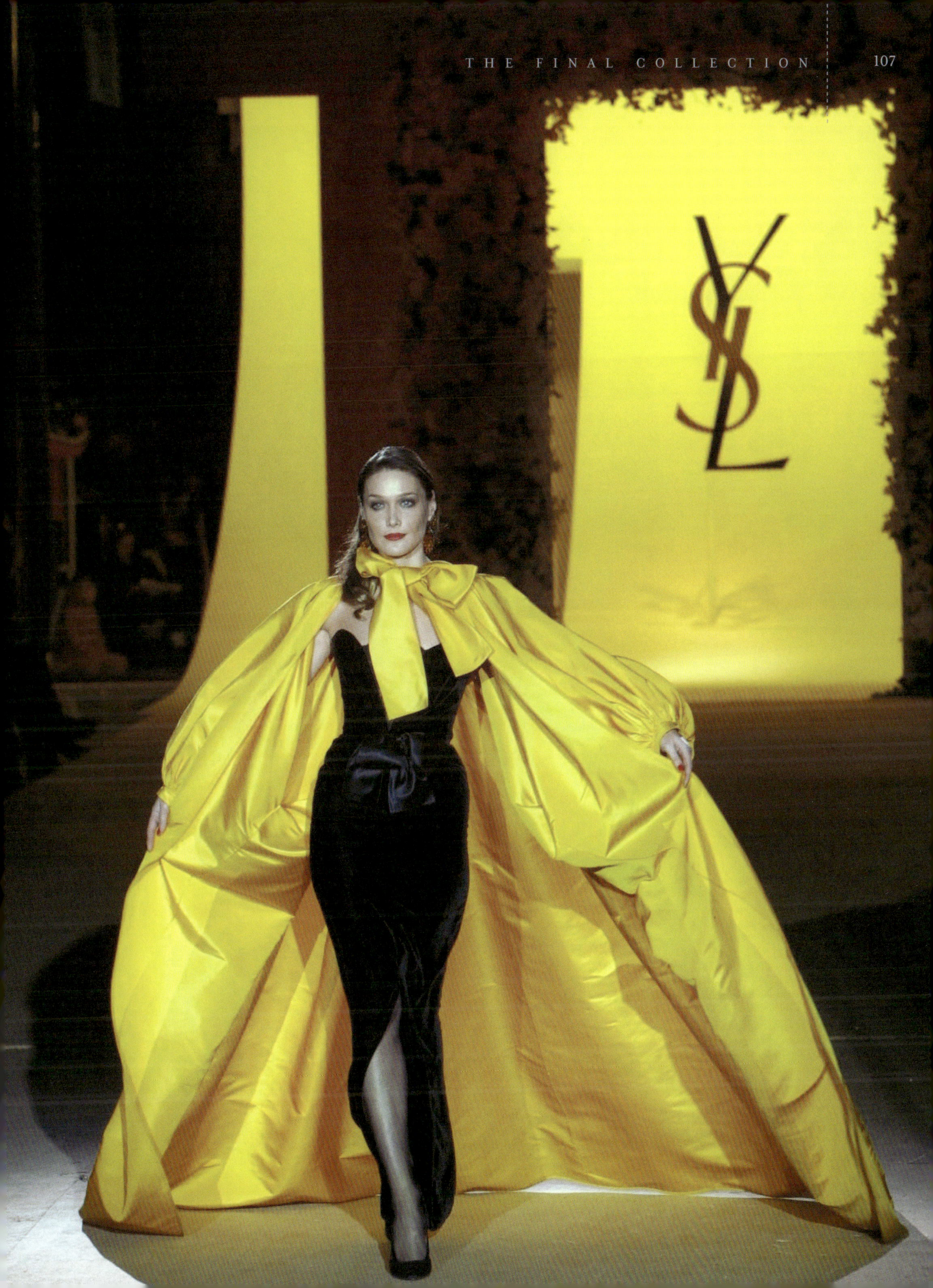
YSL

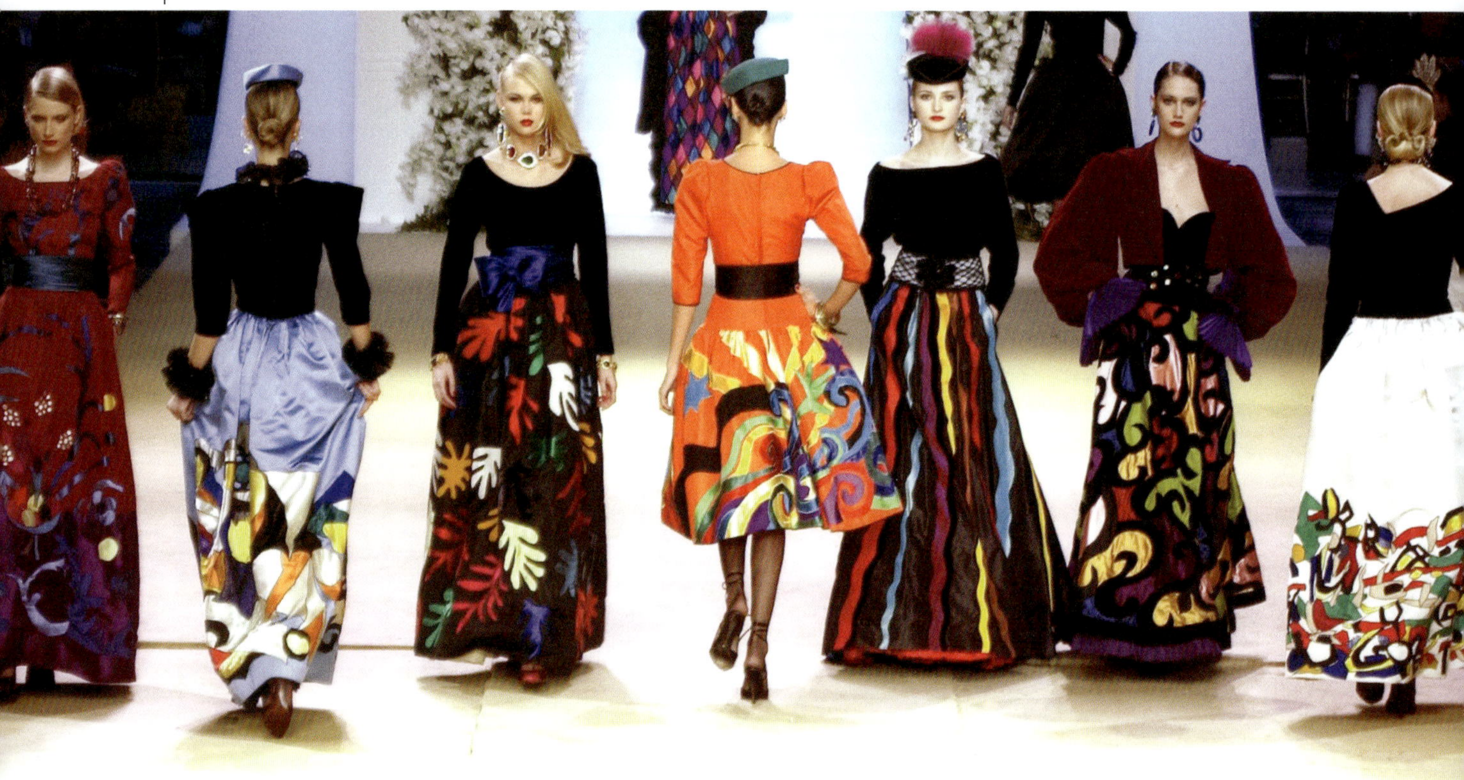

struggled with depression, anxiety and substance abuse. His overall health wasn't good which made the demands of running a fashion house — with multiple collections a year — increasingly difficult to sustain. Now in his 60s and after more than 40 years in the public eye, he was simply exhausted. Retirement would allow him to retreat from the spotlight and live a quieter life, mostly with Pierre Bergé, in Paris and Marrakech.

Although he had first spoken of his wish to step back from the label in 1999, Saint Laurent formally announced his retirement in early January 2002. His farewell runway show took place on January 23 at the Saint Laurent Couture House in Paris. The show marked the end of an era for both Saint Laurent and the fashion world, signalling the end of the legendary designer's career but also the conclusion of a legacy that had redefined the meaning of feminine elegance, modern tailoring and luxury craftsmanship. It was clear that the show would be both a celebration of Yves Saint Laurent's life's work and a personal, emotional farewell.

The models who walked the runway for this final collection included several of Saint Laurent's iconic muses, including Naomi Campbell, Jerry Hall and Katoucha. The runway was filled with both emotional tension and glamorous spectacle, as the audience – which included fashion royalty such as Anna Wintour and Carine Roitfeld - recognized the historical significance of the moment. The collection

ABOVE: Haute Couture Spring/Summer at Yves Saint Laurent's last ever show, 2002

OPP PAGE: Jerry Hall presents a gown during the retrospective part of Saint Laurent's last ever show

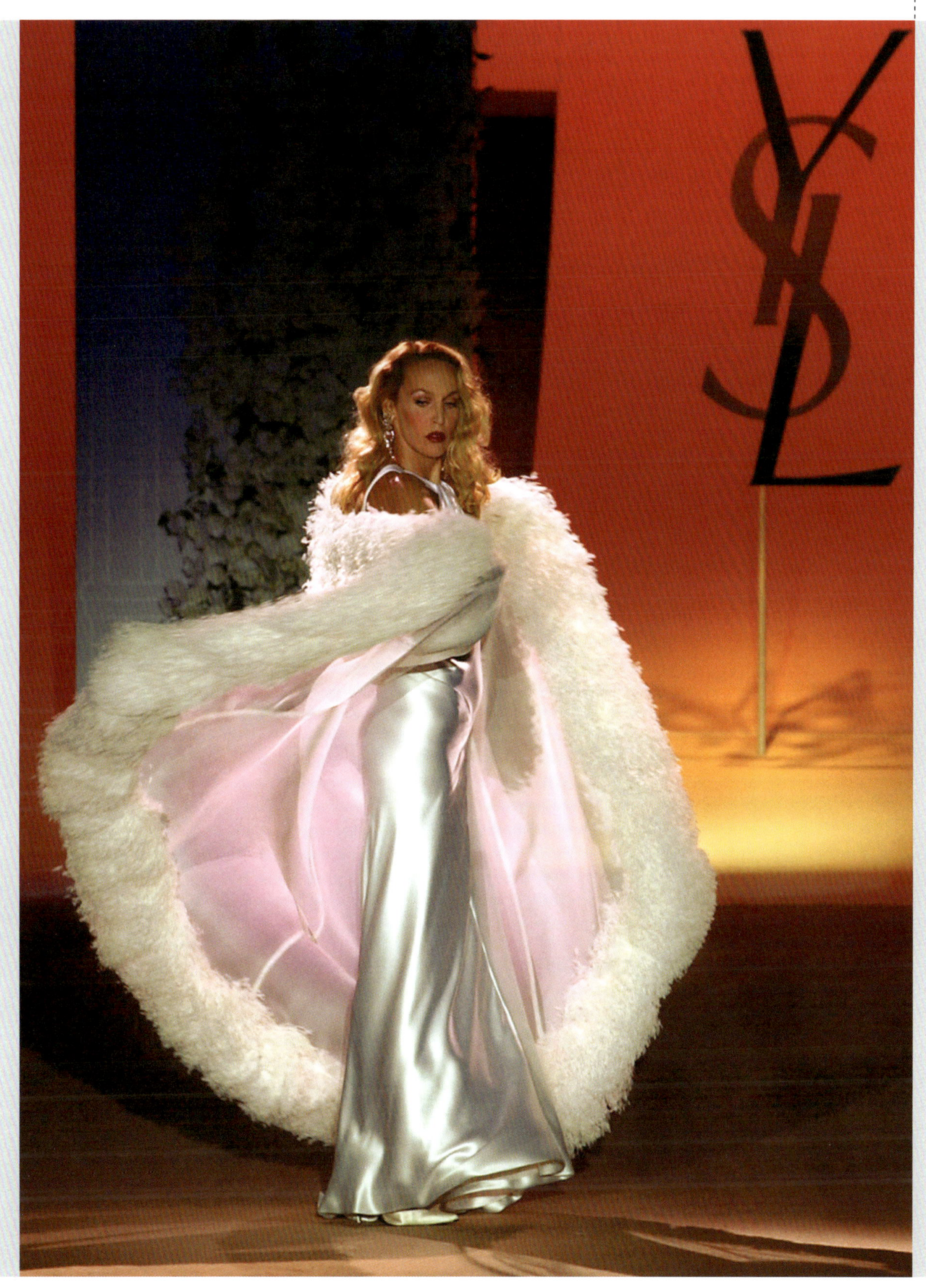

was filled with references to Yves Saint Laurent's legendary career and the various phases of his creative evolution – it was a fresh and contemporary slant on Saint Laurent's most famous and celebrated designs. There were reprises of his most iconic pieces — 'Le Smoking' tuxedo, jumpsuits, safari jackets juxtaposed with ethereal evening gowns. There were also numerous references to his African and Russian-inspired collections, demonstrating his fascination with world culture. The 2002 collection revisited these motifs, incorporating rich prints, luxurious fabrics, and voluminous silhouettes that had defined his work in the 1970s and 1980s. The colour palette of the farewell collection was a striking mix of classic YSL neutrals — blacks, whites and golds, and more vibrant tones such as rich reds, deep blues, and earthy browns. These colours reflected Saint Laurent's ability to balance luxury and restraint with bold and striking details. It was as if he were celebrating his entire body of work, from his early days of colourful excess to his more recent subdued minimalism. The silhouettes were sophisticated and powerful with a heavy emphasis on tailored suits, structured jackets, and elegant evening gowns. These looks were a testament to his lifelong dedication to the modern woman — strong, independent and graceful. In many ways, the 2002 collection marked the culmination of a lifetime's worth of innovative work, but it also showed how much Saint Laurent had shaped fashion. This final outing demonstrated how fashion could be both artistic and wearable, combining luxury with modernity and emotional depth with technical expertise. It was a poignant reminder of the power of fashion to express identity, empower women and transcend generations.

Saint Laurent's farewell collection in 2002 was a fitting end to an extraordinary career and a reminder of the transformative power of fashion. The show was a romantic celebration of Yves Saint Laurent's visionary approach to fashion, showcasing his feminine sensuality, powerful tailoring and couture artistry. For Saint Laurent himself, this collection was an emotional experience. He had always been known for his quiet and introverted personality but this show gave him the opportunity to reflect on his journey. As he sat in the front row to watch the models strut down the runway, he was clearly moved by the outpouring of admiration and respect for his work. The models, too, were visibly emotional, understanding that they were walking in one of the most significant shows in fashion history. Saint Laurent did not give a final bow at the end of the show but his presence at the event spoke volumes. It was a fitting conclusion to a career that had fundamentally shaped the world of haute couture, ready-to-wear, and the very concept of modern femininity.

Yves Saint Laurent's impact on fashion's future continued even after his departure from the industry. The iconic pieces from the collection — particularly the Le Smoking tuxedo, the safari jacket, and the tailored suit — have remained pillars of YSL's heritage and are still celebrated today.

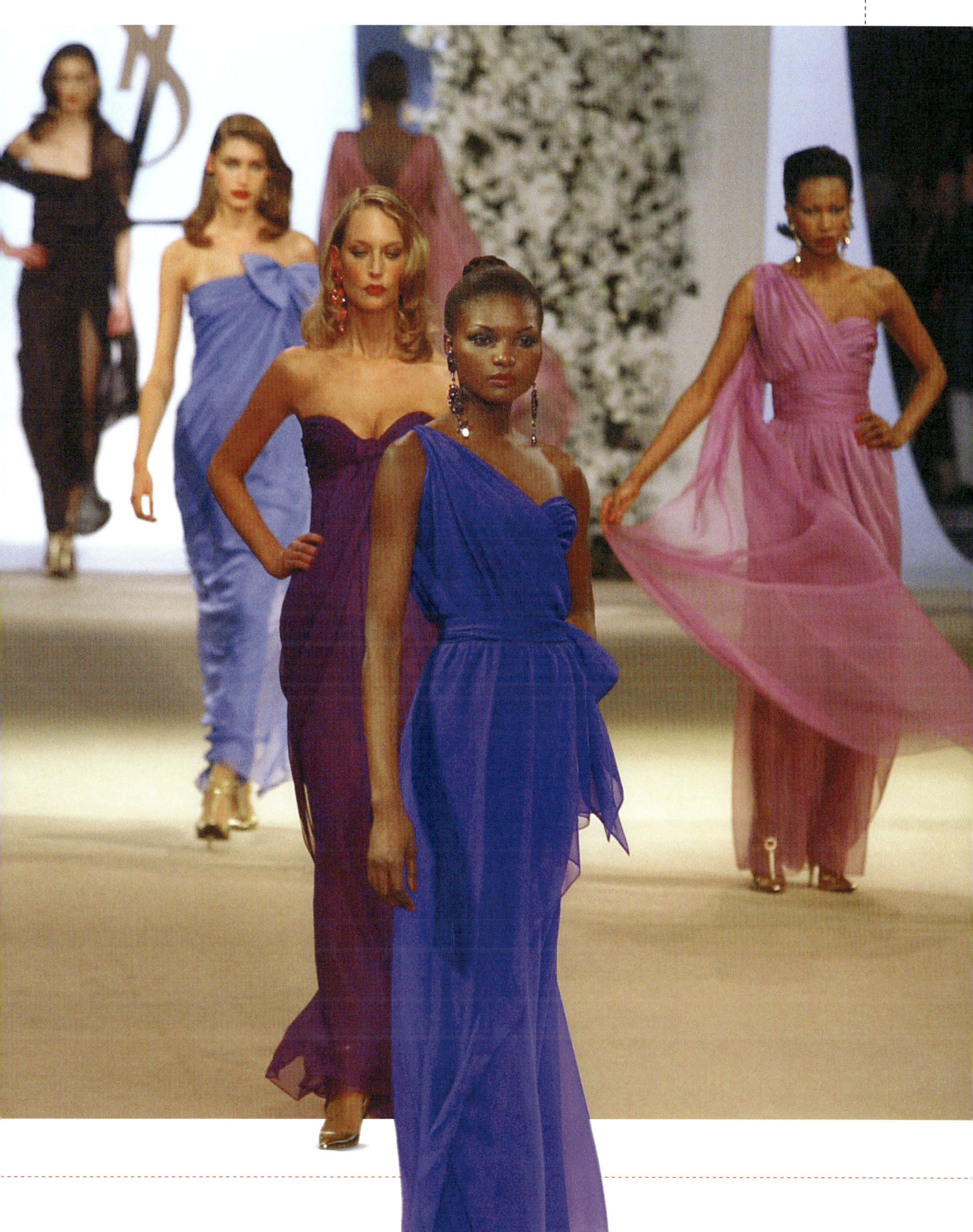

MUSES

"My muses are not mannequins. They are real women, with their own character and personality. I do not dress them to transform them but to reveal them"
Yves Saint Laurent

Yves Saint Laurent's muses were central to his creative process and legacy. More than mere models or celebrities, they were sources of inspiration, collaborators and symbols of the modern woman he designed for. They helped him push the boundaries of fashion, challenge norms and craft his unique style. Each muse embodied a different facet of femininity — elegance, rebellion, sensuality, intellect — which helped Saint Laurent explore new themes throughout his career.

VICTOIRE DOUTRELEAU

A Dior model in the 1950s, she met YSL at the beginning of his career. Striking, aristocratic, and self-possessed, she symbolized the refined yet independent, innately chic woman he loved to dress.

RIGHT: Saint Laurent poses with his models, including Victoire Doutreleau (third from left), after a Christian Dior collection show, July 1959

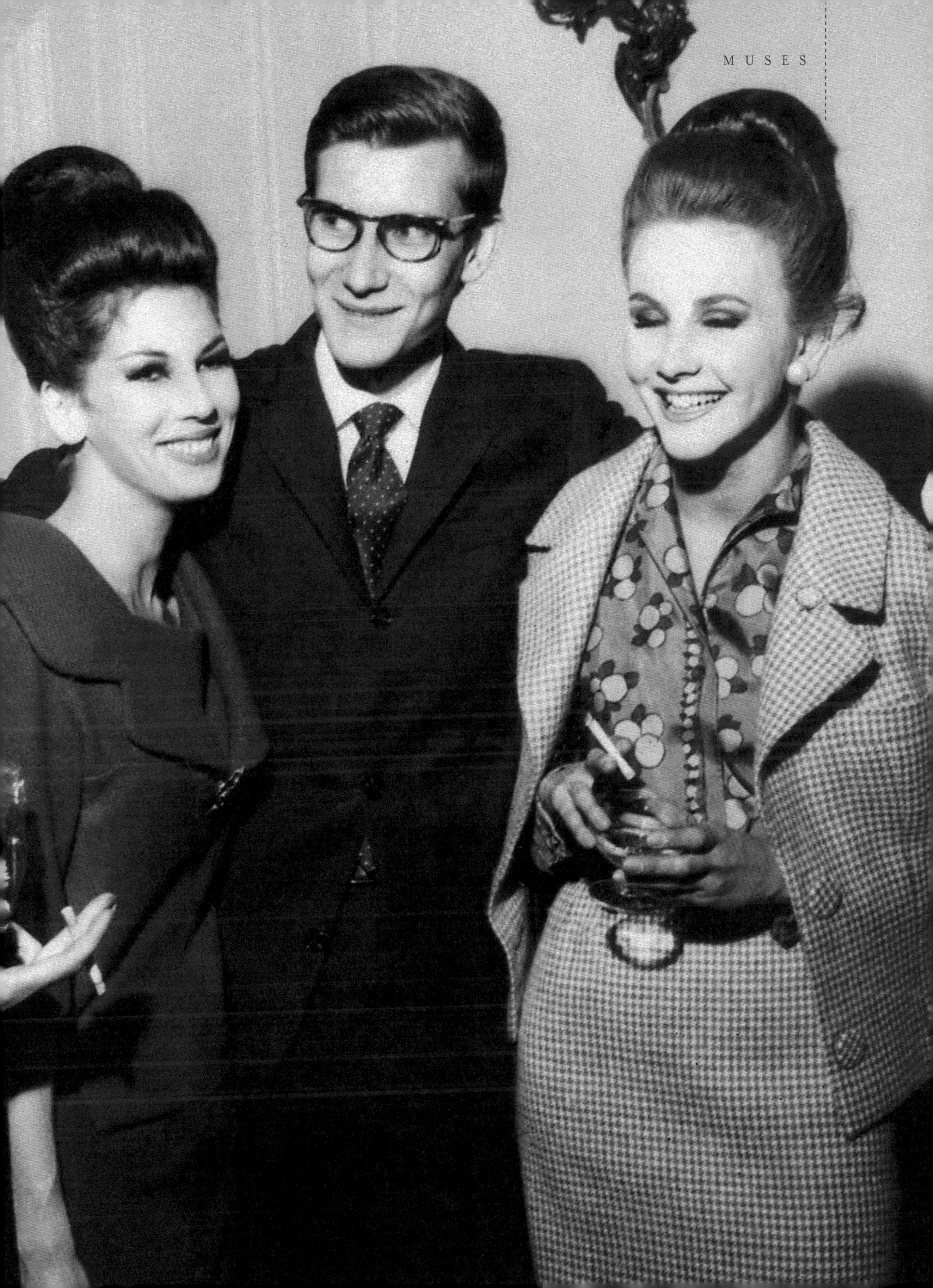

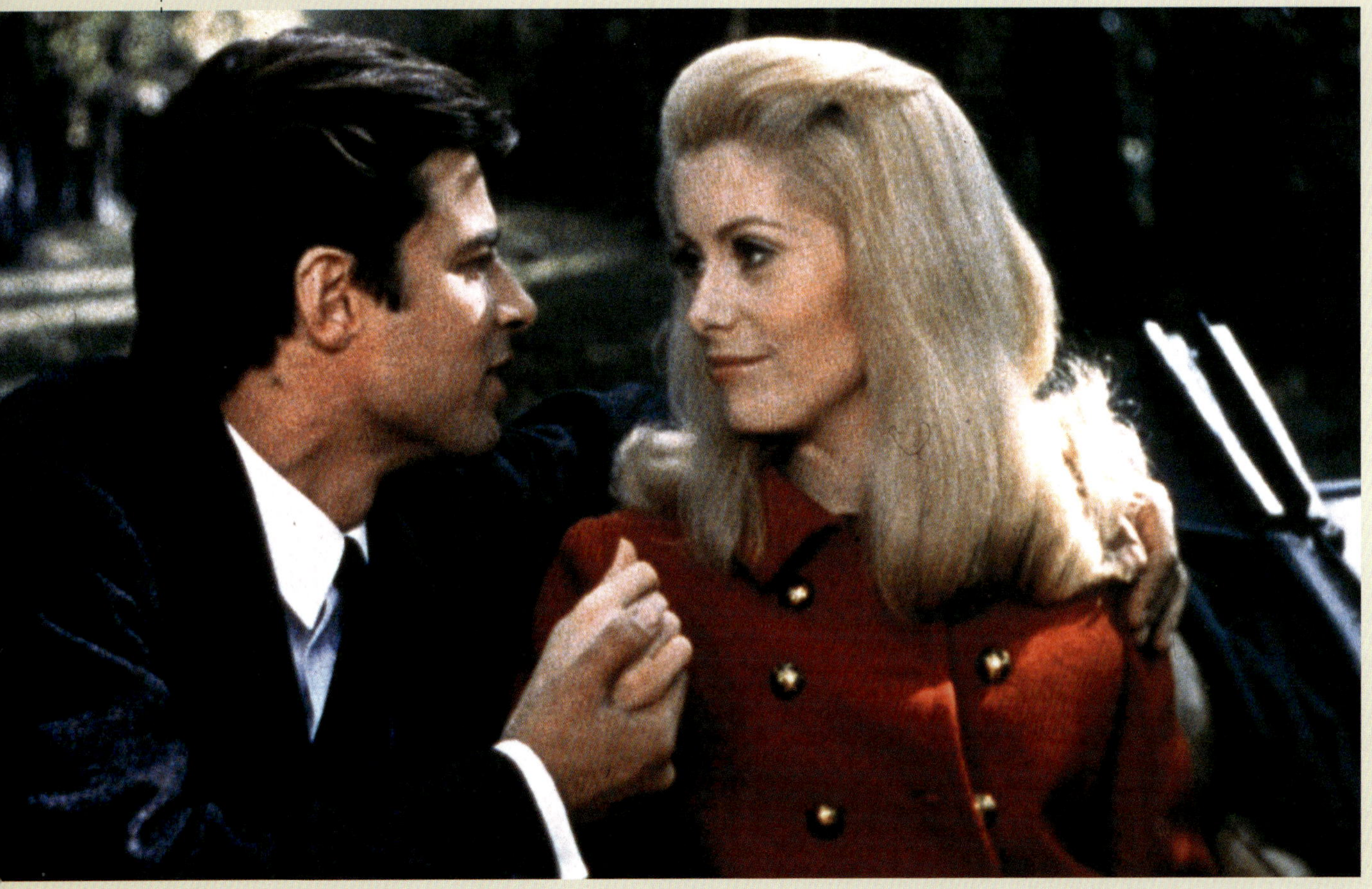

Doutreleau believed in YSL's talent before he became a global icon. She left Dior in order to follow YSL when he started his own label in 1961 and helped shape the early image of the YSL woman - confident, elegant, slightly aloof and powerful. At his first show in 1962, Victoire was the model to open for him. Though never romantically linked, although she did have a 'secret' relationship with Pierre Bergé, Doutreleau's closeness to YSL mirrored the intimacy Saint Laurent often had with his muses.

'Yves adored women, but he understood them even more,' she was later to say. *'He needed us around him — to inspire him, yes — but also to reassure him.'*

CATHERINE DENEUVE

Legendary French actress and long-time friend of YSL, Catherine Deneuve was one of his most famous muses. She often wore his designs both off and on screen, most memorably in the 1967 film 'Belle de Jour'. Her character's chic, minimalist and slightly provocative wardrobe - entirely designed by Yves Saint Laurent - became one of the most legendary fashion moments in cinema history. Deneuve remained a lifelong supporter of Saint Laurent, wearing his designs to major events, including her Oscar-nominated appearance in the 1992 film 'Indochine'.

ABOVE: Catherine Deneuve stars alongside Jean Sorel in 'Belle de Jour', 1967
OPP PAGE: (TOP) Saint Laurent and Paloma Picasso,1991 (BOTTOM) Yves Saint Laurent and Betty Catroux in 2006

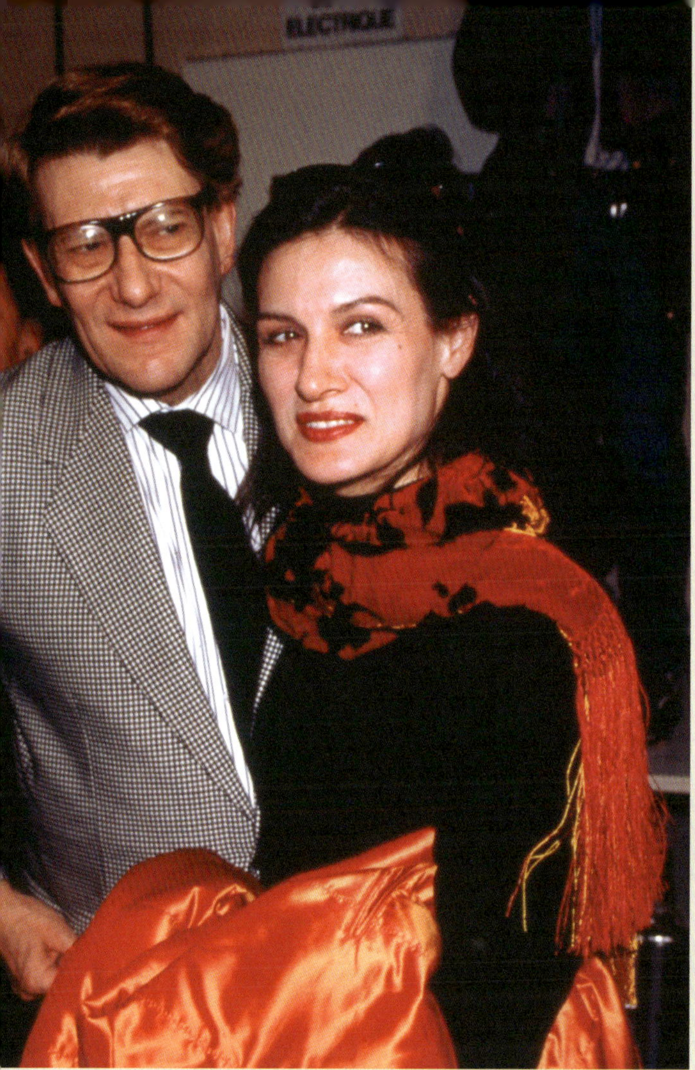

PALOMA PICASSO

The daughter of artist Pablo Picasso, Paloma was a YSL muse in the 1970s, inspiring his bold, artistic designs, especially his dramatic colour palettes and theatrical looks of that time. Paloma Picasso's signature red lips, dark hair, and dramatic personal style inspired YSL's controversial Spring/Summer 1971 haute couture 'Libération' collection. Plus her Spanish-inspired aesthetic became a recurring theme in his work. Her impact extended beyond Saint Laurent and she later became a successful designer in her own right but her fearless, theatrical fashion sense left a permanent mark on YSL's creations.

BETTY CATROUX

With her androgynous, ultra-cool style, Betty Catroux was one of YSL's closest confidantes and an inspiration for his gender-fluid silhouettes. She represented his more rebellious, rock n' roll side. One of Betty Catroux's most memorable moments with Yves Saint Laurent was her influence on Le Smoking, the iconic women's tuxedo introduced in 1966 – he felt she embodied his vision of gender-fluid, rebellious elegance, thus making her the perfect muse for this ground-breaking design. But more than mere muse, La Catroux was one of YSL's closest friends – he claimed she was himself in female form – and she influenced his creative process for over 50 years.

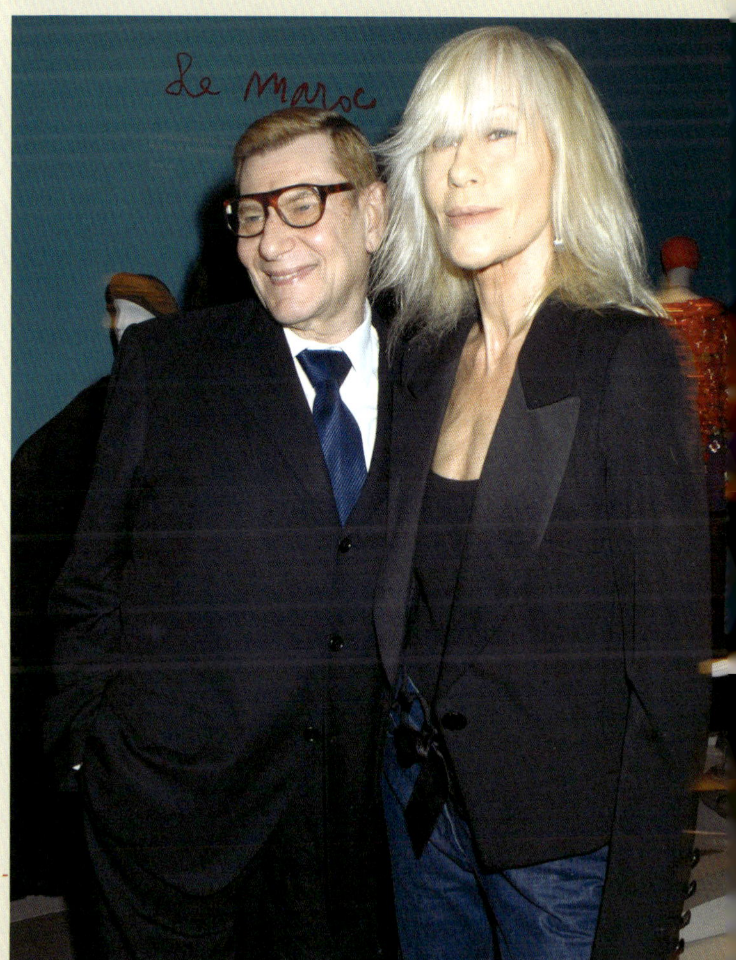

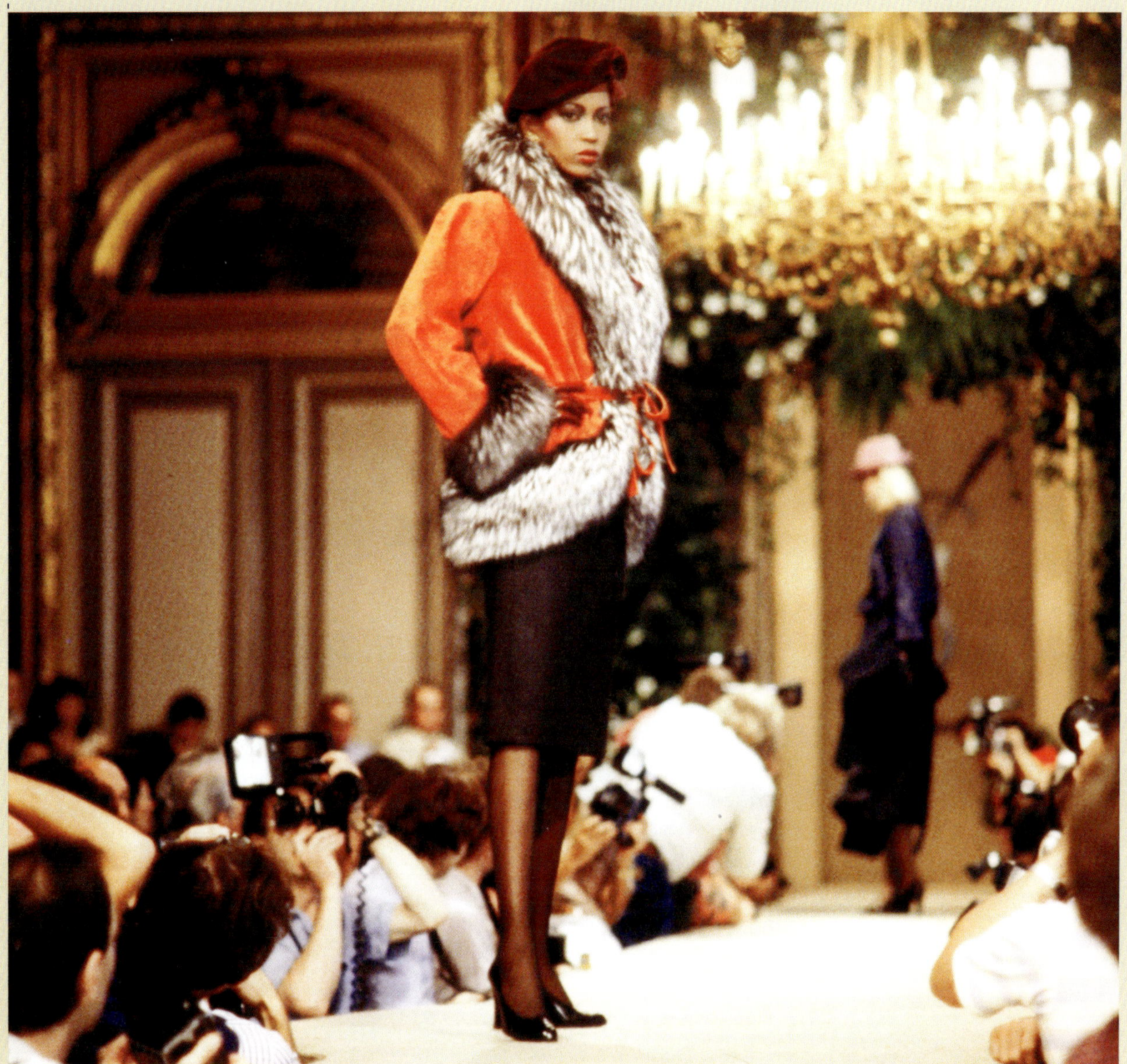

AMALIA VAIRELLI

A model of mixed French and Italian heritage, Amalia walked for YSL frequently in the 1970s and 1980s, epitomizing his classic sophistication. She was frequently seen on the runway in his dramatic evening gowns, sharp tailoring and exotically-inspired designs. Vairelli was one of the few top Black models in haute couture at the time, breaking barriers in the industry. Her presence on the YSL runway helped redefine beauty standards in high fashion, showcasing diversity before it was widely embraced. She perfectly represented the timeless, sophisticated, yet avant-garde YSL woman - making her an integral part of his brand's history.

ABOVE: Amalia Vairelli modelling Yves Saint Laurent Autumn/Winter 1980 Couture collection

OPP PAGE: Mick and Bianca Jagger stand beside the Mayor of Saint-Tropez at their wedding in 1971

BIANCA JAGGER

A style icon of the 1970s, Bianca Jagger often wore YSL's iconic 'Le Smoking' – most famously donning a white tuxedo suit at New York's Studio 54. The Nicaraguan beauty showed how effortlessly chic and rebellious women could be in menswear-inspired fashion. When Bianca Jagger married Rolling Stone Mick in 1971, she wore a YSL white tailored jacket with nothing underneath, paired with a long white skirt and a dramatic hat with a veil. The look was unconventional, modern and ultra-chic, making it one of the most famous bridal looks of all time.

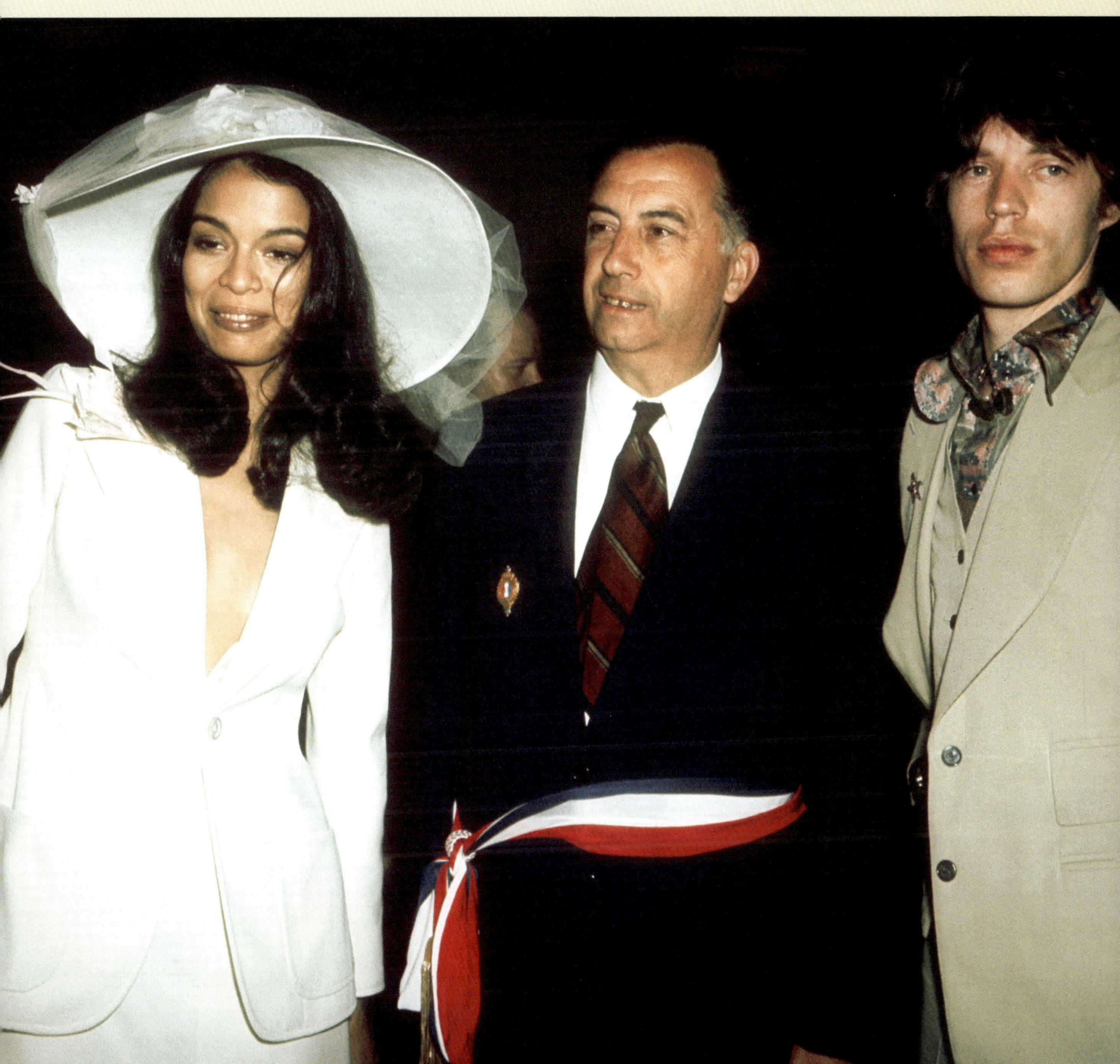

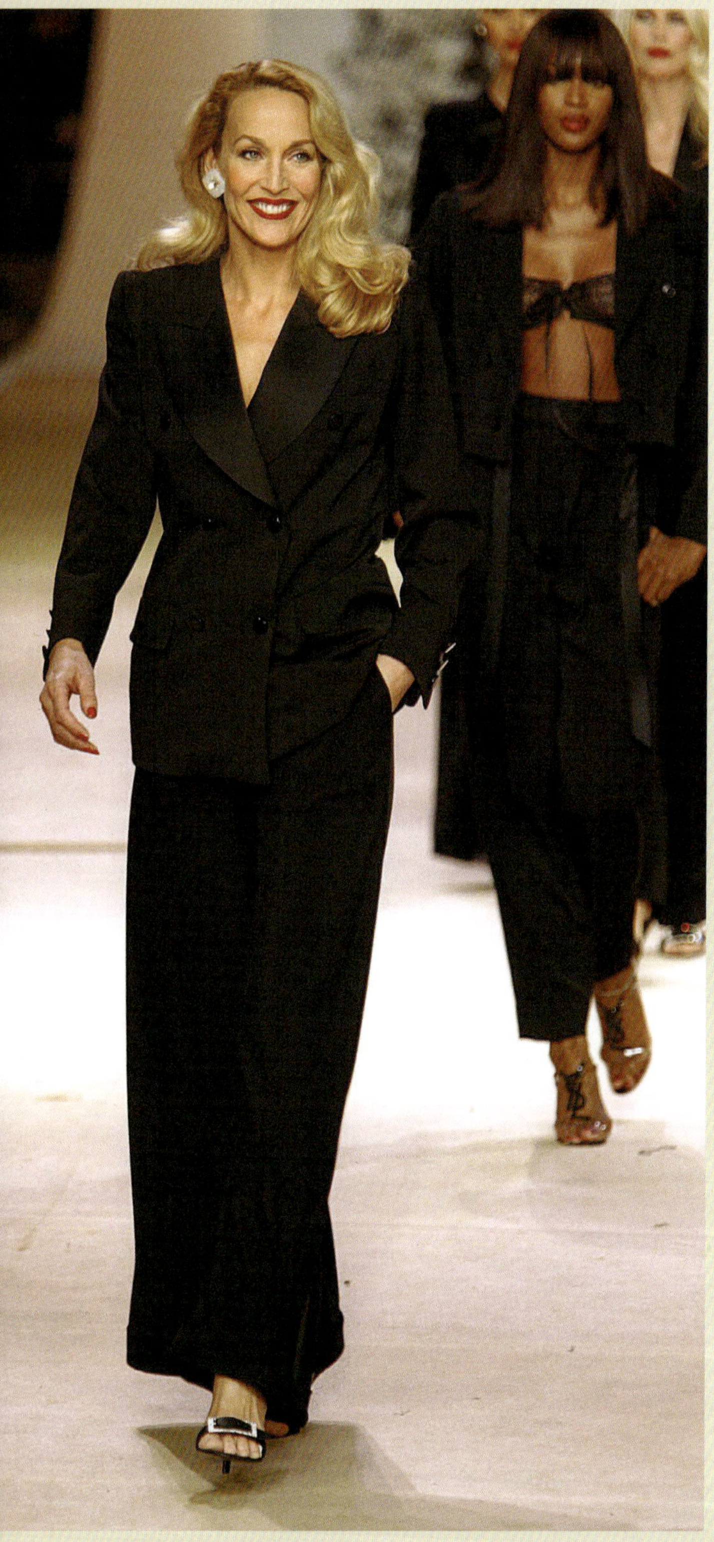

JERRY HALL

Texan model Jerry Hall was one of Yves Saint Laurent's most glamorous muses, known for her voluptuous beauty, waist-length golden hair and larger-than-life presence on the runway. She frequently modelled for his haute couture collections - often seen in dramatic evening gowns, structured tuxedos, and jewel-toned draped dresses that highlighted her statuesque frame. She was the personification of YSL's signature mix of opulence, power and sensuality. When Yves Saint Laurent launched his controversial and ultra-luxurious 'Opium' perfume in 1977, Jerry Hall was a central figure in the campaign – embodying the decadence and mystery of the fragrance. Jerry made a dramatic return to YSL's runway in 1998 for his 40th anniversary fashion show, proving that she was still an icon of the brand. She walked in a show-stopping velvet gown, exuding timeless glamour and celebrating Saint Laurent's lasting legacy in fashion.

KATOUCHA NIANE

Born in Guinea in 1960, Katoucha Niane, often simply known as Katoucha, was one of Yves Saint Laurent's most iconic muses especially during the 1980s. Like Amalia Vairelli, Katoucha was one of the first high-profile Black models to be embraced by the elite Paris fashion world - thus helping to break down more barriers in an industry that had long resisted diversity on the runway. She was known as 'La Princesse

ABOVE: Jerry Hall with a classic YSL runway look
OPP PAGE: Katoucha Niane embraces Yves Saint Laurent at his 1989 Autumn/Winter ready-to-wear fashion show in Paris

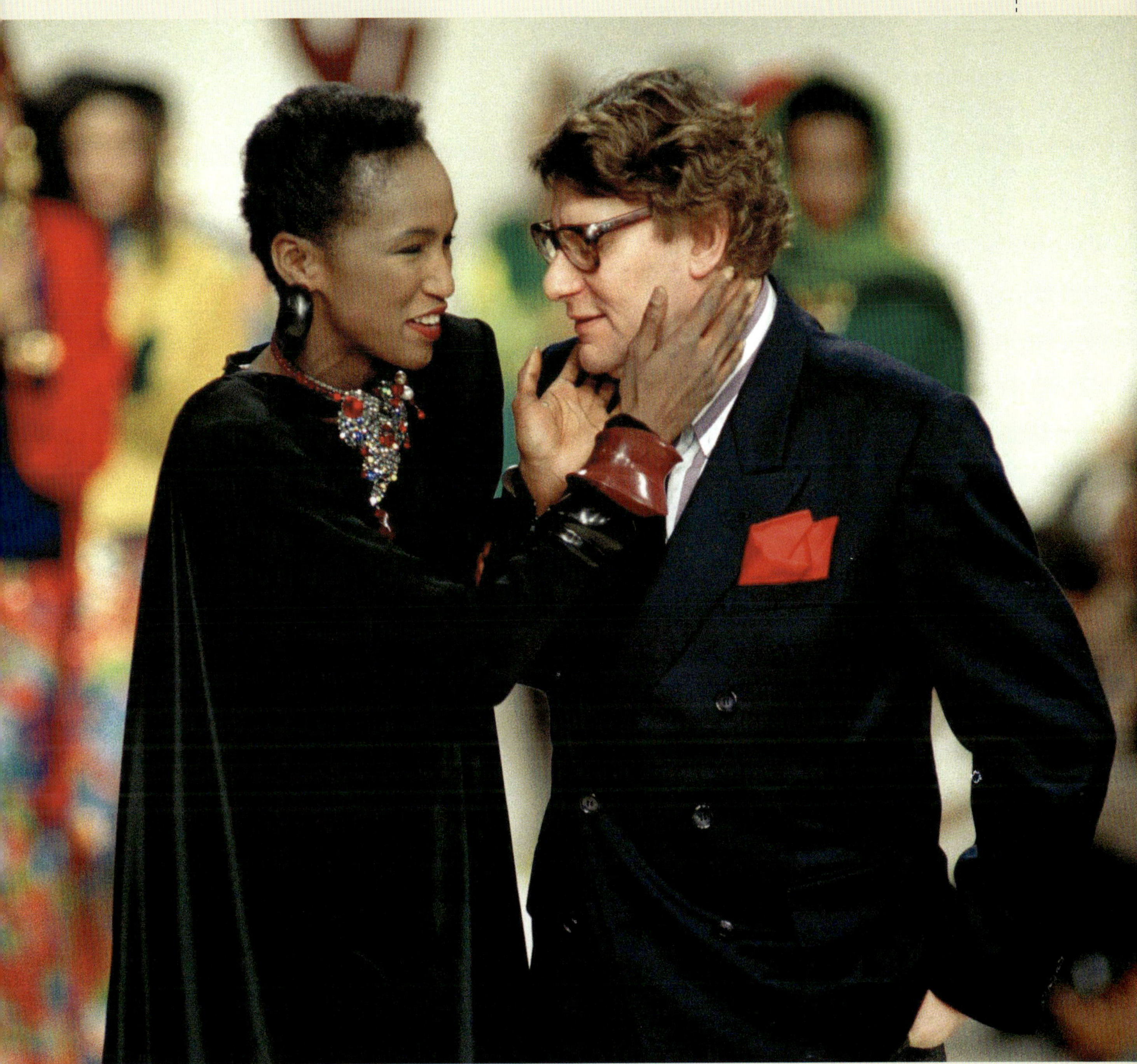

Peule', referencing her Fulani heritage and striking, aristocratic presence. Tragically, she died in Paris in 2008 under mysterious circumstances with her body later found in the river Seine. Katoucha remains a symbol of grace, power and defiance—a true muse not only for YSL but for many seeking greater representation in fashion.

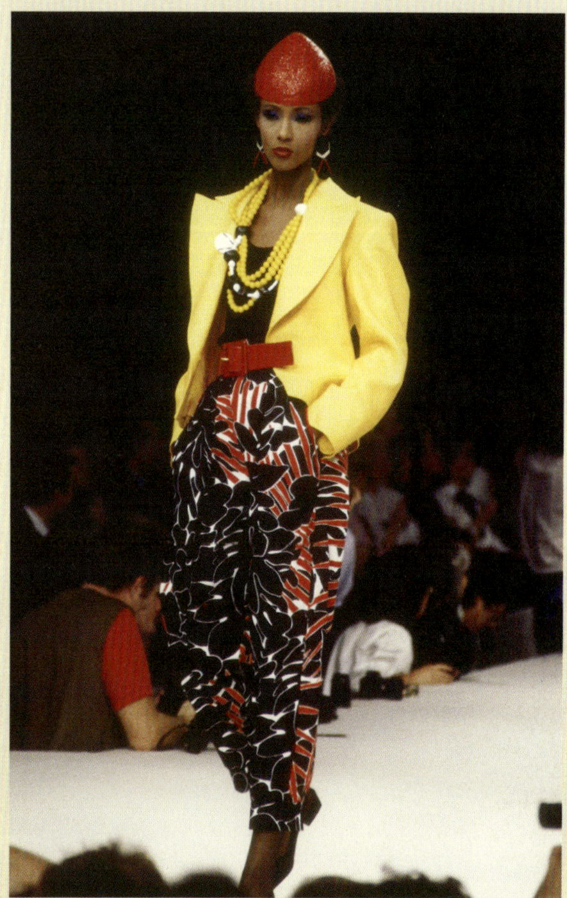

IMAN

The Somali-born supermodel, known for her striking beauty and regal presence, was a favourite of YSL and a key figure in diversifying the fashion industry. One of Iman's most legendary YSL moments was when she inspired and modelled in Yves Saint Laurent's Spring/Summer 1985 'African Queen' collection – a ground-breaking haute couture show that celebrated African beauty and culture through high fashion. In 1991, Iman became one of the faces of Yves Saint Laurent's 'Love' fragrance, further solidifying her connection to the house. In January 2002, when Yves Saint Laurent presented his final haute couture show in Paris, Iman was among the legendary YSL muse models who walked the runway to celebrate his career.

NAOMI CAMPBELL

One of the ultimate supermodels of the 1990s, Naomi Campbell frequently walked in Saint Laurent's shows and carried on his legacy of celebrating strong, glamorous women. One of Naomi Campbell's most legendary YSL moments was her runway debut for Yves Saint Laurent Haute Couture in 1988, when she was just 18 years old. Wearing a striking black gown with a sheer bodice and dramatic draping, La Campbell had well and truly arrived. That same year, she appeared on the cover of *French Vogue* for this first time – an achievement she said was down to Yves Saint Laurent. *'My first French Vogue cover ever was because of that man,'* she was to recall. *'When I said to him "Yves, they won't give me a French Vogue cover, they won't put a black girl on the cover", he was like "I'll take care of that" and he did.'* Another highlight was her appearance at the Spring/Summer 1997 haute couture show, where she wore a stunning gold strapless gown with a sculpted bodice. The look was pure Saint Laurent - elegant, sensual and regal - and Naomi's presence made it unforgettable. The look became one of the most photographed of the collection and is still referenced in YSL fashion history.

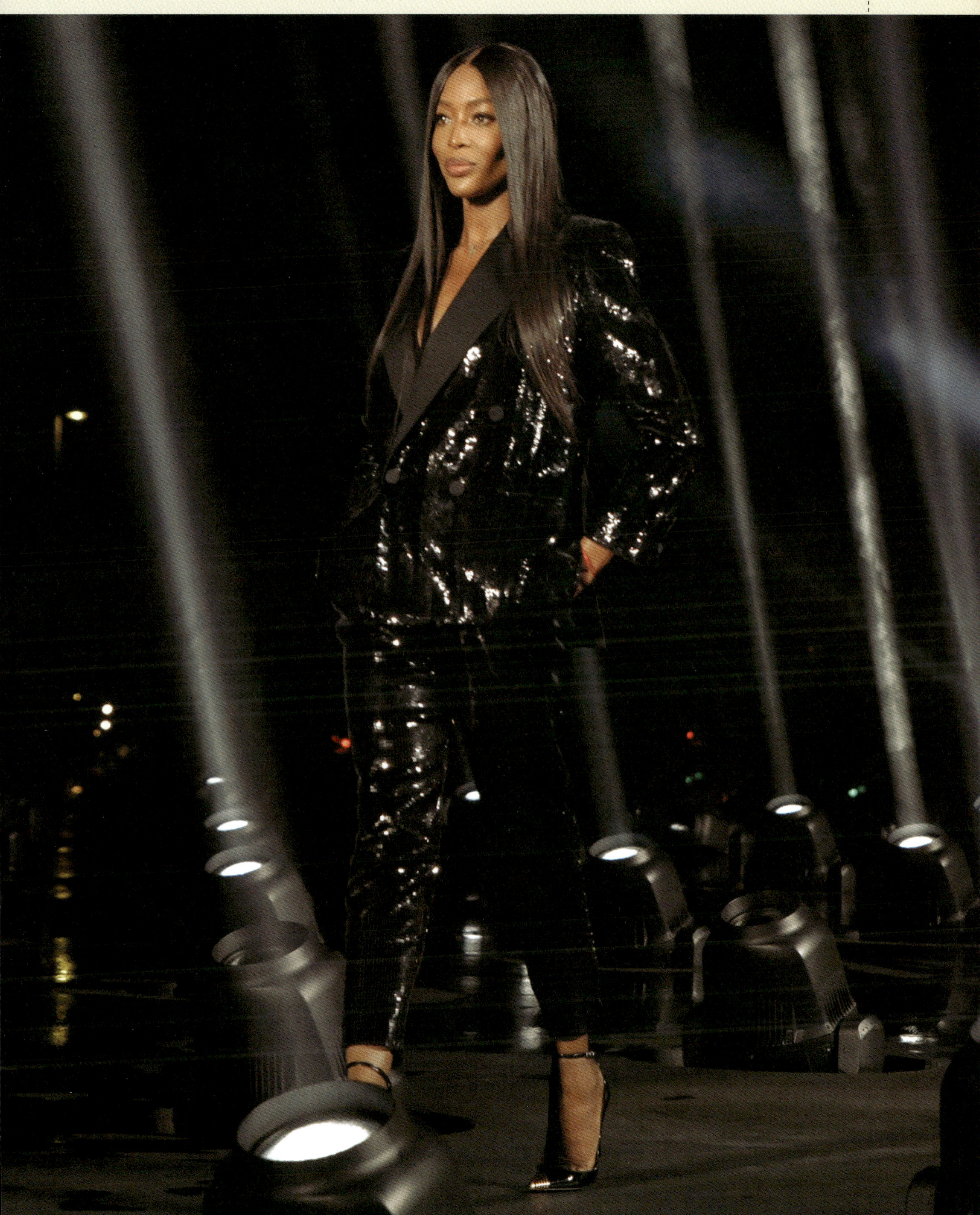

AFTER YVES

"Saint Laurent has done everything"

Stefano Pilati

Even before Yves Saint Laurent retired in 2002, it was time for YSL to begin a new chapter. While the brand remained strong, it faced the challenge of not only preserving and continuing its legacy but also ensuring the house remained relevant and innovative in the changing landscape of the fashion industry. In business terms, despite its fame and rich heritage, by the late 1990s YSL was underperforming financially. The brand had prestige but lacked profitability.

Tom Ford took over YSL Haute Couture in addition to Ready-to-Wear following Yves' departure. He would go on to create memorable and provocative collections for the brand, shaping the house's direction for the next few years. Known for his boldness, glamour and provocative aesthetic, Ford embraced a more sexy, sleek, and modern interpretation of the YSL legacy. His approach was sensual and provocative, characterised by skin-tight leather trousers, sheer tops and sassy, sultry dresses. He reimagined Yves Saint Laurent's feminine empowerment in a more contemporary and sexed-up way, making it resonate with a new generation. Ford also re-worked the iconic YSL logo, re-imagining

it for the modern era. Under Ford's direction, the brand's ready-to-wear collection expanded, gaining popularity among fashion insiders and celebrities. His advertising campaign for the YSL fragrance Opium, featuring a red-haired, suggestively-posed

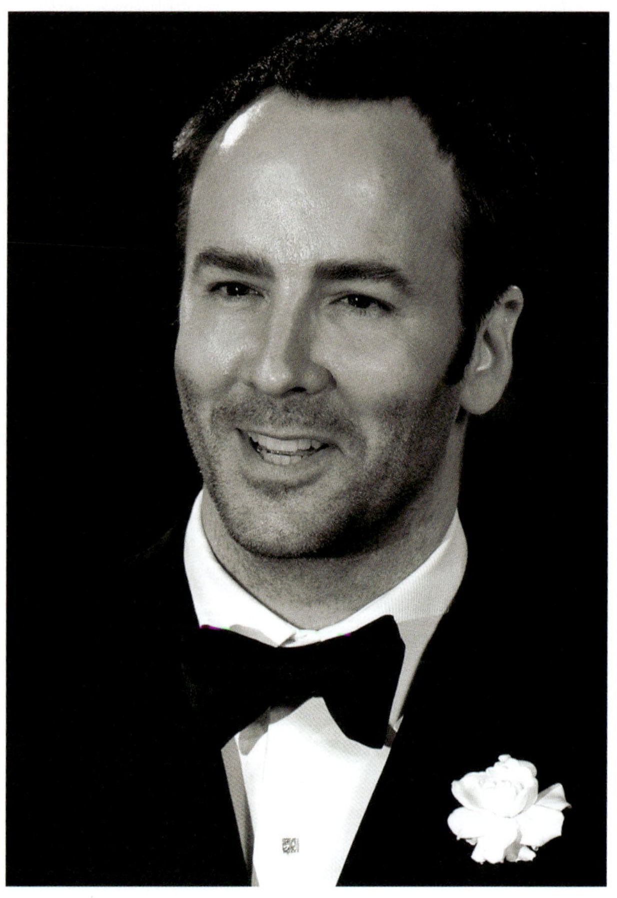

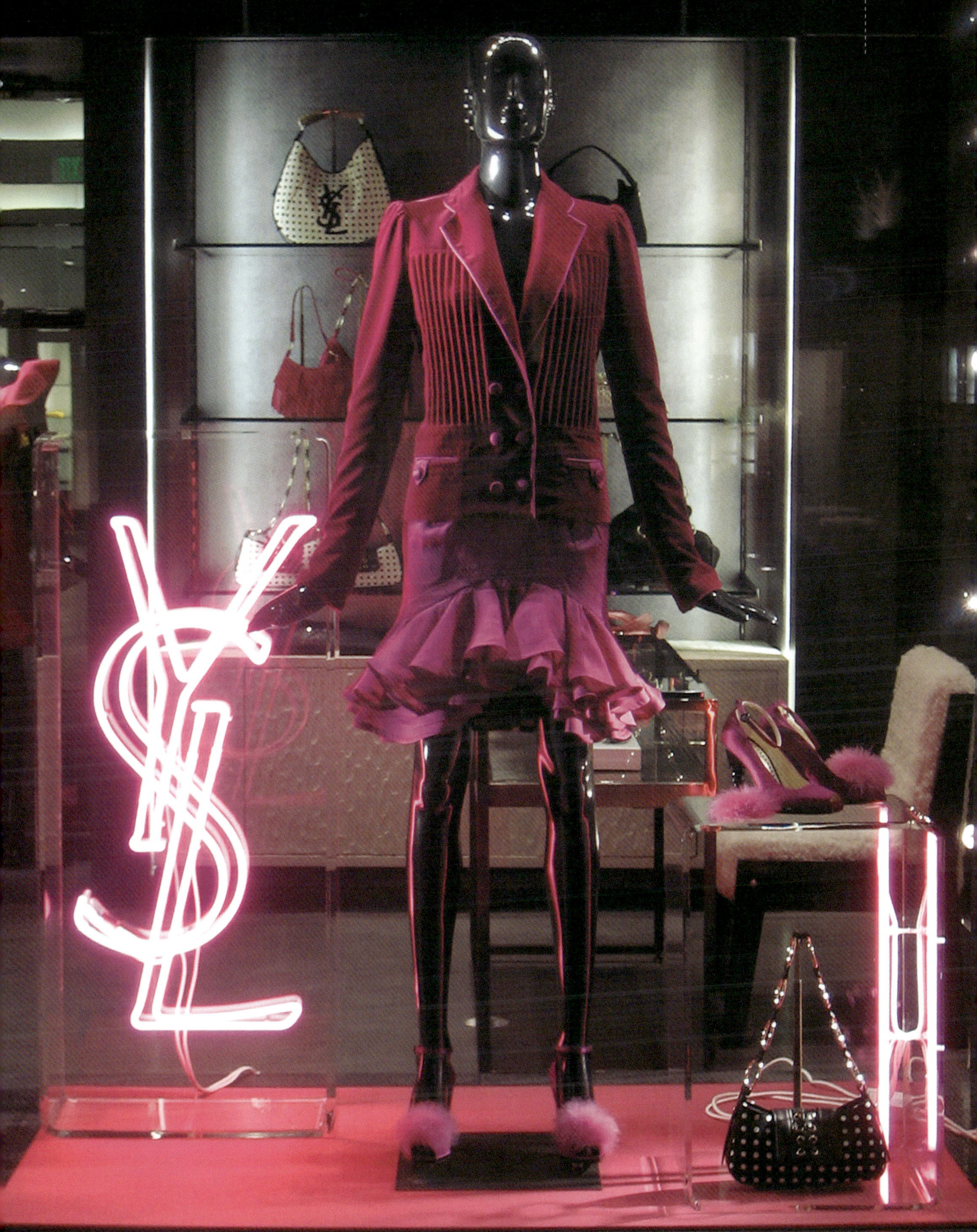

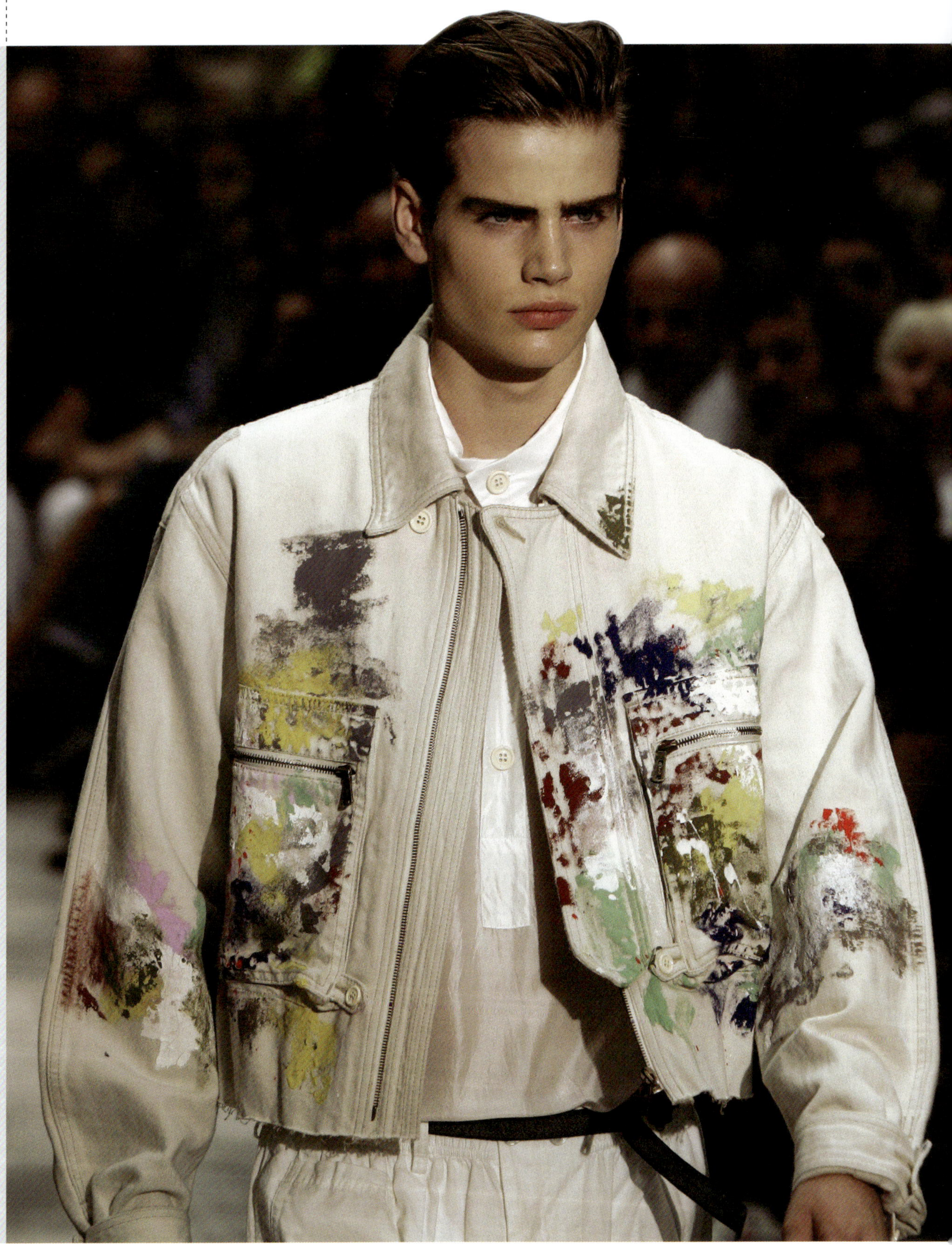

ABOVE: Part of the men's Spring/Summer 2008 collection by Stefano Pilati for Yves Saint Laurent
OPP PAGE: Dress of the Year (2004), Tom Ford for Yves Saint Laurent

Sophie Dahl naked apart from a necklace and stiletto heels, was controversial and provocative. As was the campaign for Ford-inspired cologne M7 in which martial arts champion Samuel was photographed completely naked. However, Ford understood the power of lifestyle branding and worked on elevating YSL's presence in global fashion markets. This was not entirely successful. The tension between Yves Saint Laurent himself and Ford remained. Saint Laurent had created an aesthetic universe rooted in elegance and poetry. Ford's direct, sometimes aggressive approach, represented a stark contrast. After a disagreement with Kering, YSL and Ford parted company. Saint Laurent did not hide his relief, describing Ford's tenure at the House as a damage to his legacy.

'*Finally, Ford is leaving,*' he told *Women's Wear Daily.*
'*I have suffered for what he did with my name.*
Thankfully, the damage is not irreversible.'

Ford was equally dismissive of the label claiming that, '*YSL no longer exists for me*'.

However, time is a great healer and at the Met Ball in 2024, Ford chose to wear Saint Laurent.

Stefano Pilati, who had joined YSL in 2000 to run the ready-to-wear and accessories design departments for both sexes, became the new Creative Director. The Italian approached YSL's extensive archives with reverence - acknowledging the challenge of innovating within a house where '*Saint Laurent has*

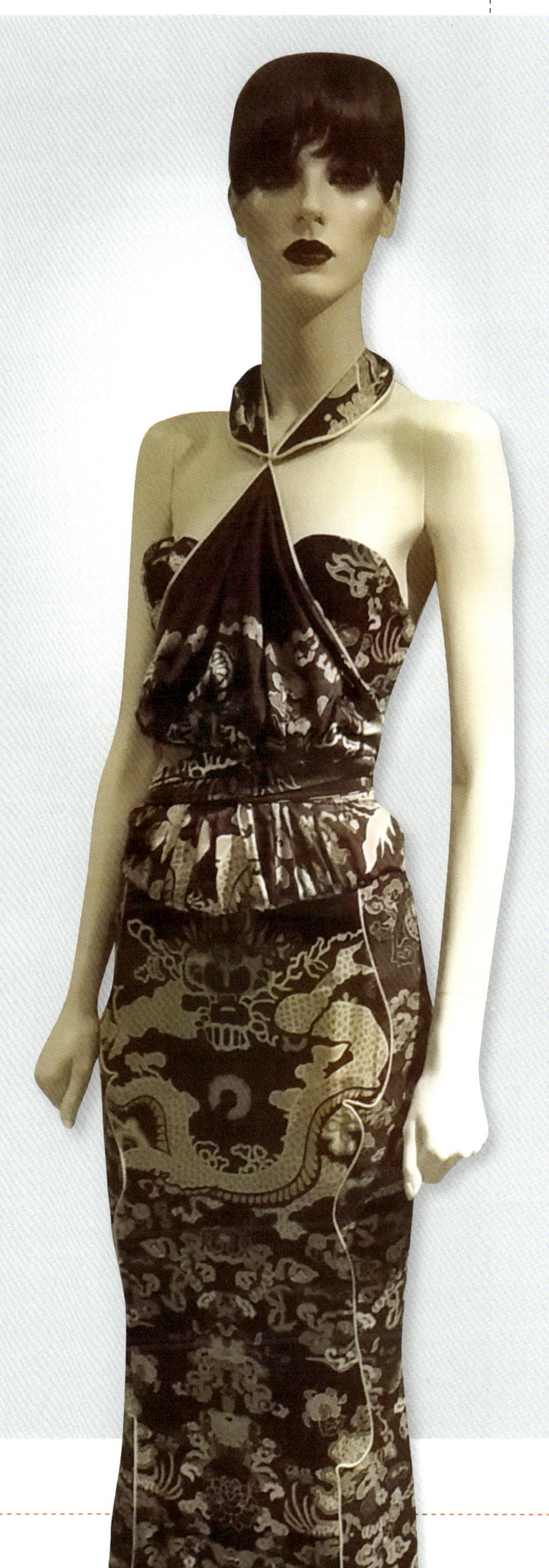

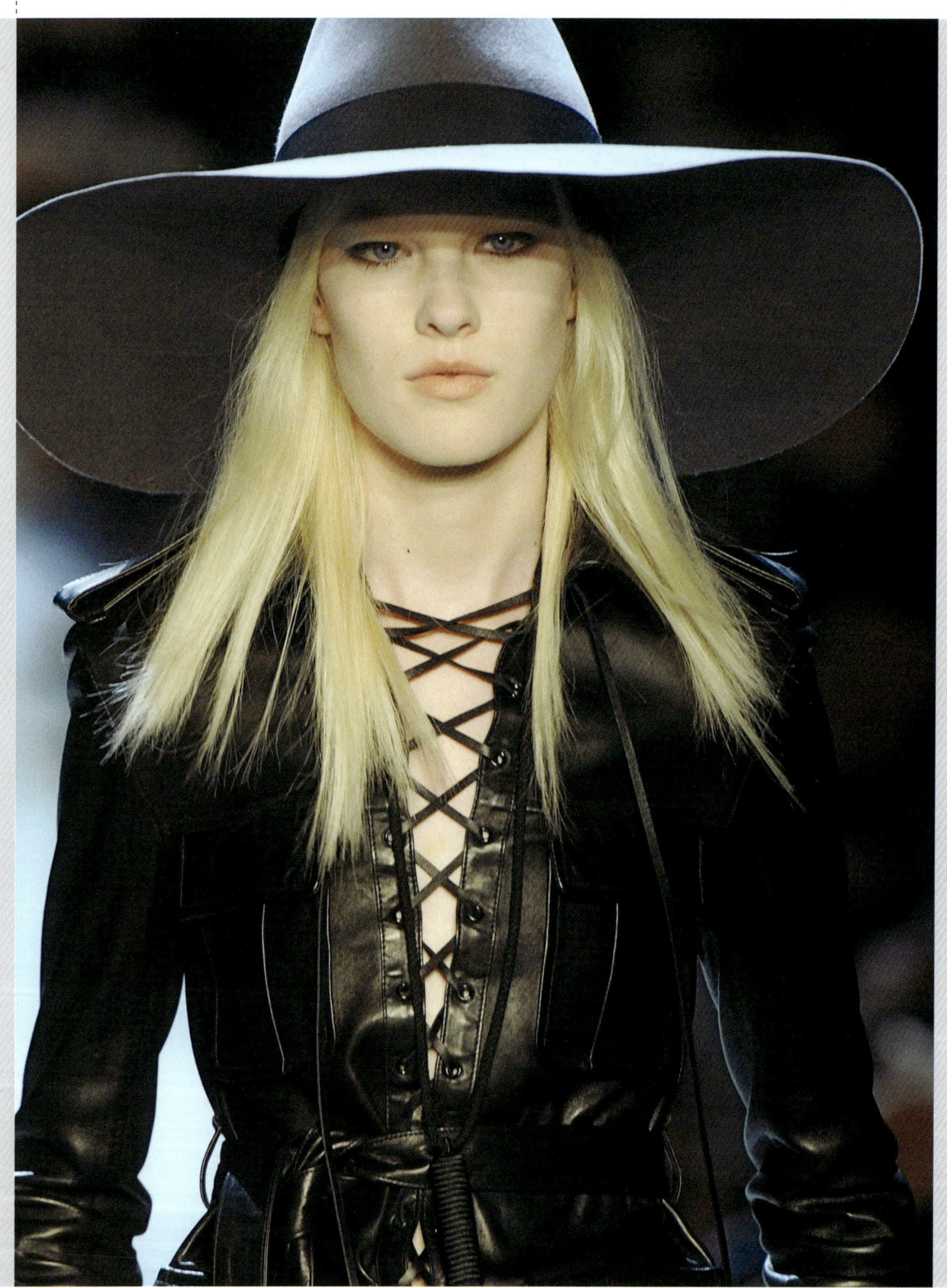

ABOVE: Yves Saint Laurent Womenswear Spring/
Summer 2013, Paris Fashion Week
OPP PAGE: Hedi Slimane

done everything'. His debut Spring/Summer 2005 collection introduced tulip skirts and polka-dot prints which received mixed reviews. However, his Fall/Winter 2005 collection, inspired by the austere aesthetics of Jansenist nuns, showcased his ability to blend historical references with modern design.

By Fall/Winter 2006, Pilati had redefined sensuality at YSL, presenting tunics over skinny pants and emphasizing subtle allure through details like garments that required assistance to unbutton. During his tenure, Pilati introduced several pieces that became synonymous with YSL's modern identity. Notably, the Muse bag and the Tribute sandal emerged as iconic accessories under his direction. He also launched the 'Manifesto' project, distributing limited-edition lookbooks directly to the public, thus making access to high fashion more democratic. Pilati's final collection for YSL in Fall 2012 was met with a standing ovation. The show featured dominatrix-inspired leather suits, chainmail dresses in jewel tones, and dark floral prints, encapsulating his signature blend of strength and elegance. Despite early scepticism, Pilati's eight-years at the helm of YSL is now recognized for its thoughtful reinterpretation of the brand's heritage and its influence on contemporary fashion. His tenure bridged the gap between the house's illustrious past and its modern evolution.

French/Tunisian designer Hedi Slimane, previously of Dior Homme, was Pilati's replacement. He lost no time in making his mark. Soon after becoming Creative Director, he rebranded the house, renaming it simply 'Saint Laurent'. The decision sparked controversy but also helped Slimane reinvent the brand for a younger, more rebellious audience. The move marked a deliberate departure from the glamour and sensuality of Ford's tenure and returned the brand to a more youthful, edgy approach. However, the iconic YSL monogram and the full 'Yves Saint Laurent' name were retained for accessories and cosmetics, preserving the brand's legacy in those areas. When it came to fashion, Slimane's focus on androgyny was consistent with Yves Saint Laurent's original spirit. He infused the brand with a sense of rock-chic, emphasizing skinny jeans, leather jackets, vintage rock band T-shirts, and sharp tailoring, all of which were directly influenced by 1970s rock culture, punk and grunge and blended with the sleek French

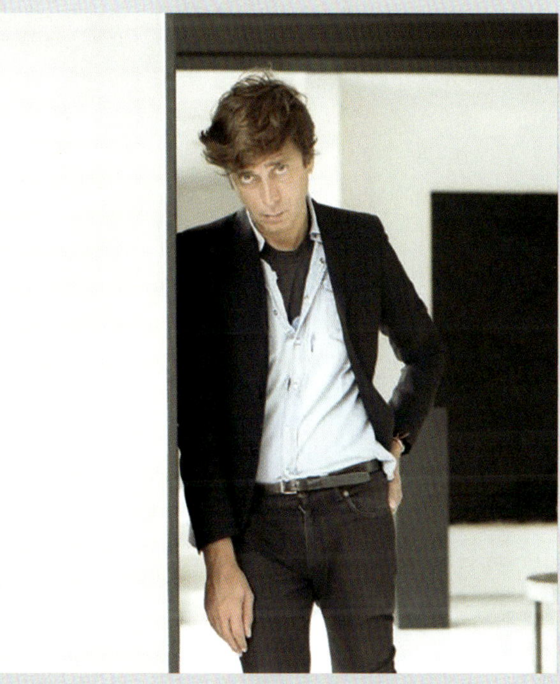

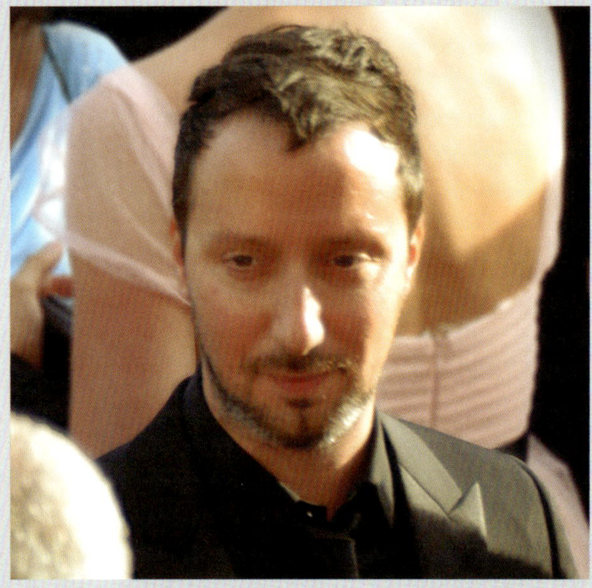

sophistication of the Saint Laurent brand. Slimane made Saint Laurent a must-have brand for young fashion enthusiasts. His approach marked a turning point for the label, placing it at the intersection of high fashion and youth culture. While Slimane's tenure alienated some long-time fans of Yves Saint Laurent's more refined and elegant approach, he successfully brought the brand into the modern fashion landscape. He revitalized ready-to-wear collections and turned Saint Laurent into one of the most coveted labels of the era, popularizing his collections through social media and celebrity endorsements.

Hedi Slimane departed from Saint Laurent in April 2016 after completing a transformative four-year tenure as the brand's creative and image director. His departure coincided with the expiration of his contract, and while specific reasons were not publicly disclosed, reports suggest that Slimane and the fashion house's parent company, Kering, were unable to reach an agreement on new terms.

In 2016, Anthony Vaccarello was appointed as the creative director of Saint Laurent Paris. Vaccarello, an Italian-Belgian-born designer who had made a name for himself with his own eponymous label and his work at Versus Versace, inherited the challenge of leading the brand through the next stage of its evolution. Vaccarello wished to reclaimed Yves' original vision. He adopted a more balanced approach than his predecessor, blending the YSL legacy with the rock-chic influence that had been established during Slimane's time. Vaccarello reintroduced a bit more glamour and refinement, but kept Slimane's edginess, creating collections that felt timeless while still appealing to modern sensibilities. Vaccarello paid homage to Yves Saint Laurent's core aesthetics — sharp tailoring, sophisticated silhouettes, and fluid, elegant lines — but updated them with a more contemporary edge, particularly focusing on luxurious evening wear, tailored suits, and rock-inspired leather pieces.

Under Vaccarello's leadership, Saint Laurent has continued to grow in global appeal, with a focus on elevating the brand's luxury status while appealing to a broader audience through ready-to-wear collections that remain relevant and desirable in the digital age. Vaccarello has continued to celebrate Yves Saint Laurent's timeless vision while making the brand feel fresh and relevant for the new generation of fashion-conscious consumers.

ABOVE: Anthony Vaccarello at Cannes, 2017
OPP PAGE: Pierre Bergé and Yves Saint Laurent attend the opening of the Yves Saint Laurent Foundation on 5 March, 2004 in Paris, France

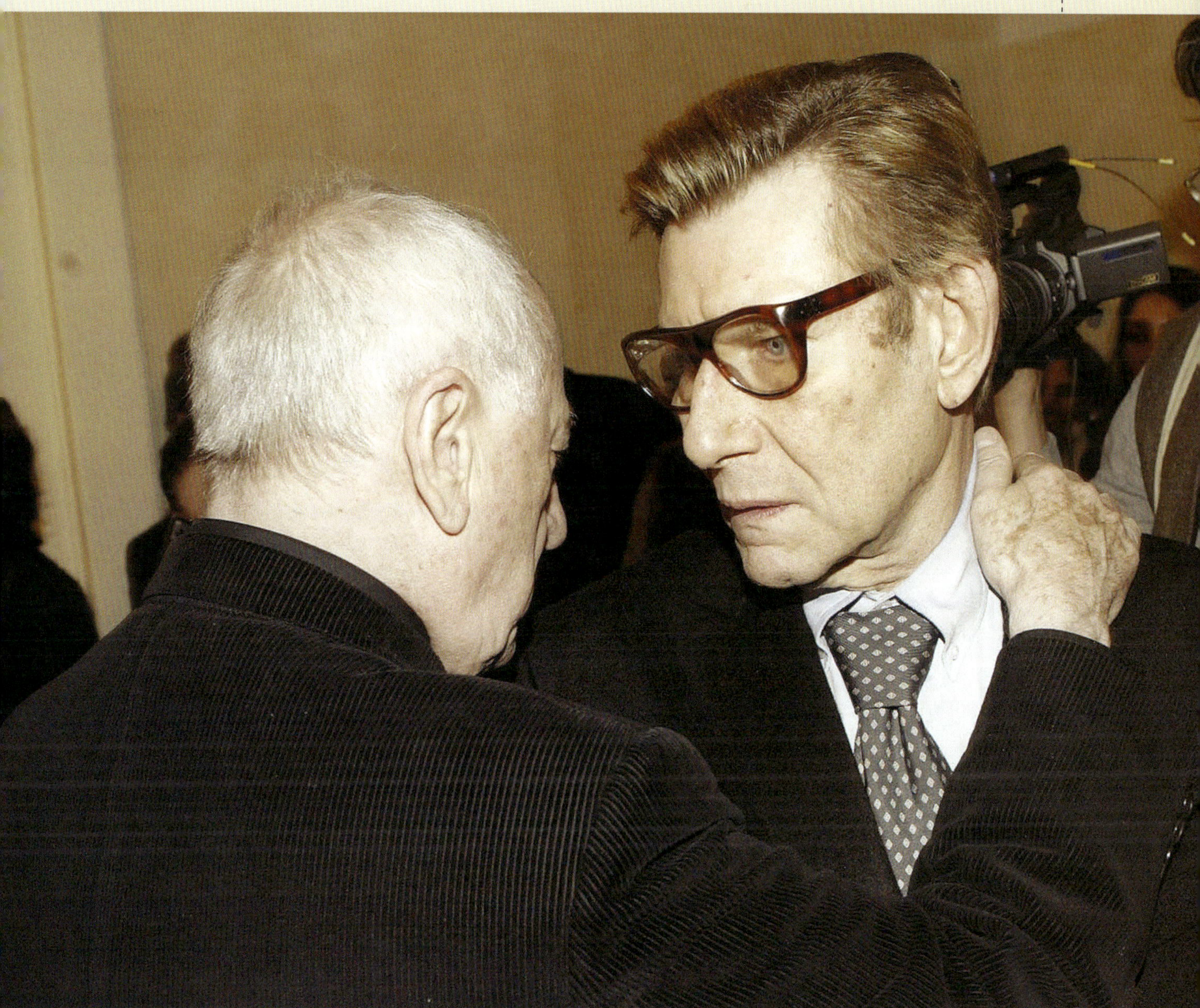

Yves Saint Laurent spent his post-retirement years with his long-time business partner and companion, Pierre Bergé. They divided their time between their homes in Paris and Morocco - Marrakech, where they owned the famous Jardin Majorelle. He focused more on his passion for art collecting. Together with Bergé, Saint Laurent amassed an extraordinary collection of art, including works by Picasso, Mondrian, and Matisse. His later years were marked by declining health. He had battled depression and substance abuse earlier in his life, and in his final years, he also faced physical health problems. Yves Saint Laurent, aged 71, died on June 1 2008, of brain cancer in Paris.

FRAGRANCE

"A woman's perfume tells more about her than her handwriting"

Yves Saint Laurent

Fragrance has always been an integral part of the Yves Saint Laurent's vision — a key element adding layers of sensuality, luxury and individuality to the brand's creations. Just as the clothes and accessories were, and are, designed to make a statement, the fragrances have become another declaration of beauty and self-expression.

From the very beginning of his fashion career, Saint Laurent understood the power of scent to evoke emotions, memories and even attitudes. Saint Laurent was a master at creating bold, daring and iconic fragrances that became instantly recognizable and eternally classic. His scents were as transformative as his designs — luxurious, provocative and timelessly modern. Saint Laurent worked closely with perfumers to create scents that embodied both boldness and sensuality. His fragrances quickly became synonymous with a kind of effortless chic. As they still are today.

Yves Saint Laurent's journey into the world of fragrance began in 1964 when he launched his first scent, 'Y'. Designed to be modern, fresh and refined, the fragrance embodied the spirit of a woman who was sophisticated yet unconventional, powerful yet subtle. Y is a woody aromatic fragrance that blends lemon, citrus, and green notes with an underlying base of vetiver and moss.

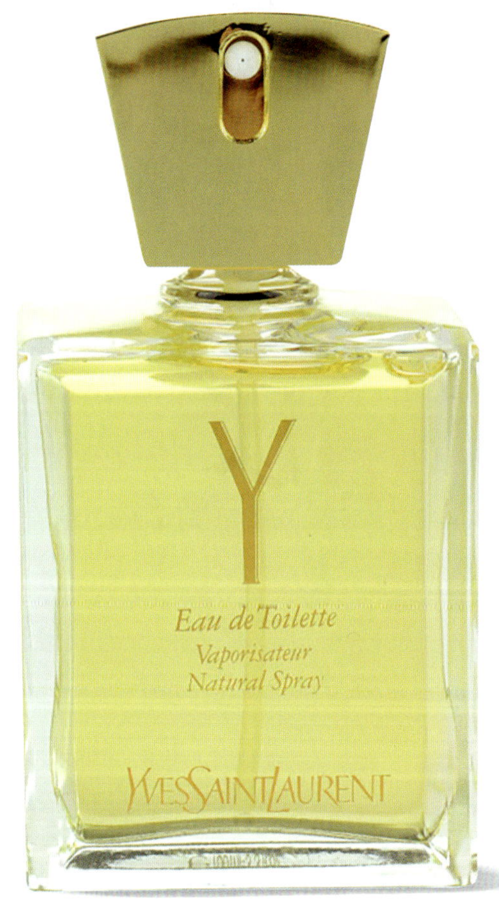

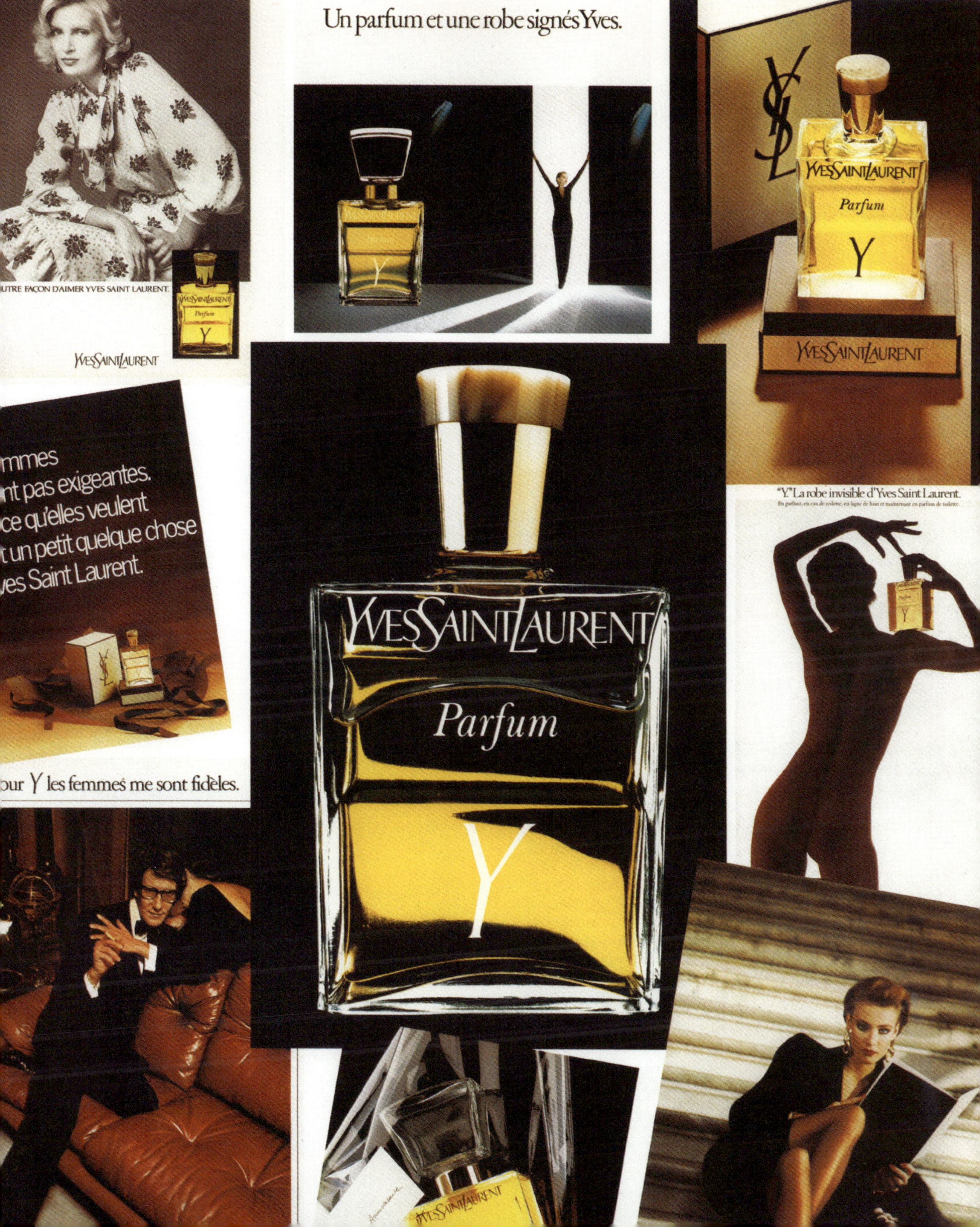
Un parfum et une robe signés Yves.

YVES SAINT LAURENT
Parfum
Y

YVES SAINT LAURENT
Parfum
Y

YVES SAINT LAURENT

YVES SAINT LAURENT
Parfum
Y

AUTRE FAÇON D'AIMER YVES SAINT LAURENT.

YVES SAINT LAURENT

mmes
nt pas exigeantes.
ce qu'elles veulent
t un petit quelque chose
ves Saint Laurent.

our Y les femmes me sont fidèles.

"Y." La robe invisible d'Yves Saint Laurent.

YVES SAINT LAURENT

Seven years later, YSL introduced 'Rive Gauche' which would go on to become one of the most iconic fragrances in history. Inspired by his ready-to-wear store of the same name, the scent captured a free-spirited, intellectual woman of the time — the kind of woman who embraced both elegance and rebellion. This fragrance opened with fresh green notes, blending beautifully with rose and jasmine. The heart of spicy patchouli and oakmoss added a sense of depth and mystery, while the base notes of amber and sandalwood gave it a warm, sensual finish. Rive Gauche was a fragrance that broke boundaries and became a symbol of modern femininity. Although not as popular as it once was, Rive Gauche is regarded as a classic in the fragrance world.

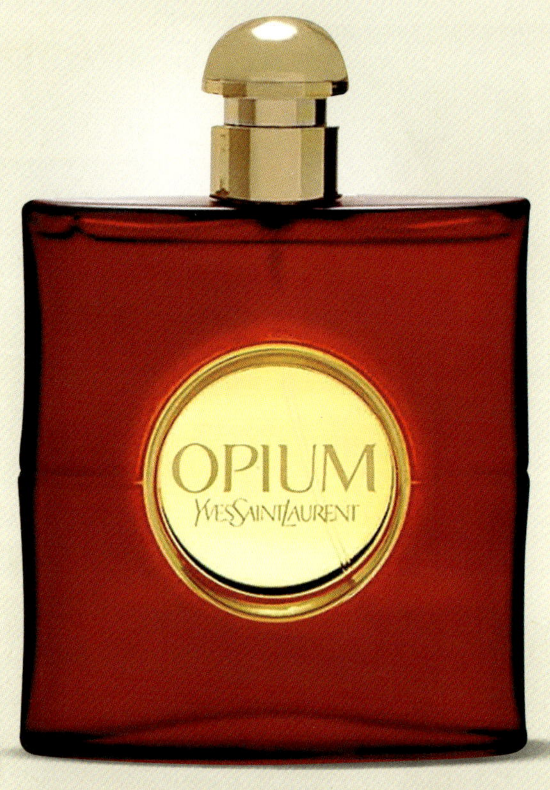

Introduced in 1977, 'Opium' is arguably the most famous of all Yves Saint Laurent fragrances. It is a spicy oriental fragrance that captured the very essence of seduction, mystery and luxury. The fragrance was named after the opulent East, inspired by the mystical, intriguing allure of Asia, and aimed to evoke a sense of dangerous sensuality. Not to mention controversy – the name of the scent sparked a backlash due to its reference to the drug, leading to bans and protests in some markets for a while. Still, this controversy also amplified its fame. With its rich blend of spices, florals, and resins, Opium became an instant classic. Notes of mandarin, clove, myrrh and sandalwood created a scent that was both euphoric and unforgettable. Opium's boldness set it apart from other perfumes of its time, making it a revolutionary fragrance embodying femininity and sensuality. It remains a symbol of unrestrained luxury and timeless elegance.

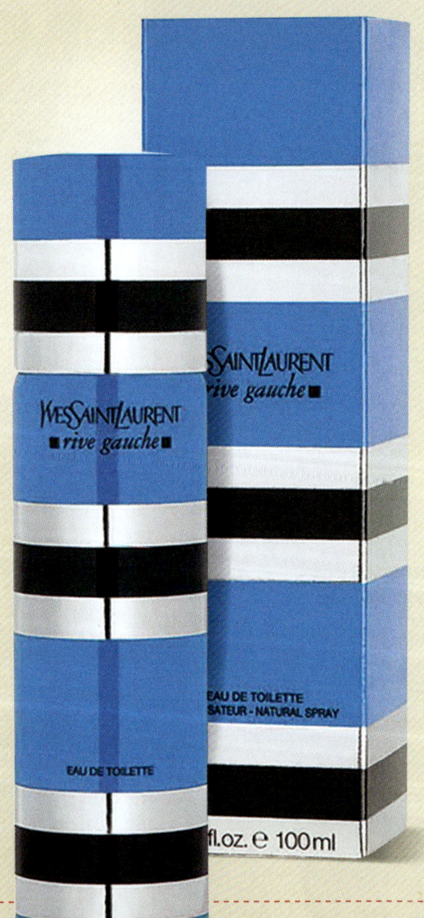

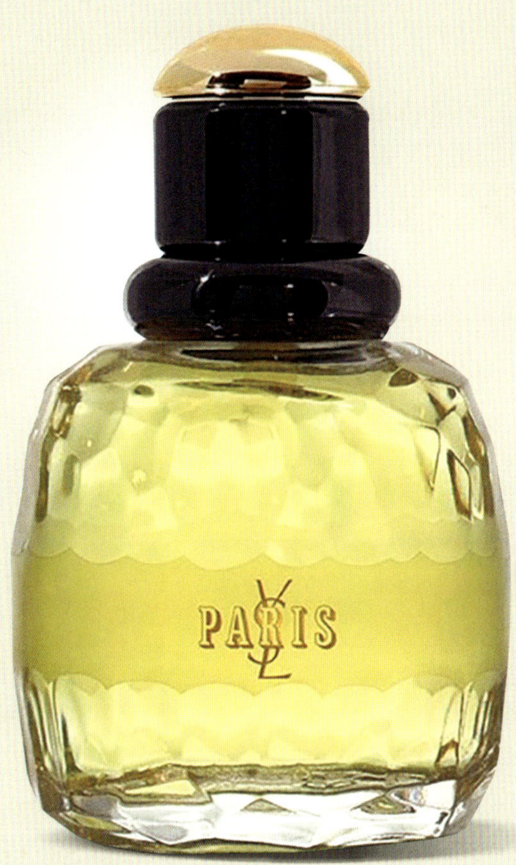

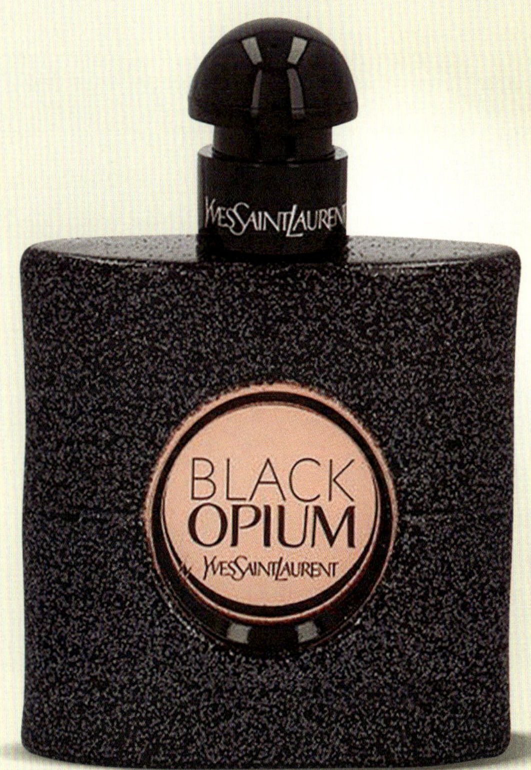

'Black Opium', launched in 2014, represents a more modern, bold, and edgy interpretation of the original Opium fragrance. It is a vibrant, seductive scent that appeals to a younger audience while still holding onto the opulence of its predecessor. The fragrance is centred around a coffee note, which combines with vanilla, white flowers, and a touch of musk. It has an addictive quality, making it an ideal fragrance for those who seek intensity and mystique.

'Paris', launched in 1983, became a celebration of everything Saint Laurent loved about the city — its romanticism, glamour and femininity. Inspired by the streets of the French capital, this fragrance was a floral tribute to the rose, one of Saint Laurent's favourite flowers. It opens with violet, orange blossom and bergamot and evolves into a heart of iris, rose and lily of the valley. Moss and amber bass notes create an earthy, timeless richness. Paris is soft, delicate, and romantic — the epitome of French elegance. It is a fragrance for those who wish to channel the allure and romance of the city, making it a true classic in the YSL fragrance collection.

Almost as important as the scents themselves are the bottles which house them. Yves Saint Laurent was known for his innovative, luxurious designs and his fragrance bottles were no exception. Each bottle was, and continues to be, crafted to reflect

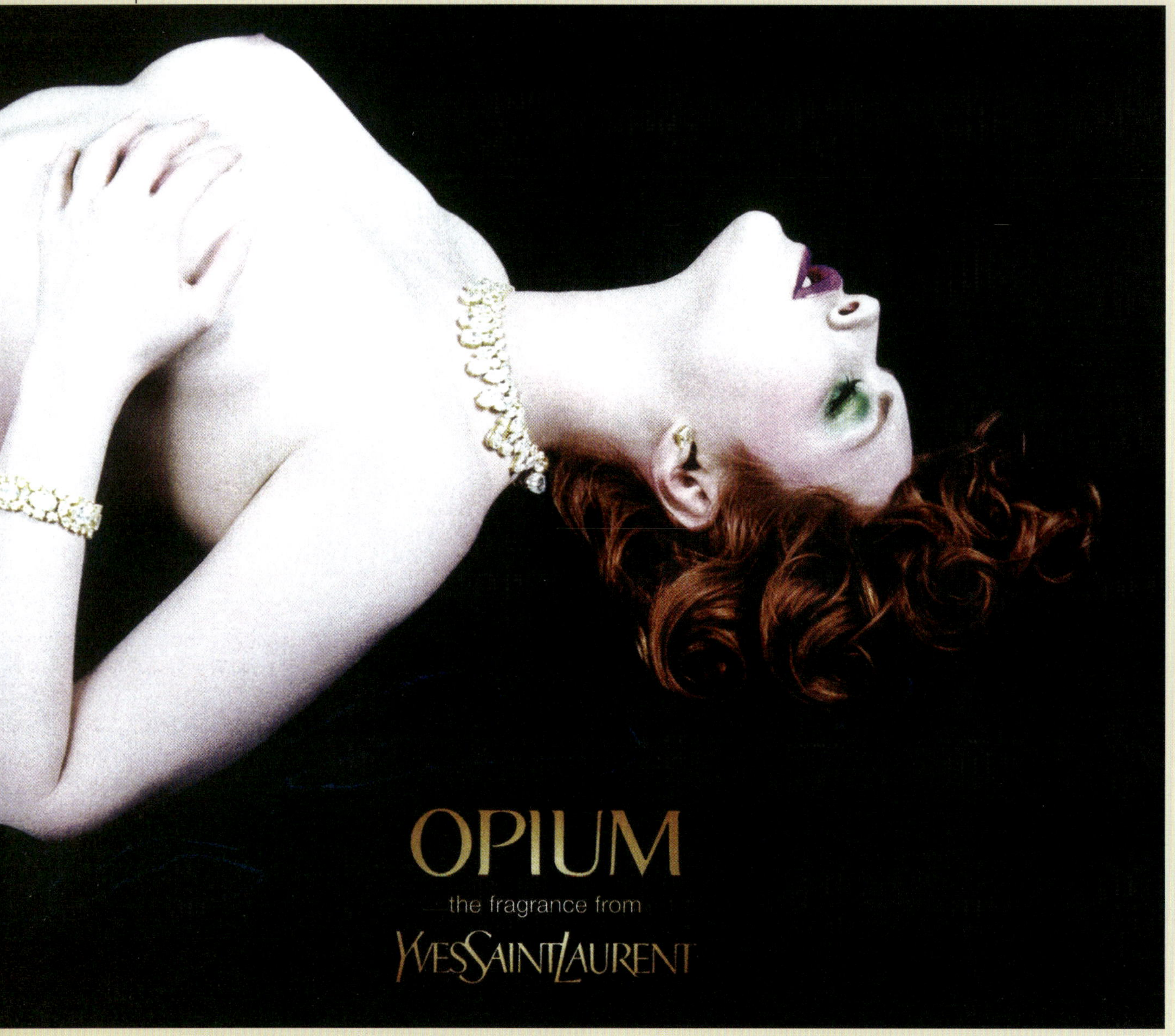

the sophistication and boldness of the scent inside. Opium's red and gold bottle, for instance, evokes an Eastern-inspired opulence while Paris' delicate, floral design embodies the romance and elegance of the fragrance. The Black Opium bottle - with its dark, glittering surface - conveys the rock-chic energy of the fragrance.

We cannot discuss YSL fragrances without mentioning the often-controversial advertising campaigns which have accompanied them - Yves Saint Laurent himself being photographed naked for his 'Pour Homme' cologne in 1971, a blissed-out Jerry Hall for the original Opium campaign, a naked Sophie Dahl in just heels and a necklace when she became

ABOVE: The iconic 2000 Yves Saint Laurent Opium Advert featuring Sophie Dahl

the face – and body - of Opium in 2000, the launch of the 'M7' cologne in 2007 with a campaign featuring the full-frontal nudity of martial arts champion Samuel de Cubber... However, these provocative initiatives have significantly contributed to the brand's visibility, allure, and sales.

Today, Yves Saint Laurent's fragrances continue to be symbols of luxury, elegance, and individual expression. The timeless classics like Opium, Paris, and Y still captivate perfume lovers worldwide, while newer creations like Black Opium and Mon Paris – a vibrantly youthful fragrance with top notes of Strawberry, Raspberry and Bergamot which was launched in 2016 - maintain the brand's innovative edge. The YSL fragrance collection is a continuing journey of exploration — a celebration of the artistry of scent and the profound impact it has on identity and self-expression. Yves Saint Laurent's legacy in fragrance is undeniable, with his perfumes remaining as relevant and desirable today as they were when first introduced.

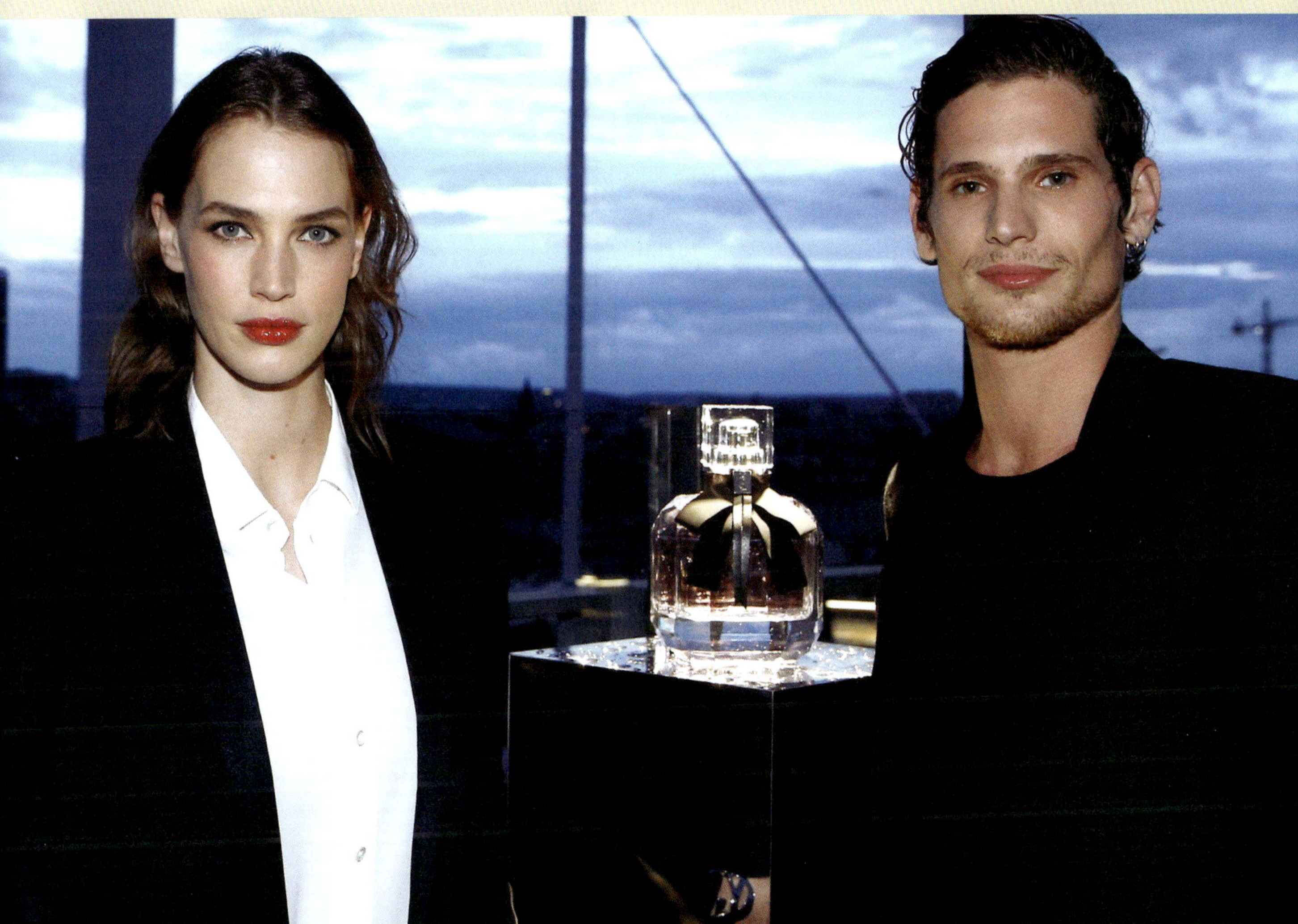

ABOVE: Model Crista Cober and actor Jeremie Laheurte attend the YSL Beauty launch of the fragrance 'Mon Paris' at Cafe Le Georges, 14 June, 2016, Paris, France

LEGACY

"Every other designer has been inspired by him in some way"

Naomi Campbell

Yves Saint Laurent, one of the most transformative figures in 20th century fashion, left an enduring legacy that continues to reverberate through the work of contemporary designers and the fashion industry at large. His visionary approach redefined the very language of style - not only in terms of aesthetics but also in how fashion intersects with gender, identity and global culture.

Saint Laurent's influence on other designers can be traced through several key innovations. Most famously, he revolutionized womenswear by adapting traditionally masculine garments for the female form. His 1966 creation of Le Smoking, the first tuxedo suit for women, challenged gender norms and became a symbol of empowered femininity. This bold move paved the way for designers like Helmut Lang, Ann Demeulemeester and Hedi Slimane, who have since explored androgyny and tailored minimalism in their own distinct ways.

He was also instrumental in democratizing fashion. As one of the first haute couture designers to launch

RIGHT: Yves Saint Laurent and Naomi Campbell attend the Miró exhibition at the Centre Pompidou, Paris, 15 January 2000

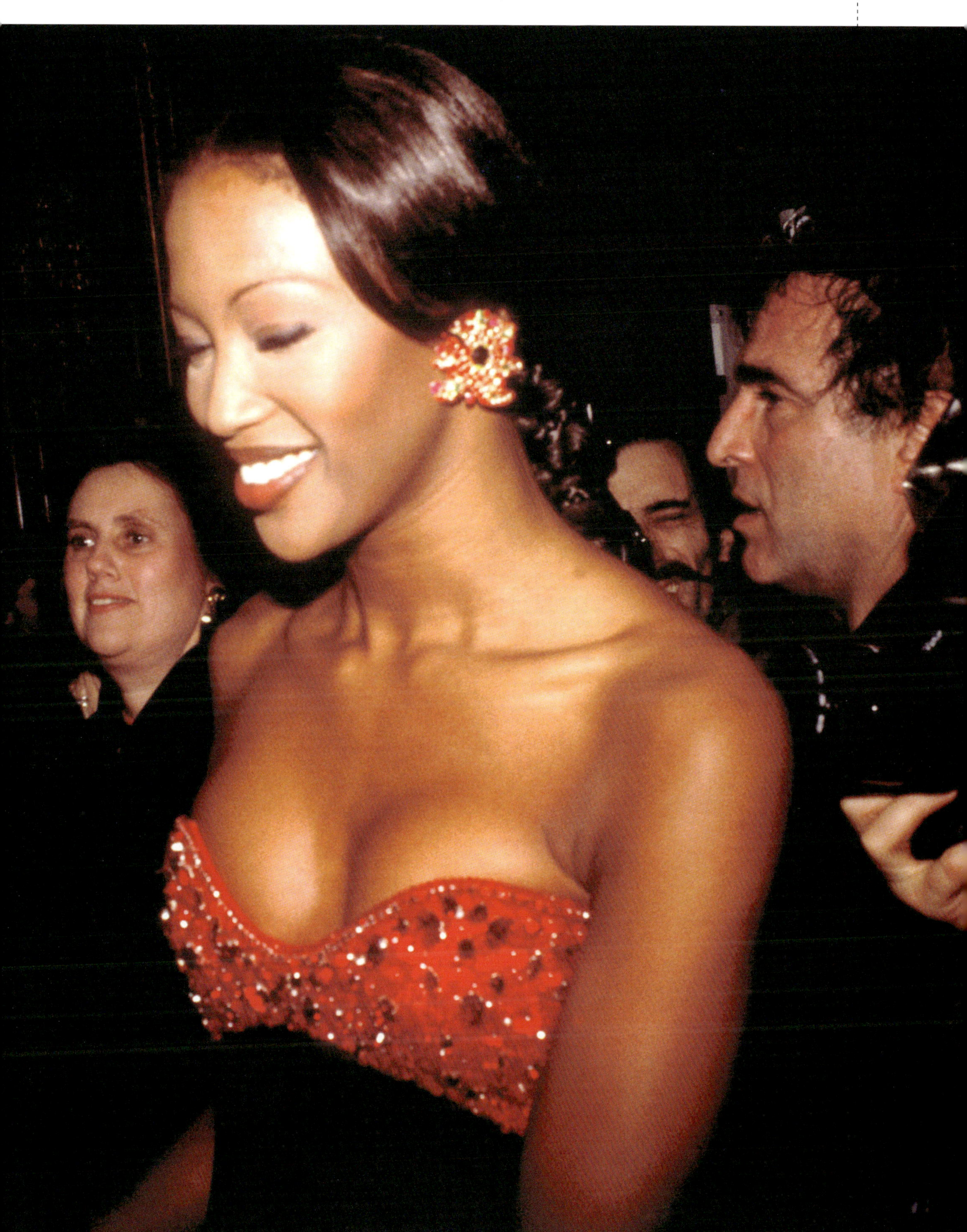

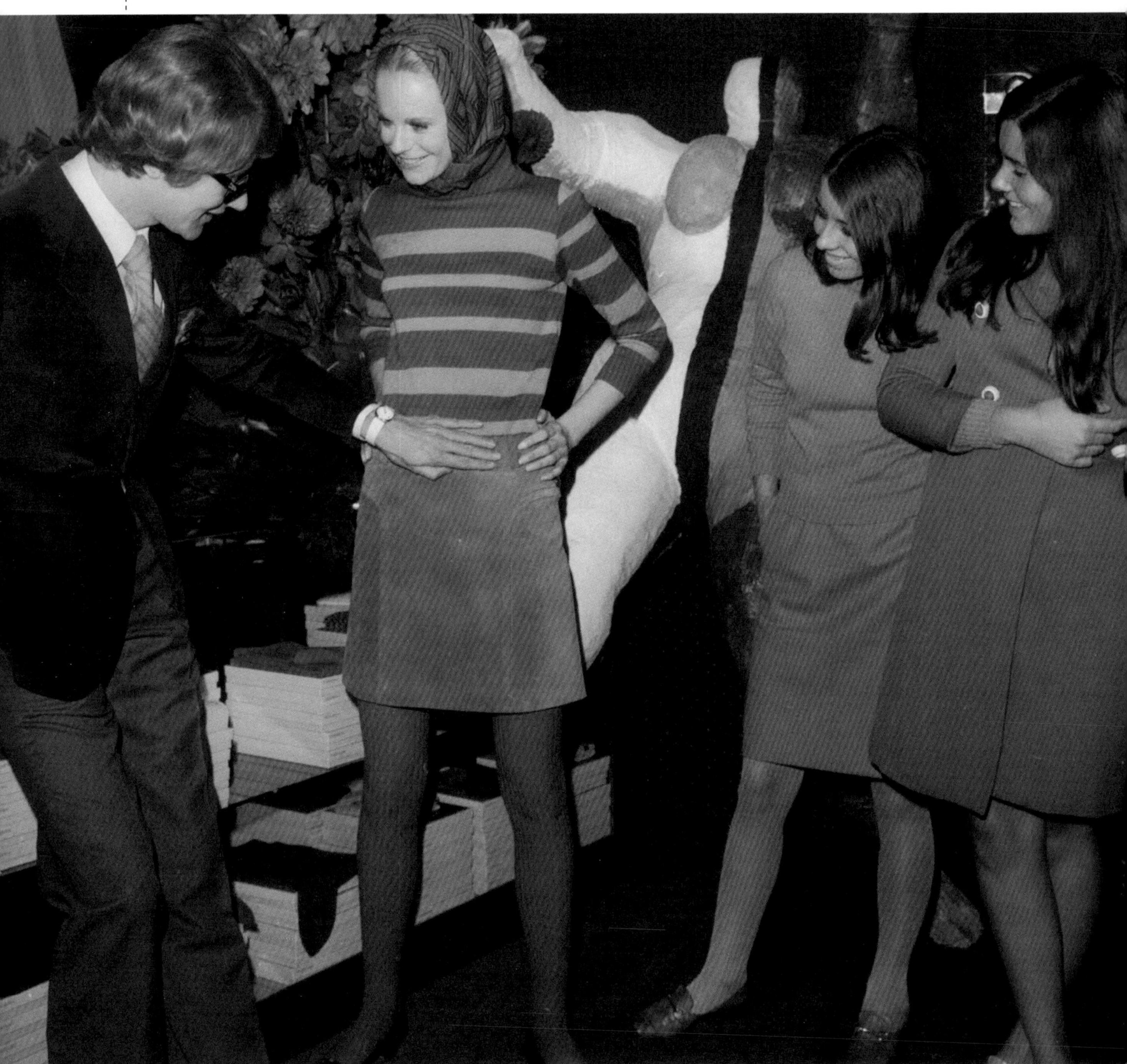

a ready-to-wear line, Rive Gauche, in 1966, he helped blur the line between elite fashion and everyday wear. This foresight anticipated today's designer collaborations, diffusion lines and the luxury-accessibility hybrid embraced by designers like Marc Jacobs and Phoebe Philo.

Saint Laurent's deeply intellectual and global

ABOVE: Yves Saint Laurent pictured with one of his models in his new boutique 'Rive Gauche', 9 September, 1966

OPP PAGE: Heart Evangelista wears a khaki off-shoulder jumpsuit from Yves Saint Laurent, 27 July, 2024

sensibility also set him apart. His collections paid homage to everything from Mondrian's abstract grids to African art, Russian costume, and Moroccan dress. This synthesis of art, history, and non-Western references made fashion a canvas for cultural storytelling - a legacy that lives on in the work of Dries Van Noten, John Galliano, and Jean Paul Gaultier.

His influence is not only preserved in the collections of modern designers but also in two remarkable institutions dedicated to his work - the Musée Yves Saint Laurent Paris and the Musée Yves Saint Laurent Marrakech. The Paris museum, located in his former couture house at 5 Avenue Marceau, offers an intimate view of his creative process and the Parisian elegance that defined much of his work. In contrast, the Marrakech museum celebrates the city that inspired his bold use of colour and love of exoticism. Together, they serve as architectural and cultural monuments to a designer who treated fashion not just as commerce, but as living art.

Ultimately, Saint Laurent's most lasting contribution is his belief that fashion can be both beautiful and meaningful - a vehicle for freedom, expression, and identity. That philosophy still resonates today, not just on runways but in the broader cultural understanding of what fashion can represent. His legacy is not merely preserved - it is actively lived, reinterpreted, and celebrated. Yves Saint Laurent once said, *'What is important in a dress is the woman who is wearing it'*. That philosophy lives on in every garment inspired by his work.

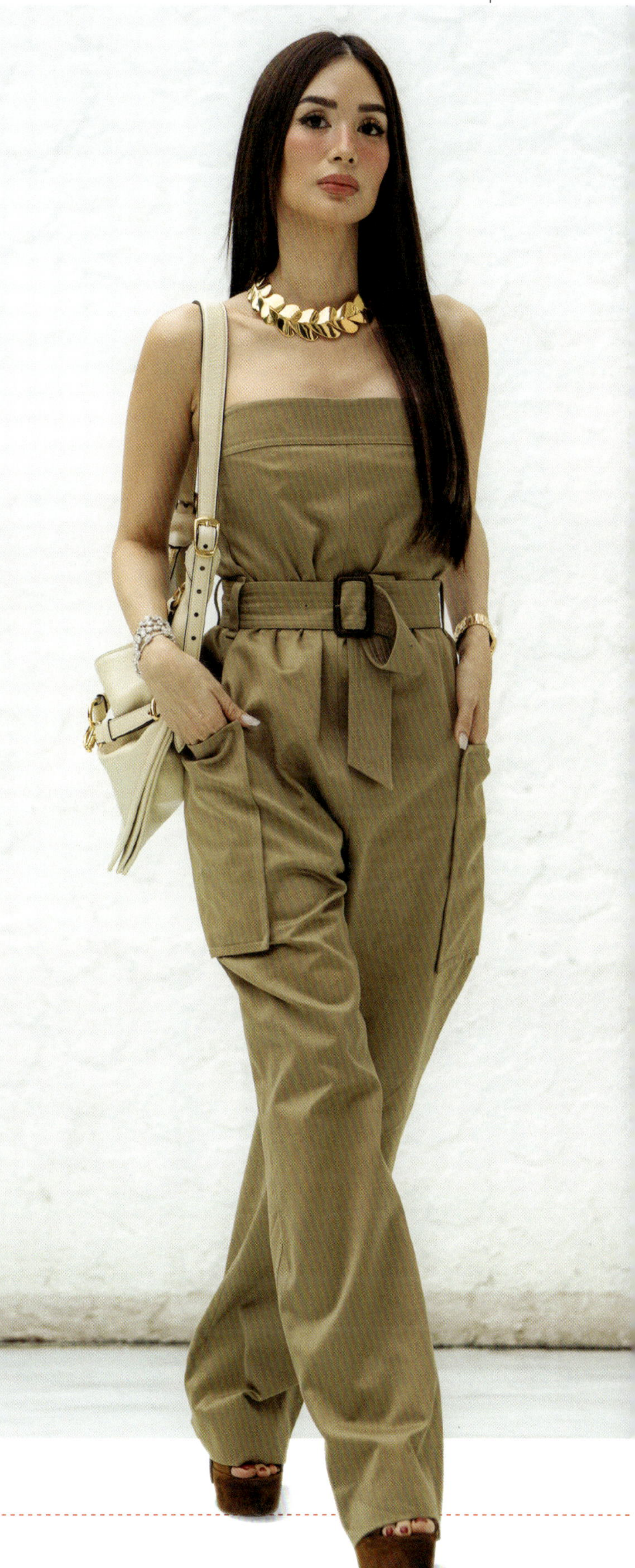

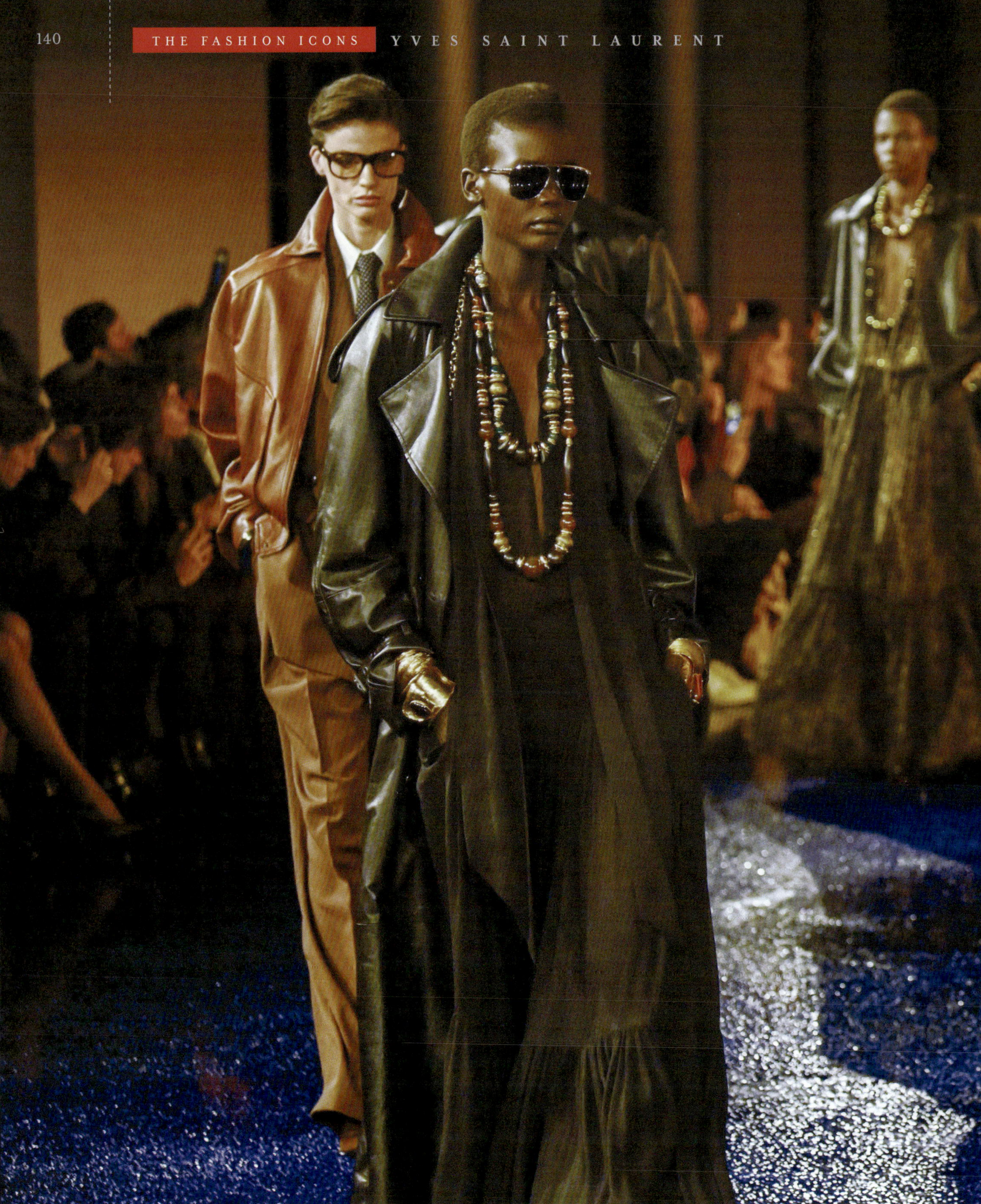

ABOVE: Yves Saint Laurent ready-to-wear Spring/ Summer 2025 fashion show as part of the Paris Fashion Week on September 24, 2024 in Paris, France

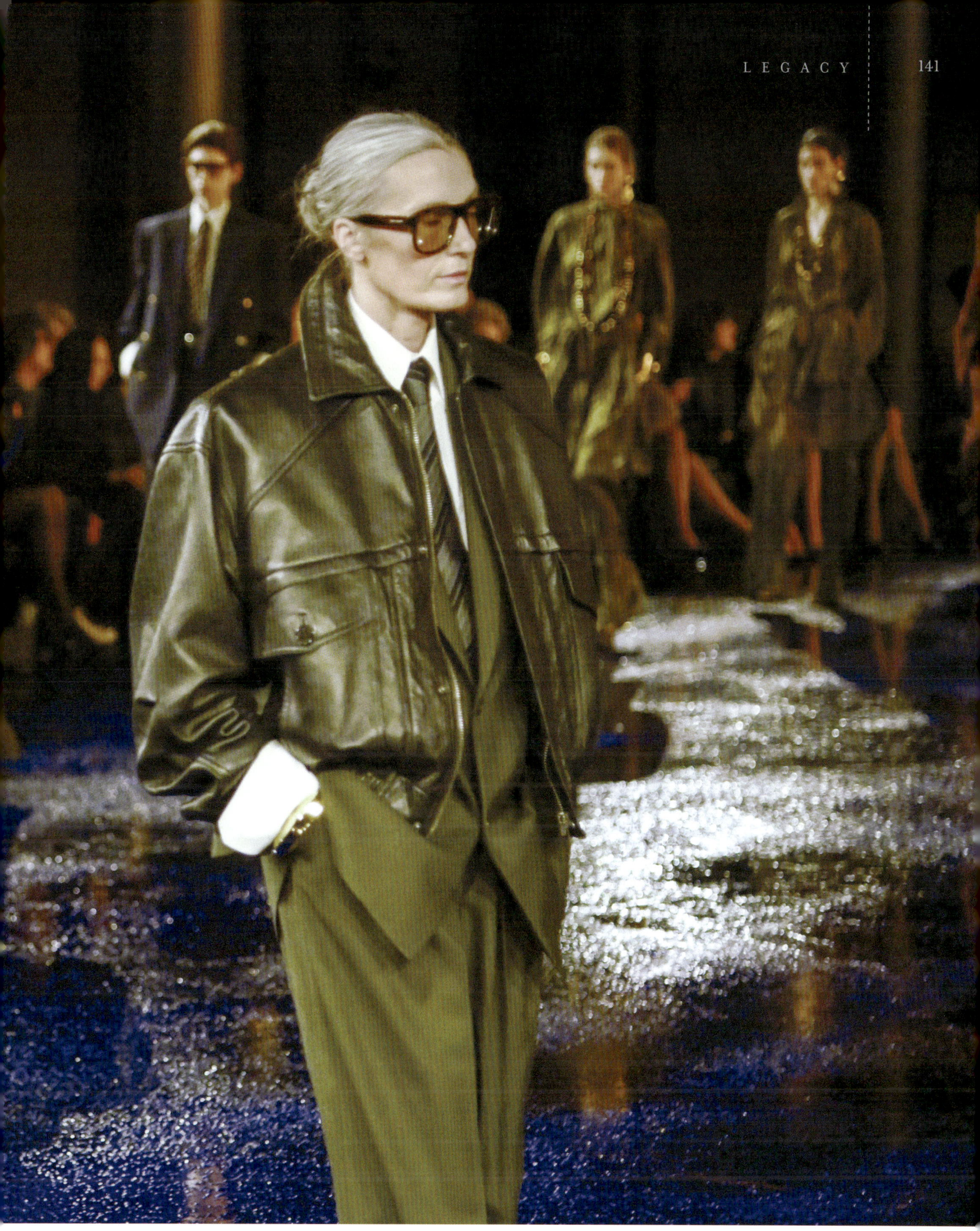

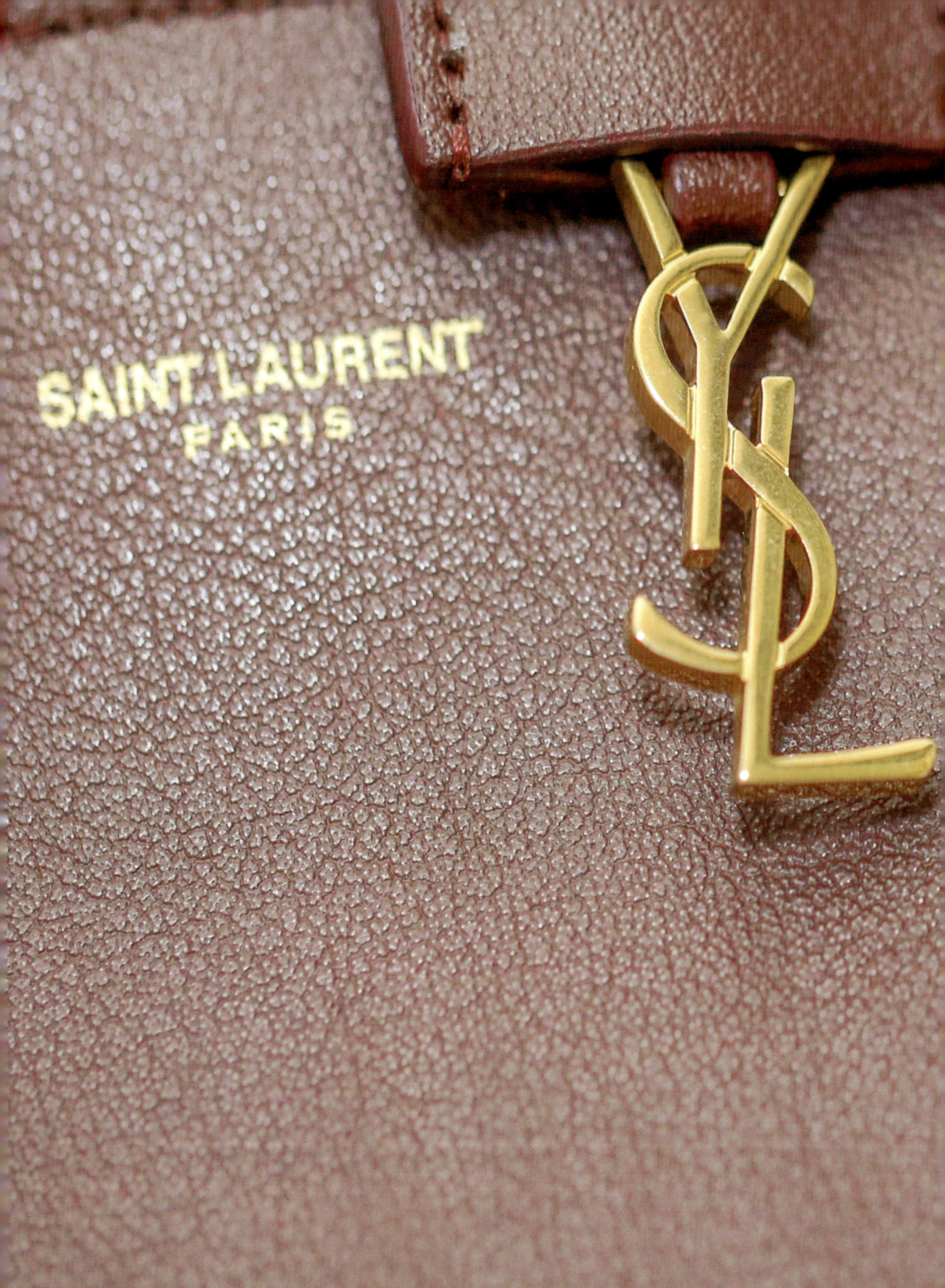

SAINT LAURENT
PARIS